LSAT
TEST PREP

The Most Complete Guide to Passing the Exam on Your First Try with the Highest Score | Includes 6 Full Exam Simulations and EXTRA Weekly Exams Based on the New LSAT Format

ETHAN STERLING

TABLE OF CONTENTS

HERE IS YOUR FREE BONUS:

Additional Full-Length Practice Test, ONE EACH WEEK

Maximize your LSAT test performance with exclusive, no-cost extras unlock them with the link or the QR code provided.

Embark on the path to LSAT mastery with our expertly crafted, free supplementary materials available for instant download. Tailored to enhance your comprehension and test-taking prowess, these indispensable resources are your key to attaining unparalleled preparedness.

CLICK HERE TO DOWNLOAD IT

OR

SCAN THE QR CODE TO DOWNLOAD IT

PREFACE

Welcome to your comprehensive guide to conquering the LSAT! Whether you are just beginning your LSAT preparation journey or are seeking to refine your skills in the final stages, this book is designed to be your ultimate resource.

The LSAT (Law School Admission Test) is a critical component of law school admissions, serving as a standardized measure of the skills necessary for success in law school and beyond. Given its importance, thorough and strategic preparation is essential. This guide aims to provide you with all the tools, techniques, and insights needed to excel on the LSAT.

This book begins by offering an overview of the LSAT, explaining its importance in law school admissions, and detailing the significant changes that will take effect from August 2024. Understanding these changes is crucial as they affect the structure and content of the test. Starting in August 2024, the LSAT will consist of two Logical Reasoning (LR) sections, one Reading Comprehension (RC) section, and one unscored section that could be either LR or RC. This adjustment, driven by rigorous research and fairness considerations, particularly in response to concerns about the Analytical Reasoning (or logic games) section, ensures the LSAT continues to measure the critical skills essential for law school success.

As you navigate this guide, you will find detailed sections dedicated to each component of the LSAT. Logical Reasoning is thoroughly covered, given its prominence in the new format. You will learn how to identify argument structures, recognize common logical fallacies, and approach different question types. The Reading Comprehension section focuses on understanding complex texts and answering related questions accurately. Additionally, the new Argumentative Writing section is explored, with guidance on analyzing issues, structuring arguments, and effectively using evidence.

Creating an effective study plan is essential for success, and this book provides a framework to help you assess your starting point, set realistic goals, and build a balanced study schedule. Regular practice is emphasized, and the guide includes multiple full-length practice tests designed to simulate real test conditions. These practice tests are invaluable for building endurance, tracking progress, and identifying areas needing further attention.

Preparing for the LSAT is not just about mastering content but also about managing the logistical and psychological aspects of the test. This guide offers insights into test registration, understanding fees, and selecting test locations, whether remote or in-person. It also addresses test day procedures, from managing anxiety to ensuring adequate rest and nutrition. Practical tips are provided to help you stay focused and calm during the test, maximizing your performance.

This book also includes a section dedicated to frequently asked questions, addressing common concerns and providing clarity on various aspects of the LSAT process. The appendices offer additional resources, including common pitfalls to avoid and further guidance to support your preparation journey.

Embarking on your LSAT preparation journey is a significant step towards achieving your law school aspirations. The process will require dedication, perseverance, and a strategic approach. This book is designed to support you every step of the way, providing the knowledge, tools, and confidence needed to succeed.

Remember, the LSAT is not just a test of knowledge but a test of skills and strategies. With the right preparation, you can master these elements and achieve your best possible score.

Good luck, and happy studying!

CHAPTER 1: Introduction to the LSAT

Overview of the LSAT

The Law School Admission Test (LSAT) is a pivotal examination for prospective law students. Administered by the Law School Admission Council (LSAC), the LSAT is a standardized test essential for admission to all American Bar Association (ABA)-accredited law schools, numerous Canadian law schools, and various international programs. The LSAT assesses key skills necessary for success in law school and the legal profession, including critical reading, logical reasoning and persuasive writing.

First introduced in 1948, the LSAT was created to standardize the admissions process across law schools, offering a common metric to objectively compare applicants from diverse educational backgrounds. Over the decades, the test has evolved, with its format and content adapting to better assess the competencies required for legal studies. The most recent significant update, effective from August 2024, reflects this ongoing evolution, emphasizing fairness and the relevance of the skills assessed.

The LSAT's primary goal is to evaluate the skills crucial for thriving in the demanding environment of law school. It measures a candidate's ability to read and understand complex texts, analyze and evaluate arguments, and develop coherent, persuasive written arguments. These skills are essential not only for academic success in law school but also for a successful legal career, where precise analysis, clear reasoning, and effective communication are indispensable.

Starting from August 2024, the LSAT underwent a significant restructuring. The test now includes two scored Logical Reasoning sections, one scored Reading Comprehension section, and one unscored section that could be either Logical Reasoning or Reading Comprehension, used to pilot questions for future tests. This new structure ensures that the LSAT continues to assess critical reasoning skills while addressing fairness concerns. These changes are designed to have minimal impact on test takers who have already begun their preparation, as they are already familiar with the Logical Reasoning section.

The LSAT is more than a test of knowledge; it is a test of skills and strategies. It assesses how well candidates can think critically and reason logically under timed conditions. Given its importance, thorough preparation is essential. This guide provides a comprehensive approach to mastering each section of the test, offering strategies, practice questions, and detailed explanations to help you build the necessary skills.

Preparation for this test involves more than just studying content; it requires developing a strategic approach to test-taking. This includes understanding the format and types of questions, practicing under timed conditions, and continuously reviewing and refining your techniques. By following a structured study plan and regularly practicing with real test questions, you can enhance your performance and boost your confidence.

The LSAT is a challenging and rigorous test that plays a pivotal role in law school admissions. This guide is designed to support you throughout your preparation journey, providing the tools and insights needed to succeed. With dedication and strategic preparation, you can master the LSAT and take a significant step towards achieving your law school aspirations and a successful legal career.

Importance of the LSAT in Law School Admissions

The LSAT plays a pivotal role in law school admissions due to its ability to provide a standardized assessment of essential skills necessary for success in legal education and the profession. This standardized measure is crucial in evaluating candidates from diverse academic and professional backgrounds, ensuring fairness and consistency in the admissions process.

One of the fundamental reasons for its importance is its standardized nature. Unlike undergraduate grades, which can vary significantly in rigor and evaluation standards across institutions, this test offers a uniform metric. This standardization helps admissions committees compare applicants on an equal footing, regardless of where they completed their undergraduate studies or what they majored in. This uniformity is essential for maintaining fairness in the highly competitive law school admissions process.

Numerous studies have demonstrated the reliability of this test as a predictor of first-year law school performance. This predictive validity is crucial for law schools as they seek to admit students who are likely to succeed academically. By assessing skills such as critical reading, analytical reasoning, and logical thinking, the test provides a clear indication of a candidate's ability to handle the demands of law school coursework. This ability to predict academic success makes the test an indispensable tool for law schools.

The test is designed to evaluate key skills that are essential for law school and legal practice. It measures a candidate's ability to read and understand complex texts, analyze and evaluate arguments, and develop coherent, persuasive written arguments. These skills are not only vital for succeeding in law school but are also fundamental to legal practice, where analyzing statutes, constructing arguments, and synthesizing large amounts of information are daily tasks. The focus on these critical skills ensures that candidates are well-prepared for the challenges they will face in their legal education and careers.

While this exam is a critical component of law school applications, it is typically considered alongside other factors such as undergraduate GPA, letters of recommendation, personal statements, and relevant work or life experiences. This holistic approach ensures that admissions committees get a well-rounded view of each candidate. However, the test often plays a decisive role, especially when comparing candidates with similar profiles. A strong score can set an applicant apart in a competitive pool, highlighting their readiness for the rigors of law school.

This assessment also serves to level the playing field among applicants. By providing a common measure, it allows students from less well-known institutions to demonstrate their abilities on the same stage as those from prestigious universities. This can be particularly advantageous for candidates who have excelled academically but may not have had the same opportunities or resources as their peers from more renowned schools. The test thus ensures that all candidates have an equal opportunity to showcase their potential.

Law schools use scores not only to assess individual candidates but also to make broader admissions decisions. Scores help schools maintain their accreditation standards, predict bar passage rates, and manage their admissions statistics to align with institutional goals. High median scores can enhance a law school's reputation and ranking, making the test scores a strategic tool in the admissions process.

Many law schools also use scores as a criterion for awarding scholarships and financial aid. High scores can make a candidate eligible for merit-based scholarships, significantly reducing the financial burden of law school. This incentive encourages students to invest time and effort into preparing for the test, further underscoring its importance.

In conclusion, the test is indispensable in the law school admissions process due to its standardization, predictive validity, and ability to assess essential skills. It ensures fairness, supports holistic admissions, and aids strategic decision-making within law schools. Performing well on this test can significantly enhance an applicant's prospects of admission and success in law school, making it a crucial step in the journey toward a legal career.

Changes to the LSAT Starting August 2024

Starting August 2024, the LSAT underwent a significant update that reflects both advancements in educational testing and a commitment to fairness for all test-takers. These changes are designed to better align the test with the skills required in law school while addressing concerns raised about the previous format.

One of the most notable changes is the removal of the Analytical Reasoning section, commonly known as logic games. This section has been replaced with a second Logical Reasoning section. The decision to eliminate logic games stems from extensive research and feedback indicating that the skills assessed by this section can be effectively measured through other parts of the test. Moreover, this change aims to ensure that the test is fair and accessible to all candidates, including those who found the diagramming aspect of logic games challenging.

The updated test now includes two scored Logical Reasoning sections, one scored Reading Comprehension section, and one unscored section that could be either Logical Reasoning or Reading Comprehension. The unscored section is used to pilot questions for future tests, ensuring that the exam remains current and valid. This new structure maintains the test's ability to assess critical reasoning and reading comprehension skills while providing a more balanced and comprehensive evaluation of a candidate's abilities.

The Logical Reasoning sections are designed to test a candidate's ability to analyze, evaluate, and complete arguments. These sections focus on assessing critical thinking skills, which are essential for success in law school. By having two Logical Reasoning sections, the test ensures that these crucial skills are thoroughly evaluated. This change also helps mitigate any potential disadvantage caused by the variability in individual section performance, providing a more reliable overall assessment.

The Reading Comprehension section remains a core component of the test, evaluating a candidate's ability to understand and analyze complex texts. This section includes a variety of passages on different topics, each followed by a series of questions. These questions test a range of skills, from basic comprehension to the ability to draw inferences and evaluate arguments. The retention of this section underscores the importance of strong reading skills in legal education and practice.

In addition to these changes, the test now features an updated scoring system. While the scoring range of 120 to 180 remains the same, the way scores are reported has been refined to provide more detailed feedback. This includes a breakdown of performance by section, helping candidates understand their strengths and areas for improvement. This transparency is designed to assist both test-takers and law schools in making informed decisions.

These changes were implemented after rigorous research and extensive consultation with educators, legal professionals, and disability advocates. The goal was to ensure that the test continues to provide a fair, valid, and reliable measure of the skills needed for success in law school. By removing the logic games and adding a second Logical Reasoning section, the test now offers a more balanced assessment that focuses on critical reasoning and reading comprehension.

Overall, the updates to the LSAT reflect a commitment to fairness and academic integrity. These changes ensure that the test remains a relevant and effective tool for law school admissions, accurately assessing the skills that are most important for future legal professionals. As candidates prepare for this new version of the test, they can be confident that it has been designed with their success in mind, providing a fair and comprehensive evaluation of their abilities.

Reasons for Removing the Logic Games Section

The decision to remove the Analytical Reasoning section, commonly known as the logic games, from the LSAT starting August 2024 was driven by several key factors aimed at improving fairness and accessibility while maintaining the test's effectiveness in assessing essential skills for law school. This change was not made lightly; it was the result of extensive research, feedback, and legal considerations.

One of the primary reasons for this change was to address accessibility concerns. In recent years, there have been growing discussions about the fairness of the logic games, especially for test-takers with visual impairments. The logic games section often required the ability to diagram and visualize spatial relationships, which could be particularly challenging for blind candidates or those with other disabilities that affect spatial reasoning. Although accommodations were available, they did not fully mitigate the inherent disadvantage faced by these individuals. By removing this section, the test aims to provide a more level playing field for all candidates, ensuring that no one is unfairly disadvantaged due to the format of a specific section.

The decision was also influenced by a settlement agreement with two blind individuals who argued that the logic games section was inherently unfair to those who could not use diagrams to solve the problems. This legal challenge highlighted the need for a more inclusive approach to testing that would allow all candidates to demonstrate their abilities without facing unnecessary obstacles. The removal of the logic games section reflects a commitment to fairness and equality, aligning the test with broader educational and legal standards that prioritize accessibility.

Extensive research was conducted to explore alternative methods for assessing the skills traditionally measured by the logic games. This research involved analyzing data from hundreds of thousands of test-takers and found that the skills assessed by the logic games could be effectively measured through other sections of the test, particularly the Logical Reasoning sections. By adding a second Logical Reasoning section, the test can still evaluate critical thinking, analytical reasoning, and deductive skills without relying on the diagrammatic nature of the logic games. This ensures that the test remains a robust and valid measure of the abilities necessary for success in law school.

Additionally, the decision to remove the logic games section was part of a broader effort to modernize the test and align it with current educational practices. The logic games, while valuable, were seen as a somewhat outdated method of assessment. Modern testing emphasizes skills that are more directly applicable to the practice of law, such as the ability to analyze complex texts, construct logical arguments, and understand nuanced reasoning. The updated test format, with its focus on Logical Reasoning and Reading Comprehension, is more reflective of the tasks and challenges faced by law students and legal professionals.

The change also benefits test-takers by simplifying the preparation process. With the removal of the logic games, candidates can focus their study efforts on developing strong reading and reasoning skills, which are directly applicable to both the test and their future legal careers. This streamlined approach to test preparation can help reduce anxiety and confusion, allowing candidates to perform at their best.

In conclusion, the removal of the logic games section from the LSAT was driven by a commitment to fairness, accessibility, and modern educational standards. By addressing accessibility concerns, responding to legal challenges, and aligning the test with the skills most relevant to law school and legal practice, this change ensures that the LSAT remains a valid, reliable, and inclusive tool for assessing the potential of future law students.

Impact on Test Preparation Strategies

The changes to the LSAT format starting August 2024 have significant implications for how prospective law students should approach their test preparation. With the removal of the logic games section and the introduction of an additional Logical Reasoning section, test-takers need to adjust their study strategies to align with the new structure and focus areas of the exam.

The elimination of the logic games section means that candidates no longer need to spend time mastering the diagramming techniques and more streamlined study plan focused on honing critical reading and logical reasoning abilities. spatial reasoning skills that were previously essential. This change allows for a Students can now redirect their preparation efforts towards developing a deeper understanding of argument structures, logical fallacies, and effective reasoning techniques, which are central to the Logical Reasoning sections.

Given that the test now includes two scored Logical Reasoning sections, it is crucial for candidates to prioritize this area in their study plans. Logical Reasoning questions assess the ability to analyze, evaluate, and complete arguments, skills that are fundamental to both the test and law school success. Effective preparation strategies include practicing with a wide range of logical reasoning questions, understanding common argument patterns, and learning to identify and avoid logical fallacies. Additionally, timed practice tests can help candidates build the stamina and pacing needed to perform well under exam conditions.

The Reading Comprehension section remains a significant component of the test, and its importance cannot be overstated. Candidates should continue to develop their ability to read and understand complex texts quickly and accurately. This involves practicing with diverse reading materials, including legal texts, scientific articles, and humanities passages, to become comfortable with different writing styles and topics. Active reading strategies, such as annotation, summarizing, and questioning, can enhance comprehension and retention of information.

With the addition of an unscored section that could be either Logical Reasoning or Reading Comprehension, candidates must be prepared for both types of questions throughout the test. This section is indistinguishable from the scored sections, so it is essential to approach every part of the exam with the same level of focus and effort. Consistent practice across all sections will ensure that candidates are well-prepared, regardless of the specific unscored section they encounter on test day.

The updated Argumentative Writing section also requires attention in preparation. Although it is not scored, the writing sample is sent to law schools as part of the application process. Candidates should practice writing clear, concise, and well-structured essays that present a coherent argument while addressing counterarguments and using evidence effectively. Understanding the common prompts and practicing under timed conditions can help build confidence and improve performance in this section.

Overall, the changes to the LSAT format necessitate a shift in preparation strategies towards a more focused and intensive practice of logical reasoning and reading comprehension skills. By adjusting their study plans to reflect the new structure, candidates can ensure they are fully prepared to excel in all aspects of the exam. Effective preparation now involves a balanced approach that prioritizes critical thinking, analytical reasoning, and comprehensive reading skills, all of which are crucial for success on the updated LSAT and in law school.

Test Structure: Breakdown of Test Sections

The LSAT is a carefully designed examination that evaluates the skills crucial for success in law school and the legal profession. The test comprises multiple sections, each targeting specific abilities that are essential for future legal professionals.

The core of the LSAT includes two Logical Reasoning sections. These sections are integral in assessing a candidate's ability to analyze, evaluate, and complete arguments. They cover a range of question types that require the test-taker to identify assumptions, evaluate evidence, and recognize logical flaws. Logical Reasoning questions are designed to mimic the kind of critical thinking and argumentation that law students and lawyers use in their work, making them a fundamental component of the exam.

In addition to Logical Reasoning, the test includes a Reading Comprehension section. This part of the exam evaluates a candidate's ability to read and understand complex texts. The passages in this section are drawn from various disciplines, including law, science, humanities, and social sciences, to ensure that candidates are well-rounded in their reading abilities. The questions following each passage test a range of skills, from basic comprehension to more complex analytical tasks, such as identifying the main idea, drawing inferences, and understanding the author's tone and purpose.

The LSAT also features an unscored section, which can be either Logical Reasoning or Reading Comprehension. This section is indistinguishable from the scored sections, ensuring that candidates approach it with the same level of seriousness. The unscored section is used to test new questions for future exams, helping to maintain the test's high standards and validity.

Another key component of the LSAT is the Argumentative Writing section. Although it is not scored, this section is an important part of the exam as it is sent to law schools as part of the candidate's application. The Argumentative Writing section presents a debatable issue and multiple perspectives on that issue. Candidates are required to take a position, construct a coherent argument, and address the various perspectives provided. This section assesses a candidate's ability to write persuasively and logically, skills that are essential for law school and legal practice.

Understanding the structure of the LSAT is crucial for effective preparation. Each section of the test is designed to evaluate different aspects of a candidate's abilities, from critical thinking and logical reasoning to reading comprehension and persuasive writing. By familiarizing themselves with the structure and purpose of each section, candidates can develop targeted study strategies that enhance their strengths and address their weaknesses.

The LSAT's structure is not arbitrary but is carefully crafted to reflect the skills needed for success in law school and beyond. Each section provides a unique lens through which to view a candidate's potential, offering law schools a comprehensive picture of an applicant's capabilities. This balanced approach ensures that the test remains a reliable and valid tool for law school admissions, helping to identify candidates who are well-prepared for the challenges of legal education and the legal profession.

Timing and Number of Questions

Understanding the timing and number of questions for each section of the test is crucial for effective preparation and time management during the exam. This aspect of the test requires strategic planning to ensure that candidates can complete each section within the allotted time while maintaining accuracy and clarity in their responses.

Each section of the test is timed, and candidates must work within these constraints to answer all questions. The Logical Reasoning sections are particularly demanding, as they require quick, critical thinking and the ability to analyze and evaluate arguments under time pressure. Each Logical Reasoning section consists of 24 to 26 questions, and candidates have 35 minutes to complete each section. This means that, on average, candidates have about 1.3 to 1.5 minutes per question. This tight timing necessitates not only a deep understanding of logical principles but also the ability to quickly identify key components of arguments and eliminate incorrect answer choices efficiently.

The Reading Comprehension section, also 35 minutes long, includes 26 to 28 questions based on multiple passages. This section challenges candidates to read complex texts and answer questions that test their comprehension, inference, and analytical skills. Given the length and complexity of the passages, time management is crucial. Candidates need to balance reading and understanding the passages with answering the questions accurately. Developing effective reading strategies, such as skimming for main ideas and annotating key points, can help manage the time constraints.

The unscored section, which can be either Logical Reasoning or Reading Comprehension, follows the same timing and structure as the scored sections. Although this section does not count towards the final score, it is essential to approach it with the same seriousness and efficiency as the scored sections, as it provides valuable practice and helps maintain a consistent pace throughout the exam.

The Argumentative Writing section, which is not timed in the same way as the multiple-choice sections, allows for 15 minutes of prewriting and 35 minutes of essay writing. During the prewriting period, candidates must analyze the given issue and the provided perspectives, plan their response, and organize their thoughts. The subsequent 35 minutes are dedicated to writing a coherent, persuasive essay. This section tests the ability to construct a well-reasoned argument and address counterarguments within a limited time frame.

Effective preparation for the exam involves familiarizing oneself with the timing and structure of each section. Practicing under timed conditions is essential to develop the pacing and endurance needed to perform well. Time management strategies, such as prioritizing easier questions, making educated guesses, and revisiting more challenging questions if time permits, can help maximize efficiency.

Furthermore, understanding the distribution of questions and the time allotted can help candidates allocate their study time effectively. Focusing on areas where they can improve speed and accuracy will contribute significantly to overall performance. Regular practice with full-length timed tests can simulate the actual exam experience, helping candidates build confidence and improve their ability to manage the pressures of test day.

Mastering the timing and number of questions for each section of the test is a critical component of effective preparation. By developing strategic approaches to time management and practicing under realistic conditions, candidates can enhance their performance and achieve their best possible scores.

Scoring System: How the LSAT is Scored

Understanding the scoring system is crucial for test-takers aiming to achieve their best performance. The scoring process is designed to provide a standardized measure of a candidate's abilities, ensuring fairness and consistency across all test administrations. Here's a detailed look at how the exam is scored and what each score represents.

The exam consists of multiple-choice sections: two scored Logical Reasoning sections, one scored Reading Comprehension section, and an unscored section that could be either Logical Reasoning or Reading Comprehension. Additionally, there is an Argumentative Writing section, which, although not scored, is sent to law schools as part of the application process.

Each multiple-choice question on the test is worth one point. There is no penalty for incorrect answers, so it is in the candidate's best interest to attempt every question. The raw score, which is the total number of questions answered correctly, is then converted to a scaled score ranging from 120 to 180. This scaling process is essential to ensure that scores are comparable across different test administrations, accounting for any variations in difficulty.

The conversion from raw score to scaled score is based on a statistical process called equating. Equating adjusts for minor differences in difficulty between different test forms. For example, a raw score of 75 might convert to a scaled score of 165 on one administration, but a slightly more challenging test might see the same raw score convert to a 167. This ensures that a score of 165 on one test has the same meaning as a 165 on another, regardless of the specific questions or their difficulty.

The scaled score is the primary score reported to law schools. It is used because it allows admissions committees to compare applicants accurately, even if they took the test at different times. The scaled score ranges from 120, the lowest possible score, to 180, the highest. Most candidates score between 140 and 160, with the median score typically around 150.

In addition to the scaled score, candidates receive a percentile rank. This rank indicates the percentage of test-takers who scored lower than a particular score. For example, a percentile rank of 90 means the candidate scored better than 90% of all test-takers. Percentile ranks are based on the scores from a pool of test-takers over the previous three testing years, providing a stable comparison.

The Argumentative Writing section is unique in that it is not scored numerically. Instead, this section is evaluated qualitatively by law school admissions committees. It provides a sample of the candidate's writing ability and reasoning skills in a context that simulates the type of written arguments required in law school. While it doesn't contribute to the numerical score, it is an important part of the application, offering schools insight into a candidate's ability to formulate coherent, persuasive arguments.

Understanding the scoring system helps candidates set realistic goals and interpret their scores effectively. A high score can significantly enhance a candidate's law school application, making a thorough understanding of the scoring process essential for strategic test preparation. Candidates should aim not only to maximize their raw scores but also to understand how these scores translate into scaled scores and percentile ranks, providing a comprehensive view of their performance relative to other test-takers.

The significance of these scores can vary depending on the law school. Highly competitive programs often look for scores in the upper 160s to 170s, while other programs may consider scores in the 150s to be strong. Understanding where a particular score falls within the score scale can help candidates gauge their competitiveness for their target schools.

By focusing on the critical components of the scoring system, candidates can better prepare for the exam, manage their expectations, and develop strategies to improve their scores. This knowledge empowers test-takers to approach the exam with confidence, knowing how their efforts translate into the scores that will ultimately be seen by law school admissions committees.

CHAPTER 2: Logical Reasoning Sections

Importance of Logical Reasoning in the LSAT

Logical Reasoning sections are a cornerstone of the LSAT, playing a crucial role in assessing the skills essential for law school and legal practice. These sections are designed to evaluate a candidate's ability to analyze, evaluate, and complete arguments, reflecting the critical thinking and analytical skills that are foundational to the study and practice of law.

One of the primary reasons for the importance of Logical Reasoning is its direct correlation with the skills used in legal practice. Lawyers must analyze complex arguments, identify strengths and weaknesses, and construct coherent, persuasive arguments. The Logical Reasoning sections mimic these real-world tasks, requiring test-takers to dissect short passages, identify assumptions, evaluate evidence, and draw logical conclusions. This direct application to legal tasks makes Logical Reasoning an invaluable component of the exam.

The sections assess a variety of reasoning skills that are critical for success in law school. These include identifying assumptions, recognizing logical flaws, evaluating the relevance and sufficiency of evidence, and determining the implications of given statements. By mastering these skills, candidates can demonstrate their ability to think critically and reason logically, both of which are vital for law school success.

Logical Reasoning also serves as a strong predictor of first-year law school performance. Numerous studies have shown that performance in these sections correlates highly with success in the first year of law school. This predictive validity is crucial for admissions committees, as it helps them identify candidates who are likely to excel academically. The ability to reason logically is essential for navigating the complex legal theories and cases that students will encounter in their coursework.

Furthermore, Logical Reasoning sections help level the playing field among applicants from diverse academic backgrounds. While undergraduate GPA can vary significantly in terms of rigor and grading standards across different institutions, Logical Reasoning provides a standardized measure that allows admissions committees to compare candidates more equitably. This standardization is essential for maintaining fairness in the competitive admissions process.

The design of these sections requires test-takers to engage in critical reading and analysis, which are skills that extend beyond law school into legal practice. Lawyers frequently need to read and interpret statutes, case law, and legal documents, all of which require a high level of analytical precision. Logical Reasoning questions train candidates in these areas, ensuring they are well-prepared for the demands of their future careers.

Additionally, preparing for Logical Reasoning sections helps develop general cognitive skills that are beneficial in many professional and academic contexts. These include critical thinking, problem-solving, and the ability to construct and deconstruct arguments. Such skills are not only crucial for legal practice but are also highly valued in other fields such as business, public policy, and academia.

Effective preparation for Logical Reasoning involves practicing with a variety of question types, developing a deep understanding of logical principles, and honing the ability to quickly identify and analyze key elements of arguments. By focusing on these areas, candidates can improve their performance and demonstrate their readiness for the challenges of law school.

These sections are essential to the exam because they assess critical skills directly applicable to law school and legal practice. They provide a standardized measure of a candidate's ability to think critically and reason logically, serving as a strong predictor of academic success and helping to ensure fairness in the admissions process. Mastery of Logical Reasoning is crucial for any prospective law student aiming to excel in their studies and future career.

Skills Assessed by Logical Reasoning

The Logical Reasoning sections are designed to evaluate a variety of critical thinking and analytical skills essential for success in law school and legal practice. These sections test an individual's ability to understand, analyze, and critically evaluate arguments, which are fundamental competencies for legal professionals.

One of the primary skills assessed is the ability to identify and understand arguments. This involves recognizing the main conclusion of an argument and the premises that support it. Candidates must discern the structure of the argument, distinguishing between evidence and assertions. This skill is crucial because legal professionals frequently need to parse complex arguments in statutes, case law, and legal briefs to understand their implications fully.

Another critical skill is evaluating the strength and validity of arguments. This requires test-takers to assess whether the premises provided logically support the conclusion. They must be able to identify any logical fallacies or weaknesses in the argument, such as assumptions that are not backed by evidence or conclusions that do not logically follow from the premises. Being adept at this skill helps in crafting stronger legal arguments and in identifying flaws in opposing arguments.

Candidates are also tested on their ability to identify assumptions within arguments. These are the unstated premises that must be true for the argument to hold. Recognizing these assumptions is vital because they often represent the weakest points in an argument. In legal practice, exposing or defending these assumptions can be pivotal in litigation and negotiation.

Detecting logical fallacies is another important skill evaluated. Logical fallacies are errors in reasoning that weaken arguments. Examples include ad hominem attacks, hasty generalizations, and false dilemmas. By identifying these fallacies, candidates demonstrate their ability to critically assess the integrity of arguments, an essential skill for constructing and deconstructing legal arguments.

The sections also measure the ability to draw valid inferences and conclusions from a set of premises. This involves understanding how different pieces of information relate to one another and what logically follows from them. In the context of law, this skill is crucial for interpreting statutes, case law, and evidence, and for making well-supported legal arguments.

Another key skill assessed is the ability to apply principles to new situations. This requires candidates to understand a general rule or principle and then apply it to a specific set of facts. This skill mirrors the legal practice of applying statutory or case law principles to the facts of a particular case, ensuring that the application is logical and consistent.

Moreover, test-takers must demonstrate their ability to compare arguments and identify similarities and differences in their logical structure and content. This comparative analysis is essential in legal reasoning, where lawyers often need to distinguish or analogize cases based on their facts and legal principles.

The ability to critically analyze complex texts is also tested. Candidates must read and comprehend dense, abstract material, which reflects the kind of reading required in law school and legal practice. This includes understanding nuanced arguments, recognizing subtleties in language, and grasping the implications of what is stated and what is left unsaid.

Overall, the Logical Reasoning sections assess a comprehensive set of skills that are foundational to legal education and practice. These skills enable candidates to think clearly, reason logically, and argue persuasively, ensuring they are well-prepared for the challenges of law school and their future careers in the legal field.

Identifying Argument Structures

Understanding how to identify argument structures is a crucial skill for those preparing for the LSAT, as it allows one to analyze and evaluate arguments effectively. Recognizing the components and framework of an argument is fundamental in assessing its validity and strength. Here, we delve into the key aspects of identifying these structures.

At the heart of any argument are its premises and conclusion. The conclusion is the main point the author is trying to prove, while the premises are the reasons provided to support this conclusion. Identifying the conclusion is the first step. It typically appears as a statement that the author wants you to accept, often signaled by words and phrases such as "therefore," "thus," "hence," "consequently," and "it follows that." Once the conclusion is identified, the premises can be recognized as the statements that provide the support for this conclusion. These are often introduced by words like "because," "since," "for," and "given that."

Understanding how these elements fit together involves recognizing the logical flow from premises to conclusion. This is the basic structure of an argument. For example, consider the argument: "All humans are mortal. Socrates is a human. Therefore, Socrates is mortal." Here, the premises are "All humans are mortal" and "Socrates is a human," leading logically to the conclusion "Socrates is mortal."

Beyond this simple structure, arguments can become more complex, incorporating multiple premises, sub-conclusions, and various forms of reasoning. Identifying these more complex structures involves looking at how different parts of the argument support each other. Sometimes, a premise supports an intermediate conclusion, which in turn supports the main conclusion. These intermediate conclusions, also known as sub-conclusions, act as both a premise for the main conclusion and a conclusion based on initial premises.

For instance, in a more complex argument: "Regular exercise leads to better health. Better health increases productivity at work. Therefore, regular exercise leads to increased productivity at work." The intermediate conclusion here is "Better health increases productivity at work," supported by the premise "Regular exercise leads to better health," and both together support the main conclusion.

Another important aspect of identifying argument structures is recognizing different types of reasoning. Deductive reasoning involves arguments where the conclusion necessarily follows from the premises. If the premises are true, the conclusion must be true. In contrast, inductive reasoning involves arguments where the premises provide some degree of support for the conclusion, but it is not guaranteed. The conclusion is likely but not certain based on the premises.

Identifying whether an argument uses deductive or inductive reasoning is crucial for evaluating its strength. Deductive arguments are evaluated based on their validity (whether the conclusion logically follows from the premises) and soundness (whether the premises are true). Inductive arguments are assessed based on the strength of the support the premises provide for the conclusion.

Another layer to consider is the identification of implicit assumptions or unstated premises. These are the underlying beliefs or statements that must be true for the argument to hold but are not explicitly stated. Recognizing these assumptions is critical, as they often represent the weakest points of an argument. If an implicit assumption is false or questionable, the argument's validity can be significantly undermined.

In practice, breaking down an argument involves carefully reading and dissecting each component, determining how each part relates to the others, and assessing the overall logical coherence. This systematic approach allows for a deeper understanding and more effective evaluation of the argument's strength and validity.

In conclusion, mastering the skill of identifying argument structures involves recognizing premises, conclusions, intermediate conclusions, and the types of reasoning used. It also requires an awareness of implicit assumptions. This comprehensive understanding enables a nuanced analysis and critique of arguments, a skill that is indispensable not only for the LSAT but also for legal education and practice.

Common Logical Fallacies

Logical fallacies are errors in reasoning that undermine the logic of an argument. Recognizing these fallacies is crucial for critically evaluating arguments and avoiding flawed reasoning in your own arguments. Here, we explore some of the most common logical fallacies.

One of the most frequent fallacies is the Ad Hominem fallacy, which occurs when an argument attacks a person's character rather than addressing the issue at hand. This is a diversion tactic that shifts the focus from the argument's validity to the individual's personal traits. For example, dismissing someone's argument on climate change because they are not a scientist does not address the actual merits of their argument.

Another prevalent fallacy is the Straw Man fallacy. This occurs when someone misrepresents an opponent's argument to make it easier to attack. By exaggerating, distorting, or outright fabricating someone else's position, the arguer creates an illusion of having refuted the original argument. For instance, if one argues that we should have more regulation on industry to protect the environment, a straw man response might be, "My opponent wants to shut down all factories and put everyone out of work," which misrepresents the original position.

The False Dilemma, or False Dichotomy, presents only two options when, in fact, more exist. This fallacy simplifies complex issues by reducing them to an either/or choice. For instance, "You are either with us, or you are against us" ignores the possibility of neutrality or alternative positions.

Slippery Slope is another common fallacy, which asserts that a relatively small first step leads to a chain of related events culminating in some significant (usually negative) effect. This assumes a drastic outcome without any evidence to support such inevitability. For example, "If we allow students to redo their assignments for a better grade, soon they will expect to pass classes without doing any work at all."

The Circular Argument, or Begging the Question, is when the conclusion is included in the premise. Instead of offering proof, the argument simply restates the conclusion in different words. An example would be, "We must trust the news because it is the most reliable source of information," where the reliability of the news is the conclusion being assumed as a given.

Hasty Generalization involves making a broad generalization based on a small or unrepresentative sample. This fallacy overlooks the diversity of data and leads to conclusions that are not statistically valid. For instance, concluding that all teenagers are irresponsible because a few you know are, is a hasty generalization.

The Red Herring fallacy introduces irrelevant information into an argument to distract from the actual issue. By diverting attention, it attempts to derail the discussion. An example is, "Why worry about environmental impacts from fracking when there are children starving in the world?" While the latter is a significant issue, it does not address the concerns about fracking.

Appeal to Authority misuses the respect people have for experts. While it is not fallacious to cite legitimate experts, it becomes fallacious when the person cited is not an authority in the field related to the argument. For instance, citing a famous actor's opinion on climate change policy does not hold the same weight as a climate scientist's research.

The Bandwagon fallacy, or Appeal to Popularity, suggests that something is true or correct because many people believe it. This fallacy assumes that popularity equates to validity. For example, "Everyone believes that this policy is beneficial, so it must be the right thing to do," does not provide actual evidence for the policy's effectiveness.

Recognizing these common fallacies can significantly enhance critical thinking and analytical skills. By understanding and identifying these errors in reasoning, one can more effectively evaluate arguments, avoid being misled by faulty logic, and construct stronger, more persuasive arguments. This skill set is not only vital for performing well on the LSAT but is also crucial for success in law school and legal practice, where clear, logical reasoning is paramount.

Types of Logical Reasoning Questions

The Logical Reasoning sections of the LSAT test various types of questions that assess a candidate's ability to analyze, evaluate, and complete arguments. Understanding these question types is crucial for developing effective strategies to tackle them efficiently.

One of the most common question types is Assumption questions. These questions require identifying an unstated premise that is necessary for the argument to hold. The ability to pinpoint what an argument relies on, but doesn't explicitly state, helps in understanding the underlying logic of the argument. For instance, if an argument concludes that a policy will succeed because a similar policy worked elsewhere, an assumption might be that the conditions in both places are comparable.

Strengthen and Weaken questions are also prominent. Strengthen questions ask you to choose an option that makes the argument more robust, while weaken questions require identifying a choice that undermines the argument. These types of questions test your ability to critically evaluate the impact of additional information on the argument's validity. For example, to strengthen an argument that a new law will reduce traffic accidents, you might choose evidence showing a similar law's success in another region. To weaken it, you might select data showing the law's ineffectiveness in a comparable scenario.

Inference questions ask you to deduce what must be true based on the given premises. These questions test your ability to draw logical conclusions from the information presented. Unlike assumption questions, which deal with unstated premises, inference questions focus on what directly follows from the stated information. For example, if given premises about demographic trends, you might be asked to infer a conclusion about future population changes.

Main Point questions require identifying the primary conclusion of the argument. This is a fundamental skill because understanding the main point is essential for analyzing the argument's structure. These questions often include distractors that might seem significant but do not represent the main conclusion. Recognizing the central thesis helps in avoiding these traps.

Flaw questions test your ability to identify errors in reasoning. These questions present arguments that contain logical fallacies or flawed logic and ask you to pinpoint these errors. Recognizing common logical fallacies, such as ad hominem attacks or false dichotomies, is key to mastering flaw questions. For example, if an argument incorrectly assumes that correlation implies causation, a flaw question would require identifying this mistake.

Principle questions involve applying a general rule or principle to a specific situation. These questions assess your ability to understand broad concepts and see how they apply in particular cases. For instance, a principle stating that "any law that infringes on individual freedoms is unjust" might be applied to determine whether a specific law is just.

Parallel Reasoning questions require you to identify an argument that is structurally similar to the one presented. This involves understanding the logical form of the argument and finding another argument that follows the same pattern. For instance, if an argument concludes that a particular outcome will happen based on a series of premises, a parallel reasoning question would ask you to find a different argument that uses the same logical structure to arrive at its conclusion.

Evaluation questions ask you to determine what information would be most useful in assessing the argument. These questions test your ability to identify gaps in the argument and understand what additional data would help in making a more informed judgment. For instance, if an argument relies on a study's results, an evaluation question might ask which aspect of the study needs further scrutiny to validate the argument.

Completing the Argument questions provide a partially completed argument and ask you to choose the best conclusion or next step. These questions test your ability to see the logical progression of an argument and understand what naturally follows from the given premises.

Mastering these question types involves not only understanding the specific skills each one tests but also developing strategies for efficiently tackling them. By familiarizing yourself with these types, you can approach the Logical Reasoning sections with greater confidence and precision, improving your overall performance on the test.

Approaches to Different Question Types

Approaching different question types in the Logical Reasoning sections requires tailored strategies to effectively analyze and answer each one. Understanding these approaches enhances your ability to tackle the questions efficiently and accurately.

For Assumption questions, start by identifying the conclusion and the premises. Look for any gaps between the premises and the conclusion—these gaps are where assumptions lie. An effective strategy is to use the "Negation Test." By negating the potential assumption and checking if the argument falls apart, you can confirm whether it is indeed necessary for the argument to hold.

When dealing with Strengthen and Weaken questions, focus on how new information impacts the argument. For strengthen questions, look for choices that provide additional support to the premises or reinforce the link between the premises and the conclusion. For weaken questions, identify options that introduce new evidence or highlight flaws in the argument. It helps to anticipate possible weaknesses or strengths before examining the answer choices.

Inference questions require drawing conclusions from given premises. Approach these by treating the premises as facts and determining what must be true based on them. Avoid extreme language in the answer choices, as correct inferences are typically conservative conclusions that can be directly supported by the given information.

For Main Point questions, distinguish between the primary conclusion and supporting information. Focus on the author's overall message rather than specific details. The correct answer will encapsulate the main argument without introducing new elements or distorting the original meaning.

Flaw questions involve identifying errors in reasoning. Familiarize yourself with common logical fallacies, such as ad hominem attacks, false dilemmas, and hasty generalizations. When analyzing the argument, pinpoint where it deviates from logical principles. The correct answer will clearly articulate this flaw.

In Principle questions, you need to apply a general rule to a specific situation. Understand the principle being stated and ensure that the chosen answer accurately applies it to the scenario presented. These questions often test your ability to abstractly think about how general rules govern particular cases.

Parallel Reasoning questions demand recognizing the logical structure of the argument and finding another argument with the same structure. Break down the argument into its core components (premises and conclusion) and look for answer choices that mirror this pattern. Ignore the subject matter and focus solely on the logical framework.

Evaluation questions ask you to determine what information would be most useful in assessing the argument. These questions test your ability to identify what's missing or what additional data would clarify the argument. Consider what kind of evidence would directly impact the argument's strength or validity.

For Completing the Argument questions, identify the logical flow of the argument and predict what comes next. The correct answer will logically extend the premises to the conclusion, maintaining coherence and logical consistency.

To master these question types, practice is key. Work on a variety of questions to become familiar with different argument structures and logical principles. Time yourself to build speed and ensure you can apply these strategies under test conditions. Regular review of explanations for both correct and incorrect answers will deepen your understanding and help you recognize patterns.

In summary, each question type in the Logical Reasoning sections demands a specific approach. By understanding and practicing these strategies, you can effectively navigate the complexities of the test, enhancing your critical thinking skills and improving your performance.

Tips for Eliminating Wrong Answers

When tackling the LSAT, one of the most effective strategies is to eliminate wrong answers. This approach not only narrows down your choices but also increases your chances of selecting the correct answer. Here are several tips to help you efficiently eliminate incorrect options.

Firstly, carefully read the question stem to understand exactly what is being asked. Misinterpreting the question can lead to confusion and mistakes. Once you have a clear grasp of the question, it's easier to recognize irrelevant or incorrect answers.

Next, focus on understanding the argument presented. Identify the conclusion and the premises supporting it. This foundational understanding helps you spot answers that do not align with the argument's logic or structure. For instance, if a question asks for an assumption, any answer that introduces new information or strays from the argument's core elements can be eliminated.

Look out for extreme language in the answer choices. Words like "always," "never," "all," or "none" often indicate answers that are too broad or absolute, which are rarely correct in logical reasoning questions. The LSAT typically favors more nuanced and moderate language. Therefore, answers with extreme statements are usually good candidates for elimination.

Another useful tactic is to identify answer choices that are too specific or too general compared to the argument's scope. If an argument makes a general statement, an answer choice that narrows it down too much is likely incorrect. Conversely, if the argument is specific, an overly broad answer is probably wrong.

Pay attention to answers that introduce completely new concepts not mentioned in the argument. These choices often serve as distractors, diverting your focus from the core issue. An answer must be directly related to the premises and conclusion to be correct.

For certain question types, such as weaken or strengthen questions, eliminate answers that have no impact on the argument. These neutral choices do not affect the argument's validity or strength, making them incorrect. Focus on how each option influences the argument, and discard those that leave it unchanged.

When dealing with complex wording or convoluted answer choices, simplify them. Break down complicated sentences into simpler terms to understand their true meaning. This simplification process can reveal whether the choice aligns with the argument or not.

Consider the relevance of each answer choice. Answers that go off on tangents or discuss aspects unrelated to the argument's main point are generally incorrect. Stay focused on the argument's primary issue and eliminate choices that divert from it.

Use the process of elimination actively. As you go through each choice, cross out those that are clearly wrong. This physical or mental act of eliminating wrong answers keeps you organized and helps avoid second-guessing.

Sometimes, two answer choices might seem correct. In such cases, compare them directly to see which one better addresses the question. Look for subtle differences and consider which choice more precisely aligns with the argument's logic.

Lastly, practice makes perfect. Regular practice with LSAT questions helps you become familiar with common distractors and improves your ability to quickly identify and eliminate wrong answers. Review explanations for both correct and incorrect choices to understand the reasoning behind them.

By applying these strategies, you can systematically eliminate wrong answers, narrowing your choices and enhancing your chances of selecting the correct answer. This methodical approach is key to improving accuracy and efficiency on the LSAT.

Common Pitfalls and How to Avoid Them

Preparing for the LSAT can be a daunting task, and many test-takers encounter common pitfalls that can hinder their performance. Understanding these pitfalls and knowing how to avoid them can make a significant difference in achieving a high score.

One of the most frequent mistakes is **inadequate time management**. The LSAT is a timed test, and each section has a strict time limit. Many candidates spend too much time on difficult questions, leaving less time for easier ones. To avoid this, practice pacing yourself during practice tests. Develop a strategy to move on if you're stuck on a question, and return to it if time permits. Regular timed practice can help you get a feel for the pacing required to complete each section effectively.

Another common issue is **misreading or misunderstanding questions**. The questions can be complex and often include subtle nuances. It's crucial to read each question carefully, paying close attention to the wording. Misinterpreting a single word can change the entire meaning of the question and lead to incorrect answers. Train yourself to read slowly and deliberately, especially under timed conditions, to ensure you fully understand what is being asked.

Overlooking details in the passages is another pitfall, particularly in the reading comprehension section. Many test-takers skims through the passages and miss key details. To avoid this, practice active reading techniques such as underlining or noting significant points in the margins. This helps in retaining crucial information and makes it easier to refer back to the text when answering questions.

Falling for trap answers is a common issue in multiple-choice tests. The LSAT is designed with distractor options that seem plausible but are incorrect. These options often include partial truths or common misconceptions. To avoid falling for these traps, practice critical analysis of each answer choice. Eliminate options that are clearly wrong first, and then scrutinize the remaining choices for subtle differences that align with the question stem.

Neglecting the importance of logical reasoning skills can be a significant hindrance. The test heavily emphasizes the ability to analyze and evaluate arguments. Many candidates focus too much on memorizing content rather than developing their reasoning skills. Engage in activities that enhance critical thinking, such as reading editorials, solving puzzles, or discussing complex topics. These practices help in honing the analytical skills required for the test.

Inconsistent study schedules can also be detrimental. Sporadic studying leads to uneven progress and retention. Establish a regular study routine and stick to it. Consistent practice over time is far more effective than cramming. Set specific goals for each study session and track your progress.

Ignoring the importance of review and reflection is another common mistake. Simply completing practice questions without reviewing mistakes leads to repeated errors. After each practice session, spend time reviewing incorrect answers and understanding why they were wrong. This reflection helps in identifying patterns in your mistakes and addressing them.

Underestimating the importance of mental and physical preparation can also affect performance. Stress and anxiety can significantly impact test performance. Incorporate stress-relief techniques such as exercise, meditation, or deep-breathing exercises into your routine. Ensure you get adequate sleep, especially in the days leading up to the test, and maintain a healthy diet to keep your mind sharp.

Failing to take full-length practice tests under realistic conditions can leave you unprepared for the endurance required on test day. Regularly taking full-length, timed practice tests helps build stamina and gives you a realistic sense of what to expect.

In conclusion, avoiding these common pitfalls involves strategic preparation, consistent practice, and self-awareness. By managing your time effectively, reading questions carefully, honing your reasoning skills, maintaining a consistent study schedule, and taking care of your mental and physical health, you can significantly improve your chances of achieving a high score on the LSAT.

Practice Drills with Detailed Explanations

Effective preparation for the LSAT involves extensive practice with various types of questions. Practice drills are crucial in this process, providing opportunities to apply learned strategies and improve critical thinking skills. Detailed explanations accompanying these drills offer insight into the reasoning behind each answer, deepening understanding and correcting misconceptions.

When working through practice drills, simulate real test conditions as closely as possible. Time yourself strictly to mirror the constraints you'll face on test day. This not only builds your time management skills but also helps you get accustomed to the pressure of the actual test environment. Set aside a quiet space, avoid distractions, and treat each practice session with the seriousness of the actual exam.

As you complete each drill, take detailed notes on your thought process. Record why you chose each answer and why you eliminated others. This reflective practice helps reinforce your understanding and makes it easier to identify patterns in your reasoning, both correct and incorrect.

For instance, let's consider a sample logical reasoning question:

Practice Prompt:

"Many studies have shown that people who exercise regularly have lower stress levels. Therefore, if companies provided time for exercise during work hours, their employees would experience less stress."

Question: Which of the following, if true, would most weaken the argument?

A) Regular exercise can sometimes lead to increased fatigue.
B) Employees are generally more productive when they are less stressed.
C) Many employees prefer to exercise outside of work hours.
D) The studies did not consider the effect of different types of exercise on stress levels.
E) Providing time for exercise during work hours could reduce the total number of hours employees work.

Answer: E) Providing time for exercise during work hours could reduce the total number of hours employees work.

Detailed Explanation:

This question asks you to identify the choice that most weakens the argument. The conclusion is that allowing time for exercise during work hours would reduce employee stress. To weaken this argument, you need to show that this intervention might not have the intended effect. Option E suggests that providing exercise time could reduce total work hours, potentially leading to negative consequences that might outweigh the benefits of reduced stress. This undermines the conclusion directly, making it the correct answer.

After finishing a set of questions, review each one thoroughly. For every question, whether you got it right or wrong, read the detailed explanation carefully. These explanations are invaluable—they reveal the logic behind the correct answer and explain why other choices are incorrect. Understanding the reasoning is more important than simply knowing the right answer.

Use these explanations to develop a checklist of common pitfalls and successful strategies. For instance, you might note that extreme language in answer choices is often a red flag, or that arguments with more than one logical flaw require careful parsing. Regularly review this checklist to keep these insights fresh in your mind.

In addition to individual question reviews, periodically analyze your overall performance. Look for trends in the types of questions you struggle with and those you excel at. This meta-analysis can inform your study plan, allowing you to allocate more time to areas needing improvement. For example, if you find that you consistently miss questions related to identifying logical fallacies, you can focus more practice on that specific skill.

Group study sessions can also be beneficial. Discussing questions and explanations with peers can provide new perspectives and insights. Teaching others what you've learned can reinforce your understanding and reveal gaps in your knowledge. Additionally, group sessions can introduce you to alternative strategies that might work better for you.

Finally, ensure that your practice includes regular full-length practice tests. These comprehensive drills help integrate all the skills you've developed and provide a more accurate measure of your readiness. After each full-length test, conduct a thorough review just as you would with shorter drills, analyzing both individual questions and your overall performance.

By incorporating diverse practice drills, simulating test conditions, taking detailed notes, thoroughly reviewing explanations, and regularly analyzing performance, you can effectively prepare for the LSAT. This disciplined and reflective approach to practice will enhance your critical thinking skills, improve your test-taking strategies, and ultimately boost your confidence and performance on test day.

CHAPTER 3: Reading Comprehension Section

Importance of Reading Comprehension in the LSAT

Reading comprehension is a crucial component of the LSAT, reflecting its fundamental importance in both legal education and practice. This section assesses a candidate's ability to read, understand, and analyze complex texts—skills that are essential for success in law school and the legal profession. The focus on reading comprehension is justified by the nature of legal work, which often involves interpreting dense and intricate documents, such as statutes, case law, and legal briefs.

One primary reason for the emphasis on reading comprehension is its role in developing critical thinking skills. Legal education and practice require the ability to understand nuanced arguments, identify underlying assumptions, and evaluate the validity of different points of view. This section of the test challenges candidates to dissect passages, understand the main ideas, and grasp the subtle implications of the text. Such skills are indispensable for law students, who must navigate a vast array of legal texts and develop well-reasoned arguments based on their readings.

Moreover, reading comprehension on the LSAT helps predict a candidate's academic performance in law school. Studies have shown a strong correlation between LSAT reading comprehension scores and first-year law school grades. This predictive validity underscores the importance of this skill in the legal academic setting. By performing well in this section, candidates demonstrate their readiness to handle the demanding reading and analytical tasks they will encounter in their courses.

The ability to read and comprehend complex texts also translates into effective communication, both written and oral. Lawyers must be adept at interpreting legal documents and conveying their analyses clearly and persuasively. Reading comprehension exercises train candidates to pay attention to detail, recognize the structure of arguments, and articulate their understanding accurately. These skills are crucial not only for academic success but also for professional competence in legal practice.

In addition, the reading comprehension section fosters a thorough and methodical approach to problem-solving. Legal problems often require sifting through vast amounts of information to find relevant facts and precedents. This section simulates this process by presenting candidates with lengthy and detailed passages on diverse topics, from humanities and social sciences to natural sciences and law. Candidates must learn to extract pertinent information quickly and accurately, a skill that is directly applicable to legal research and case preparation.

Furthermore, the variety of passages in the reading comprehension section exposes candidates to different writing styles and content areas. This diversity mirrors the multifaceted nature of legal practice, where lawyers must be prepared to engage with a broad range of subjects and perspectives. By tackling passages on unfamiliar topics, candidates develop the flexibility and adaptability needed to thrive in the dynamic field of law.

Preparation for the reading comprehension section also encourages disciplined study habits and time management. Given the time constraints of the LSAT, candidates must learn to read efficiently without sacrificing comprehension. This balance is critical in law school, where students are often required to digest large volumes of reading material within limited time frames. Practicing reading comprehension helps develop the stamina and concentration needed for sustained intellectual effort.

In conclusion, reading comprehension holds a place of paramount importance in the LSAT due to its role in developing critical thinking, predicting academic success, enhancing communication skills, fostering a methodical approach to problem-solving, and promoting flexibility in handling diverse topics. These attributes are essential for both legal education and practice, making this section a vital part of the LSAT. Candidates who excel in reading comprehension are well-positioned to meet the challenges of law school and to succeed in their future legal careers.

Different Types of Passages

In the LSAT's reading comprehension section, candidates encounter a variety of passages that test their ability to understand and analyze complex texts. These passages cover diverse topics, each designed to assess different aspects of reading and analytical skills. Understanding the types of passages you may encounter and developing strategies to approach them is crucial for success.

One common type of passage is the **humanities passage**. These passages often focus on topics related to literature, art, philosophy, and history. They typically require an understanding of the main ideas and themes, as well as the ability to interpret the author's tone and intent. For instance, a passage might discuss the impact of a particular literary movement on modern writing, requiring you to identify key influences and the author's perspective on the subject. Humanities passages often use sophisticated language and intricate arguments, demanding careful attention to detail and subtle nuances.

Another frequent type is the **social sciences passage**. These passages cover subjects like psychology, sociology, economics, and political science. They often present theories, research findings, or case studies, requiring you to evaluate evidence, understand research methods, and recognize implications. For example, a passage might explore the effects of social media on political engagement, asking you to analyze various studies and draw conclusions based on the presented data. Social sciences passages necessitate a keen ability to synthesize information from multiple sources and apply it to broader contexts.

The **natural sciences passage** is also a staple of the reading comprehension section. These passages deal with topics in biology, chemistry, physics, and environmental science. They typically present factual information, describe experiments, or explain scientific phenomena. You might encounter a passage detailing the process of photosynthesis, requiring you to understand complex biological processes and the implications of scientific findings. Natural sciences passages often include technical terminology and detailed descriptions, challenging you to comprehend and retain specific information accurately.

Legal and law-related passages are particularly relevant to the LSAT, given its focus on legal education. These passages may discuss legal principles, landmark cases, or issues in jurisprudence. They require an understanding of legal reasoning, the ability to follow complex arguments, and the skill to apply legal concepts to hypothetical situations. For instance, a passage might analyze a Supreme Court decision, asking you to evaluate the reasoning behind the judgment and its broader implications. Legal passages demand a precise reading of arguments and an ability to discern the logical flow of legal reasoning.

In addition to these broad categories, some passages may combine elements from multiple disciplines, presenting interdisciplinary topics that require a comprehensive approach. For example, a passage might discuss the economic impacts of climate change, integrating concepts from both natural sciences and social sciences. These interdisciplinary passages challenge you to draw connections between different fields and understand how various factors interplay.

When approaching different types of passages, it's essential to adjust your reading strategies accordingly. For humanities passages, focus on grasping the main ideas, themes, and author's intent. For social sciences, pay attention to the structure of arguments, the validity of evidence, and the conclusions drawn. For natural sciences, concentrate on understanding technical details and the implications of scientific findings. For legal passages, emphasize the logical structure of arguments and the application of legal principles.

Developing familiarity with these different types of passages through practice is crucial. Regularly reading diverse materials, such as scientific journals, legal opinions, and literary critiques, can help you build the skills needed to tackle each type effectively. Additionally, practicing active reading techniques, such as annotating the text, summarizing paragraphs, and questioning the author's arguments, can enhance your comprehension and retention.

The reading comprehension section of the LSAT includes a variety of passage types, each designed to assess different reading and analytical skills. By understanding the characteristics of humanities, social sciences, natural sciences, and legal passages, and adapting your reading strategies accordingly, you can improve your performance and approach this section with confidence.

Understanding Complex Texts

This is a critical skill, especially when preparing for the LSAT. Complex texts are characterized by dense information, sophisticated vocabulary, intricate arguments, and nuanced implications. To excel in reading comprehension, it's essential to develop strategies for navigating these challenging materials effectively.

First, it's important to **approach complex texts with a clear mind and focus**. Begin by previewing the text to get a general sense of its structure and main ideas. Skimming headings, subheadings, and any introductory or concluding paragraphs can provide a roadmap of the content. This preliminary scan helps in forming a mental framework for understanding the detailed information that follows.

While reading, **active engagement** with the text is crucial. This means interacting with the material rather than passively reading it. Annotate as you go along, underlining key points, highlighting unfamiliar terms, and jotting down brief notes or questions in the margins. These annotations serve as mental bookmarks, helping you to track the argument's flow and locate important sections quickly during review.

Breaking down sentences and paragraphs is another effective strategy. Complex texts often contain long, intricate sentences packed with information. Identify the subject, verb, and object in each sentence to simplify its structure. This grammatical parsing helps in understanding the main action or idea being conveyed. Similarly, summarize each paragraph in a few words to capture its essence. These summaries can then be linked together to form a cohesive understanding of the entire passage.

Pay close attention to **transitional words and phrases**. Words like "however," "therefore," "in contrast," and "additionally" signal changes in direction, conclusions, or the introduction of new points. Recognizing these cues can help in following the logical progression of arguments and understanding how different parts of the text are connected.

Contextual understanding is vital when dealing with complex texts. Many challenging readings assume a certain level of background knowledge. If you encounter unfamiliar concepts or references, take a moment to look them up. Understanding the broader context in which the text is situated can provide clarity and deepen your comprehension.

Developing critical thinking skills is also essential. Complex texts often present multiple viewpoints, implicit assumptions, and hidden implications. Question the author's motives, the evidence provided, and the conclusions drawn. Consider what might be missing or what counterarguments could be made. This analytical approach not only helps in understanding the text better but also prepares you for answering questions that test your ability to evaluate arguments critically.

Visualization techniques can be particularly useful. When reading descriptions of processes, scientific phenomena, or detailed scenarios, try to create a mental image of what is being described. Drawing diagrams or flowcharts can also aid in visualizing complex relationships and processes, making abstract concepts more concrete and easier to understand.

Another key aspect is **managing your reading speed**. While it might be tempting to rush through difficult passages to save time, it's more effective to read slowly and carefully. Speed reading techniques can be counterproductive when dealing with complex texts that require a deep level of comprehension. Instead, focus on thorough understanding, even if it means reading more slowly than usual.

After reading, **summarize the text in your own words**. This exercise forces you to process the information actively and ensures that you have a clear grasp of the main ideas and arguments. Summarizing also aids in retention and makes it easier to recall information during test preparation or when answering related questions.

Finally, **practice regularly with diverse and challenging materials**. The more you expose yourself to complex texts, the more comfortable you will become with their structure and style. Regular practice enhances your ability to parse intricate sentences, understand sophisticated arguments, and retain detailed information.

Understanding complex texts requires active engagement, critical thinking, and strategic reading techniques. By previewing, annotating, summarizing, and questioning the material, you can navigate even the most challenging passages with confidence and clarity. Regular practice and a disciplined approach to reading will strengthen these skills, making you well-prepared for the reading comprehension section of the LSAT and beyond.

Types of Questions Asked in Reading Comprehension

The reading comprehension section of the LSAT includes various types of questions that assess a candidate's ability to understand, analyze, and interpret complex texts. These questions test different skills and require distinct strategies to answer effectively. Familiarizing yourself with these question types and developing specific approaches for each can significantly improve your performance.

One common type is the **main idea question**. These questions ask you to identify the primary purpose or central theme of the passage. To answer effectively, focus on the overall argument or narrative presented. Begin by skimming the introduction and conclusion, as these sections often contain the thesis or summary. Look for repeated ideas or phrases emphasized throughout the text. Summarizing the passage in your own words before reviewing the answer choices can help solidify your understanding and pinpoint the main idea, ensuring a more accurate response.

Another frequent type is the **detail question**. These require you to locate specific information within the passage. They often use phrases like "according to the passage" or "the author states." To answer effectively, use keywords from the question to locate the relevant section. Skimming and scanning techniques are useful here. Quickly reviewing your annotations and underlined sections can help you find the relevant details. Once you find the information, read a few lines before and after the highlighted text to ensure contextual accuracy. Cross-check your findings with the answer choices to ensure accuracy.

Inference questions are another staple of reading comprehension, asking you to draw logical conclusions based on the provided information. These questions test your ability to read between the lines and understand implications, focusing on the author's tone, assumptions, and underlying themes. Since the answers are not directly stated, look for subtle hints and cues in the passage that suggest deeper meanings. It's essential to distinguish between what is directly stated and what is implied to accurately deduce the correct information.

Function questions ask about the role or purpose of a specific part of the passage, such as a paragraph or a sentence. To answer these, consider how the section contributes to the overall argument or narrative. Identify whether it introduces a new idea, provides evidence, counters an argument, or summarizes points. Understanding the passage's structure and the logical flow of arguments is crucial. These questions require you to determine how each part fits into the whole, making it essential to grasp the broader context of the passage.

Author's attitude or tone questions require you to determine the author's perspective or emotional stance towards the subject. Pay attention to descriptive language and subjective comments, as words conveying emotions, judgments, or biases are key indicators of tone. Understanding whether the tone is positive, negative, critical, enthusiastic, or neutral will guide you to the correct answer. Identifying these emotional cues helps accurately assess the author's perspective, which is crucial for answering these questions correctly.

Analogy questions ask you to compare situations, ideas, or arguments in the passage to other scenarios. They test your ability to recognize similarities in different contexts. To tackle them, break down the core elements of the comparison in the passage and match them to the most analogous choice. Focus on parallel structures and relationships rather than surface-level similarities. By understanding the underlying concepts and relationships, you can accurately identify the correct analogy and apply it to the given question.

Application questions, though less common, may appear in the reading comprehension section. They require you to apply information or concepts from the passage to new situations, assessing your ability to extend your understanding beyond the text. To answer these effectively, ensure a deep comprehension of the main ideas and arguments. Then, use this understanding to infer how the concepts would apply in different contexts. By thoroughly grasping the passage's key points, you can accurately apply the information to novel scenarios presented in these questions.

Weaken and strengthen questions evaluate your critical thinking by asking you to identify which statements would undermine or support the passage's arguments. These often appear in the context of scientific studies or logical arguments. To answer, determine the central claim and the supporting evidence, then assess how additional information would impact the argument's validity. By understanding the main argument and the evidence provided, you can accurately determine how new information would either weaken or strengthen the argument. This assessment is crucial for addressing these question types effectively.

Finally, **Global structure questions** ask about the organization and flow of the passage, requiring an understanding of how different parts of the text relate to each other. Identifying the main sections, their purposes, and transitions between ideas is essential. This holistic view of the passage helps in answering questions about its overall structure. By comprehending how various components fit together and contribute to the passage's argument or narrative, you can accurately address these questions and demonstrate a thorough understanding of the text's organization.

In summary, the reading comprehension section includes a variety of question types that test different aspects of understanding and analyzing texts. By recognizing these types and employing specific strategies for each, you can enhance your ability to answer them accurately and efficiently. Regular practice with diverse passages and question sets will further refine these skills, preparing you for success on the LSAT.

Speed Reading Tips

Speed reading can be a powerful tool when preparing for the LSAT, particularly for the reading comprehension section. The ability to read quickly while retaining comprehension can save valuable time and reduce stress during the exam. Here are several tips to help you enhance your speed-reading skills effectively.

First and foremost, practice active reading. This involves engaging with the text more interactively by asking questions, making predictions, and summarizing information as you go. Active reading keeps your mind focused and helps you process information more efficiently. Before you start reading, take a moment to preview the passage. Skim the introduction, headings, subheadings, and any highlighted or italicized text. This gives you a sense of the structure and main points, helping you anticipate the content and read more purposefully.

Another critical aspect of speed reading is minimizing sub vocalization, which is the habit of silently pronouncing each word as you read. This can significantly slow you down. Instead, try to see words as images or concepts. Practice reading blocks of words or entire phrases at a time, rather than focusing on individual words. This technique, known as chunking, allows you to process information more rapidly and improves your overall reading speed.

Eye movement also plays a crucial role in speed reading. Avoid fixating on each word and train your eyes to move smoothly across the page. Use a pointer, such as your finger or a pen, to guide your eyes and keep them moving steadily. This method, known as meta-guiding, can help reduce distractions and increase reading speed. Additionally, practice widening your peripheral vision to capture more words in a single glance. This technique enables you to read multiple words at once, further enhancing your reading efficiency.

Improving your reading speed also involves building a robust vocabulary. The more words you recognize instantly, the less time you spend decoding unfamiliar terms. Regularly practice with vocabulary-building exercises and familiarize yourself with common terminology used in the LSAT passages. This preparation will make you more comfortable and quicker at understanding complex texts.

Comprehension is just as important as speed. To ensure you retain the information you read quickly, practice summarizing paragraphs or sections in your own words. This reinforces your understanding and helps you recall key points more effectively. Additionally, after reading a passage, take a moment to review and mentally outline the main ideas and arguments. This reflection consolidates your comprehension and prepares you for answering related questions.

Using technology can also aid in improving your speed-reading skills. Several apps and online tools are designed to train your eyes and brain for faster reading. Programs like Spreeder and Spritz display text in a way that encourages rapid consumption and comprehension. Regular use of these tools can gradually increase your reading speed and confidence.

It's essential to practice speed reading regularly and track your progress. Set aside dedicated time each day to practice with various texts, gradually increasing the difficulty level. Measure your reading speed and comprehension accuracy to identify areas for improvement. Consistent practice will lead to gradual improvement in both speed and understanding.

Balancing speed with comprehension is the key to effective speed reading. It's not just about reading as fast as possible but ensuring that you fully grasp and retain the information. By incorporating these tips into your study routine, you can enhance your reading efficiency, better manage your time during the LSAT, and improve your overall performance on the exam.

Annotation and Note-taking Strategies

These skills help organize thoughts, retain key information, and enhance overall understanding of complex texts. Developing a systematic approach to annotating and taking notes can significantly improve performance on the exam.

One effective annotation strategy involves marking up the text as you read. This process starts with identifying the main idea of each paragraph and underlining or highlighting it.

Focus on key points, arguments, and evidence presented by the author. Highlighting keywords and phrases can help you quickly locate important information later. Use symbols or shorthand to denote important concepts, such as an asterisk for key points, a question mark for areas of confusion, or an exclamation point for surprising information.

Creating marginal notes is another crucial aspect of annotation. Writing brief summaries or comments in the margins helps reinforce understanding and recall. For example, if a paragraph presents an argument, note the main claim and supporting evidence in the margin. These notes serve as a quick reference when answering questions about the passage. Additionally, jotting down any questions or thoughts that arise while reading can aid in deeper comprehension and critical analysis.

Note-taking is equally important and complements annotation. Developing a structured system for organizing notes can greatly enhance your study sessions. One effective method is the Cornell Note-Taking System, which divides the page into three sections: a narrow left-hand column for cues or questions, a larger right-hand column for detailed notes, and a summary section at the bottom. This format encourages active engagement with the material and facilitates quick review.

When taking notes, focus on capturing the main ideas, supporting details, and any inferences or conclusions drawn by the author. Avoid transcribing large portions of text verbatim; instead, paraphrase the information in your own words. This practice aids in understanding and retention. Additionally, organizing notes by section or theme can help create a coherent summary of the passage, making it easier to review later.

Incorporating visual aids into your notes can also be beneficial. Diagrams, charts, and mind maps can help illustrate complex relationships and structures within the text. For instance, creating a flowchart to outline the progression of an argument or a Venn diagram to compare and contrast different perspectives can provide a clearer understanding of the material.

Reviewing and refining your notes regularly is crucial for retention. After completing a reading session, take a few minutes to review and organize your annotations and notes. Summarize the key points and arguments in a concise manner. This process reinforces what you have learned and helps identify any gaps in understanding that may need further attention.

Using digital tools can further enhance your annotation and note-taking practices. Applications like Evernote, OneNote, or Notion allow for organized, searchable notes and annotations. These tools often include features such as tagging, linking, and highlighting, which can streamline the study process and make it easier to manage large amounts of information.

Effective annotation and note-taking are not just about marking up the text but about engaging actively with the material. By developing a consistent approach to these practices, you can improve your comprehension and retention of complex texts, ultimately enhancing your performance on the LSAT. With diligent practice and refinement of these strategies, you will be better equipped to handle the demands of the reading comprehension section and achieve your desired score.

Practice Drills with Questions and Explanations

Effective practice drills are essential for mastering the reading comprehension section of the LSAT. Engaging in regular practice not only familiarizes you with the types of questions you'll encounter but also helps you refine your strategies and improve your accuracy. Here, we will explore practice drills with questions and detailed explanations to help you hone your skills.

To start, select a variety of passages covering different topics. This ensures exposure to a range of content and difficulty levels. For each passage, follow these steps:

1. **Read the Passage Carefully**: Begin by reading the passage thoroughly. Pay attention to the main ideas, supporting details, and the author's tone. Make annotations to highlight key points and summarize paragraphs in the margins.
2. **Answer the Questions**: After reading the passage, proceed to the questions. Attempt to answer each question based on your understanding of the passage. Avoid referring back to the text immediately; rely on your initial comprehension.
3. **Review and Refine**: Once you've answered all the questions, review each one carefully. Go back to the passage to verify your answers and understand any mistakes you made. This step is crucial for learning and improvement.

Practice Prompt with Detailed Explanation

Passage Example: Read the following passage and answer the questions that follow.

"The industrial revolution, which began in the late 18th century, marked a significant turning point in history. It transformed economies that had been based on agriculture and handicrafts into economies based on large-scale industry, mechanized manufacturing, and the factory system. New machines, new power sources, and new ways of organizing work made existing industries more productive and efficient. However, the industrial revolution also had a profound impact on the social, economic, and cultural conditions of the times. While it brought about significant technological advancements, it also led to harsh working conditions, environmental degradation, and social upheaval."

Question 1: What is the primary purpose of the passage?

A. To describe the technological advancements of the industrial revolution.
B. To highlight the social and economic impacts of the industrial revolution.
C. To explain the causes of the industrial revolution.
D. To discuss the agricultural practices before the industrial revolution.

Explanation: The primary purpose of the passage is to highlight the social and economic impacts of the industrial revolution. While the passage mentions technological advancements, the emphasis is on the broader changes and consequences. Thus, the correct answer is **B**.

Question 2: According to the passage, which of the following was NOT a result of the industrial revolution?

A. Increased productivity in existing industries.
B. Improved working conditions for factory workers.
C. Environmental degradation.
D. Social upheaval.

Explanation: The passage states that the industrial revolution led to harsh working conditions, environmental degradation, and social upheaval. It does not mention improved working conditions. Therefore, the correct answer is **B**.

Question 3: The author's tone in the passage can best be described as:

A. Neutral and informative.
B. Critical and pessimistic.
C. Enthusiastic and supportive.
D. Indifferent and uninterested.

Explanation: The author's tone is neutral and informative. The passage presents both the positive and negative aspects of the industrial revolution without showing bias. Thus, the correct answer is **A**.

Question 4: Which of the following can be inferred about the author's view on technological advancements during the industrial revolution?

A. The author believes they were entirely beneficial.
B. The author thinks they were mostly detrimental.
C. The author acknowledges both benefits and drawbacks.
D. The author is indifferent to their impacts.

Explanation: The author acknowledges both benefits (increased productivity and efficiency) and drawbacks (harsh working conditions, environmental degradation). Thus, the correct answer is **C**.

Creating Your Own Drills

1. **Select Diverse Passages**: Choose passages from various sources such as historical texts, scientific articles, and literary excerpts. This diversity helps in dealing with different writing styles and topics.
2. **Formulate Questions**: Develop a set of questions for each passage, including main idea, detail, inference, and tone questions. Ensure a mix of question types to cover all aspects of reading comprehension.
3. **Timed Practice**: Simulate test conditions by timing your practice sessions. This helps improve your speed and efficiency under exam conditions.
4. **Detailed Review**: After completing the practice, review each question and answer thoroughly. Understand the rationale behind correct answers and learn from any mistakes.

Regular practice with well-crafted drills and thorough explanations can significantly enhance your reading comprehension skills. By understanding the reasoning behind each question and answer, you can refine your strategies and approach the LSAT with confidence.

CHAPTER 4: LSAT Argumentative Writing

Purpose of the Argumentative Writing Section

The purpose of the Argumentative Writing section on the LSAT is to assess a candidate's ability to construct a coherent, logical, and persuasive argument. This section, which has been updated to better reflect the skills necessary for success in law school and legal practice, requires examinees to analyze a given issue, consider multiple perspectives, and articulate their own position clearly and effectively.

This section serves several important functions in the context of law school admissions. Firstly, it provides a standardized measure of a candidate's writing and reasoning abilities. Law schools seek students who can think critically and express their ideas clearly and persuasively, as these skills are crucial for success in legal education and practice. The Argumentative Writing section offers admissions committees a consistent and objective way to evaluate these abilities across all applicants, regardless of their undergraduate background or previous writing experience.

Secondly, this section simulates the kind of writing that law students and lawyers do regularly. Legal professionals must often construct arguments, address counterarguments, and support their positions with evidence. By asking candidates to engage in this type of writing, the test helps identify those who are well-prepared for the rigors of legal education and the demands of the profession. The ability to write a well-reasoned argument is not only vital for law school exams but also for tasks such as drafting legal briefs, memos, and court documents.

Moreover, the Argumentative Writing section encourages critical thinking and the ability to engage with complex issues. Candidates are presented with a debatable topic and must consider various viewpoints before articulating their own stance. This process of analyzing different perspectives and constructing a persuasive argument mirrors the kind of analytical thinking required in law school. It challenges test-takers to go beyond mere opinion and develop well-reasoned, evidence-based arguments.

Additionally, this section offers insight into a candidate's ability to handle pressure and manage time effectively. Test-takers must read, analyze, and write within a limited timeframe, which reflects the time-constrained environment of law school exams and the legal profession. The ability to think quickly, organize thoughts efficiently, and communicate effectively under pressure is a valuable skill that the Argumentative Writing section seeks to measure.

The updated format of this section, introduced in 2024, reflects a more holistic approach to assessing writing skills. Unlike the previous format, which was more narrowly focused on pure logical reasoning, the new Argumentative Writing section provides a clearer and more authentic writing purpose. Test-takers are given a debatable issue along with multiple perspectives that provide additional context. They must then draft an essay taking a position on the issue, while addressing some of the arguments and ideas presented by the other perspectives. This approach allows for a broader assessment of decision-making skills, rhetorical techniques, and evidentiary strategies.

The Argumentative Writing section is a critical component of the LSAT, designed to evaluate essential skills needed for law school and legal practice. It measures a candidate's ability to construct logical, coherent, and persuasive arguments, simulates the writing tasks common in the legal profession, encourages critical thinking, and assesses the ability to perform under pressure. By providing a standardized and objective measure of these skills, the Argumentative Writing section plays a vital role in the law school admissions process, helping to identify candidates who are well-prepared for the challenges of legal education and beyond.

Analyzing the Given Issue

Analyzing the given issue in the LSAT Argumentative Writing section requires a systematic approach to understand and engage with the topic thoroughly. This process involves several key steps: understanding the prompt, identifying the central issue, considering various perspectives, and formulating a clear, structured response.

First, carefully read the prompt to grasp the main question or issue presented. This initial step is crucial because it sets the foundation for your entire essay. Take note of any specific instructions or particular angles that the prompt emphasizes. Understanding the exact requirements will help you stay focused and relevant in your response.

Next, identify the central issue or debate. This usually involves pinpointing the main conflict or question at the heart of the prompt. Consider why this issue is significant and what broader implications it might have. By clarifying the core issue, you can ensure that your essay remains centered on the most important aspects of the topic.

Once you have identified the central issue, consider the various perspectives presented in the prompt. These perspectives offer different viewpoints on the issue and provide a basis for your analysis. Take the time to understand each perspective, noting the key arguments and evidence used to support them. This understanding will allow you to address these viewpoints effectively in your essay.

After considering the perspectives, begin formulating your own position on the issue. This involves developing a clear thesis statement that outlines your stance and provides a roadmap for your argument. Your thesis should be concise and specific, clearly indicating the position you will defend throughout your essay.

With your thesis in place, start constructing your argument by organizing your main points logically. Each paragraph should focus on a single idea or piece of evidence that supports your thesis. Begin each paragraph with a topic sentence that introduces the main point, followed by supporting details and examples. Use the perspectives provided in the prompt to enhance your argument, either by aligning them with your position or by addressing and refuting them.

When addressing opposing viewpoints, it's essential to engage with them respectfully and thoughtfully. Acknowledge the validity of these perspectives where appropriate, but also highlight their weaknesses or limitations. This balanced approach demonstrates critical thinking and shows that you have considered the issue from multiple angles.

Throughout your essay, use clear and precise language to articulate your ideas. Avoid vague or overly general statements, and ensure that each point you make is supported by specific evidence or examples. This clarity and specificity will make your argument more compelling and easier for the reader to follow.

In addition to constructing a solid argument, pay attention to the overall flow and coherence of your essay. Use transitional phrases and sentences to connect your ideas and ensure a smooth progression from one point to the next. This coherence helps maintain the reader's engagement and reinforces the logical structure of your argument.

Finally, conclude your essay by summarizing your main points and restating your thesis in a new light, considering the analysis you have provided. A strong conclusion reinforces your argument and leaves a lasting impression on the reader.

Analyzing the given issue in the LSAT Argumentative Writing section involves understanding the prompt, identifying the central issue, considering various perspectives, and constructing a clear, logical argument. By following these steps and maintaining a focus on clarity and coherence, you can effectively engage with the topic and demonstrate your analytical and writing skills.

Exploring Different Perspectives

Exploring different perspectives is a crucial aspect of the LSAT Argumentative Writing section. This process involves understanding various viewpoints on a given issue, analyzing their strengths and weaknesses, and using this analysis to construct a well-rounded and compelling argument. Engaging with multiple perspectives not only enriches your argument but also demonstrates your ability to think critically and empathetically.

To begin, carefully read the prompt and identify the different perspectives provided. These perspectives offer a range of viewpoints on the issue at hand, each backed by specific arguments and evidence. Take the time to thoroughly understand each perspective, noting the key points and underlying assumptions. This initial analysis sets the stage for a more in-depth exploration of the issue.

Next, evaluate the strengths and weaknesses of each perspective. Consider the evidence and reasoning used to support each viewpoint. Are the arguments logically sound? Is the evidence reliable and relevant? Identifying the strengths of a perspective helps you appreciate its validity, while recognizing its weaknesses allows you to critically engage with it. This balanced evaluation is essential for developing a nuanced understanding of the issue.

In addition to evaluating the arguments, consider the underlying values and assumptions of each perspective. Understanding these deeper elements provides insight into why individuals might hold certain views. For instance, one perspective might prioritize economic efficiency, while another might emphasize social justice. By acknowledging these values, you can better appreciate the motivations behind different viewpoints and address them more effectively in your argument.

As you analyze the perspectives, think about how they relate to each other. Are there common themes or points of agreement? Where do they diverge significantly? This comparative analysis helps you identify areas of overlap and conflict, which can be useful in constructing your argument. Highlighting these relationships demonstrates your ability to see the issue from multiple angles and integrate various viewpoints into a coherent discussion.

When formulating your argument, use the insights gained from exploring different perspectives to support your position. Refer to the strengths of perspectives that align with your argument, and address the weaknesses of opposing viewpoints. This approach not only strengthens your argument but also shows that you have considered the issue comprehensively. For example, if one perspective emphasizes the economic benefits of a policy, you might use this to support your argument if you also prioritize economic considerations. Conversely, if another perspective raises valid concerns about social impact, addressing these concerns in your argument demonstrates your ability to engage with counterarguments thoughtfully.

Moreover, incorporating different perspectives into your argument adds depth and complexity to your discussion. Rather than presenting a one-sided view, you create a more dynamic and persuasive argument by acknowledging and responding to various viewpoints. This approach reflects the kind of critical thinking and analytical skills valued in law school and legal practice, where understanding multiple sides of an issue is essential for effective advocacy and decision-making.

In writing your essay, ensure that each perspective is represented accurately and fairly. Misrepresenting or oversimplifying opposing viewpoints weakens your credibility and undermines your argument. Instead, strive for an honest and balanced portrayal of each perspective, even if you ultimately disagree with it. This integrity in your analysis builds trust with your reader and enhances the persuasiveness of your argument.

Exploring different perspectives is a fundamental aspect of the LSAT Argumentative Writing section. By understanding, evaluating, and integrating various viewpoints, you can construct a well-rounded and compelling argument. This process not only enriches your discussion but also demonstrates the critical thinking and analytical skills essential for success in law school and beyond. Engaging with multiple perspectives thoughtfully and respectfully is a key to mastering the Argumentative Writing section and excelling in your legal education and career.

Writing the Essay: Structuring Your Argument

Structuring your argument effectively is crucial when writing the essay for the LSAT's Argumentative Writing section. A clear, logical structure not only makes your argument more persuasive but also easier for the reader to follow. Here's a detailed guide on how to structure your argument to create a compelling and coherent essay.

Start with a strong introduction. This is where you set the stage for your argument. Begin by briefly introducing the topic and stating the issue at hand. Clearly articulate your thesis statement, which is the central argument or position you will be defending throughout your essay. Your thesis should be specific and concise, providing a clear roadmap for your essay. For example, if the prompt discusses whether a city should invest in public transportation or road infrastructure, your thesis might state that investing in public transportation is more beneficial for the city's long-term growth.

Following your introduction, develop your argument in the body paragraphs. Each paragraph should focus on a single point that supports your thesis. Start each paragraph with a topic sentence that clearly states the main idea of the paragraph. This helps the reader understand the direction of your argument and how each point connects to your overall thesis.

Provide evidence and examples to support each point. This is crucial for making your argument convincing. Use data, facts, and examples relevant to the issue to back up your claims. For instance, if arguing for public transportation, you might cite statistics showing reduced traffic congestion and pollution levels in cities with robust public transit systems. Ensure that your evidence is credible and directly related to the point you are making.

In addition to providing evidence, explain how it supports your thesis. Don't assume that the connection between your evidence and your argument is obvious. Clearly explain the relevance of each piece of evidence and how it strengthens your position. This analysis is where you demonstrate your critical thinking skills, showing that you can not only present information but also interpret and apply it effectively.

Address counterarguments to strengthen your essay further. Acknowledging opposing viewpoints shows that you have considered multiple sides of the issue and are not blindly advocating for your position. Identify potential objections to your argument and refute them with evidence and reasoning. This not only demonstrates thorough understanding but also reinforces the validity of your own argument. For example, if you acknowledge that road infrastructure is also important, you might counter by arguing that public transportation has a more significant overall impact on reducing urban congestion and pollution.

Use transitional phrases and sentences to ensure smooth flow between paragraphs and ideas. Transitions help guide the reader through your argument, making it easier to follow. Phrases like "furthermore," "in addition," "however," and "conversely" can signal shifts in your argument and connect your ideas logically.

Conclude your essay by summarizing your main points and restating your thesis in light of the evidence and analysis you've presented. The conclusion should reinforce the strength of your argument, leaving the reader with a clear understanding of your position and its justification. Avoid introducing new information in the conclusion; instead, focus on tying together the points you've already made.

Finally, ensure that your writing is clear and concise. Avoid unnecessary jargon or overly complex sentences that could confuse the reader. Clarity and precision are key to effective communication, especially in a persuasive essay.

In summary, structuring your argument in the LSAT's Argumentative Writing section involves starting with a strong introduction, developing body paragraphs that each focus on a single supporting point, providing clear evidence and explanations, addressing counterarguments, using transitions for coherence, and concluding with a powerful summary. This structured approach ensures that your essay is logical, persuasive, and easy to follow, demonstrating your ability to construct a well-reasoned argument.

Addressing Counterarguments

Addressing counterarguments is a critical component of constructing a persuasive and robust argumentative essay. It demonstrates your ability to consider and critically engage with opposing viewpoints, strengthening your overall position. To address counterarguments effectively, follow these guidelines:

First, acknowledge the counterarguments. This step shows that you have a comprehensive understanding of the issue and are not ignoring opposing views. Introducing counterarguments can be done with phrases like "Some may argue that..." or "A common objection is...". For instance, if your essay argues for increased public transportation funding, you might acknowledge that some believe investing in road infrastructure is more beneficial.

After acknowledging the counterarguments, clearly present them. Ensure that you represent these opposing views fairly and accurately. Misrepresenting or creating a straw man argument can weaken your essay, as it may appear that you cannot engage with the strongest points of the opposition. For example, state clearly that those who support road infrastructure investment argue it will reduce traffic congestion and boost economic growth in specific areas.

Next, critically evaluate the counterarguments. This involves examining the logic and evidence behind these opposing views. Point out any flaws, inconsistencies, or weaknesses in the arguments. For example, you could argue that while road infrastructure might reduce congestion in the short term, it is a less sustainable solution compared to public transportation, which offers long-term environmental and economic benefits.

Support your evaluation with evidence. Use data, statistics, expert opinions, or real-world examples to refute the counterarguments. This not only strengthens your rebuttal but also reinforces the credibility of your own position. If arguing against road infrastructure investment, you might cite studies showing that cities with robust public transit systems experience less pollution and traffic over time, compared to those that rely heavily on road infrastructure.

Explain why your position remains stronger despite the counterarguments. Emphasize the benefits and strengths of your argument, highlighting why it is more convincing and beneficial in the context of the issue. For instance, reiterate that public transportation not only addresses congestion and environmental concerns but also promotes greater social equity by providing affordable mobility options to all residents.

Integrate the counterarguments and your responses smoothly into your essay. Use transitions to connect these sections logically, ensuring a coherent flow of ideas. Phrases like "However," "Nevertheless," or "Despite these arguments" can help to seamlessly integrate your rebuttal into the overall structure of your essay.

Finally, ensure that addressing counterarguments does not overshadow your main argument. While it is important to engage with opposing views, your essay should remain focused on defending your thesis. Balance the discussion of counterarguments with a strong emphasis on your own points and supporting evidence.

Addressing counterarguments involves acknowledging opposing views, presenting them accurately, critically evaluating their merits, supporting your evaluation with evidence, and reinforcing the strengths of your own argument. This approach not only demonstrates critical thinking and fairness but also enhances the persuasiveness and robustness of your essay. Engaging with counterarguments thoughtfully and respectfully ensures that your position is well-rounded and compelling, ultimately leading to a more convincing argument.

Effective Use of Evidence

Effective use of evidence is crucial in constructing a compelling argumentative essay. Evidence provides the backbone for your claims, lending credibility and support to your arguments. To use evidence effectively, one must consider several key strategies that enhance the strength and persuasiveness of the essay.

Firstly, selecting relevant evidence is essential. The evidence should directly support the claim you are making. Whether it's statistics, expert opinions, research findings, or real-world examples, ensure that it is pertinent to the argument. Irrelevant or tangential evidence can confuse the reader and weaken your position. For example, if you are arguing for the benefits of renewable energy, citing data on the efficiency and cost-effectiveness of solar panels would be more relevant than discussing general environmental issues.

Once relevant evidence is selected, it's important to integrate it smoothly into your writing. Evidence should be woven into your argument rather than presented as an isolated fact. This involves explaining how the evidence supports your claim. Simply presenting a statistic or a quote without context or explanation leaves the reader to make the connection themselves, which may not always be clear. For instance, after presenting a statistic on the reduction of carbon emissions due to renewable energy, you should explain how this supports the broader argument about the environmental benefits of renewable energy sources.

Using a variety of evidence types strengthens your argument by showing a well-rounded understanding of the topic. Different types of evidence, such as quantitative data, qualitative anecdotes, and authoritative quotes, provide multiple angles of support for your claims. This variety not only makes your argument more robust but also more interesting to the reader. For example, a balanced argument for renewable energy might include statistical data on energy output, testimonials from communities benefiting from renewable projects, and quotes from experts in environmental science.

Proper citation of evidence is another crucial aspect. Crediting your sources not only avoids plagiarism but also enhances your credibility. It shows that your arguments are grounded in research and respected authorities. When citing sources, be sure to follow the appropriate citation style as required. Additionally, ensure that your sources are reliable and current. Using outdated or dubious sources can undermine the credibility of your entire essay.

Addressing potential counterarguments with evidence further strengthens your position. By acknowledging opposing viewpoints and using evidence to refute them, you demonstrate critical thinking and a comprehensive understanding of the issue. For example, if there is a counterargument that renewable energy is too expensive, you could present recent data showing the decreasing costs of renewable technologies and their long-term economic benefits.

Moreover, it's important to analyze and interpret the evidence rather than just presenting it. Critical analysis involves discussing the implications of the evidence, drawing connections between different pieces of evidence, and explaining how it fits into the overall argument. This deeper engagement with the evidence shows a higher level of understanding and helps to persuade the reader more effectively.

Avoiding overreliance on a single source or type of evidence is also vital. Relying too heavily on one source can create a biased perspective. Instead, draw from a range of sources to provide a balanced and comprehensive argument. This approach not only enhances the credibility of your essay but also demonstrates your ability to synthesize information from various perspectives.

Effective use of evidence is about more than just including facts and figures in your essay. It involves selecting relevant evidence, integrating it smoothly, using a variety of sources, properly citing them, addressing counterarguments, analyzing and interpreting the evidence, and avoiding overreliance on a single type. By mastering these strategies, you can construct a compelling and persuasive argument that is well-supported and credible.

Practice Exercises: Sample Prompts and Essays

Engaging in practice exercises is crucial for excelling in the LSAT's argumentative writing section. By working with sample prompts and crafting well-structured essays, you develop the skills needed to present clear, logical, and persuasive arguments. Here's a detailed guide on how to approach these exercises effectively.

Sample Prompt Analysis

Prompt: "Governments should prioritize renewable energy sources over fossil fuels to address climate change. Discuss the extent to which you agree or disagree with this statement. Support your position with reasons and examples from your own experience, observations, or reading."

Understanding the Prompt

Start by thoroughly understanding the prompt. Identify the key issue: whether governments should prioritize renewable energy sources over fossil fuels. Note that you need to discuss both sides of the argument and support your position with concrete examples.

Brainstorming and Planning

Before writing, spend a few minutes brainstorming. Consider the benefits of renewable energy: reduced greenhouse gas emissions, sustainability, and energy security. Contrast these with the advantages of fossil fuels: current infrastructure, economic benefits, and reliability.

Create an outline to organize your thoughts. Your essay should have a clear introduction, body paragraphs for each main point, and a conclusion. For instance:

- **Introduction:** Introduce the topic and state your thesis.
- **Body Paragraph 1:** Benefits of renewable energy.
- **Body Paragraph 2:** Advantages of fossil fuels.
- **Body Paragraph 3:** Addressing counterarguments.
- **Conclusion:** Reinforce your thesis and summarize key points.

Writing the Essay

Introduction:

"Climate change is a pressing global issue that requires immediate and sustained action. While some argue that fossil fuels remain essential for economic stability, I believe that governments should prioritize renewable energy sources. By reducing greenhouse gas emissions, promoting sustainability, and ensuring long-term energy security, renewable energy is crucial for addressing climate change."

Body Paragraphs:

Benefits of Renewable Energy:

"Firstly, renewable energy significantly reduces greenhouse gas emissions, which are the primary cause of global warming. For instance, wind and solar power generate electricity without emitting carbon dioxide. This shift towards cleaner energy sources is essential for mitigating the adverse effects of climate change. Moreover, renewable energy promotes sustainability. Unlike fossil fuels, which are finite, renewable sources such as wind, solar, and hydro are abundant and can be replenished naturally. This ensures a continuous supply of energy for future generations."

Advantages of Fossil Fuels:

"On the other hand, fossil fuels currently play a critical role in the global economy. The existing infrastructure for oil, coal, and natural gas is extensive and well-developed, providing reliable energy supply. Fossil fuels also contribute significantly to economic growth and job creation, particularly in industries related to extraction, refining, and distribution. For example, many regions depend on coal mining and oil drilling for employment and revenue."

Addressing Counterarguments:

"However, the long-term environmental and economic costs of fossil fuels outweigh their short-term benefits. While transitioning to renewable energy may require substantial initial investments, the long-term savings from reduced health costs due to pollution and the avoidance of climate-related damages justify these expenses. Additionally, advancements in technology are making renewable energy more cost-effective and reliable. Countries like Germany and Denmark have successfully integrated a high percentage of renewables into their energy mix, demonstrating that a transition is feasible."

Conclusion:

"In conclusion, while fossil fuels have historically driven economic growth and development, the urgent need to address climate change necessitates a shift towards renewable energy sources. By reducing greenhouse gas emissions, promoting sustainability, and ensuring energy security, renewable energy presents a viable solution for the future. Governments should, therefore, prioritize the development and implementation of renewable energy policies to safeguard the planet for future generations."

Review and Revision

After writing, take time to review and revise your essay. Check for clarity, coherence, and logical flow. Ensure your evidence supports your thesis and that you have addressed counterarguments effectively. Look for grammatical errors and awkward phrasing.

Practicing Regularly

Engaging with multiple prompts will improve your ability to think critically and articulate your arguments. Regular practice helps you become familiar with various topics and refine your writing style.

By consistently working on practice prompts and reviewing model essays, you can develop the skills needed to excel in the argumentative writing section of the LSAT. This approach not only prepares you for the test but also enhances your overall ability to construct and defend arguments, a crucial skill in legal education and practice.

Detailed Feedback and Critique

Providing detailed feedback and critique is an essential part of improving writing skills, particularly for those preparing for the LSAT's argumentative writing section. Constructive criticism helps identify strengths and weaknesses, guiding students to refine their arguments, structure, and overall writing style. Here's a comprehensive approach to offering effective feedback and critique:

Clarity and Focus

First, assess the clarity and focus of the essay. An effective argument must have a clear thesis statement that directly addresses the prompt. Examine whether the writer has clearly stated their position and maintained focus throughout the essay. Any deviations from the main argument should be noted, as they can confuse the reader and weaken the overall impact.

Example Feedback: "Your thesis is clear and directly answers the prompt, which provides a strong foundation for your essay. However, in the third paragraph, the discussion about renewable energy subsidies seems tangential. Consider tightening this section to maintain focus on your main argument."

Structure and Organization

Evaluate the structure of the essay. A well-organized essay should have a logical flow, with each paragraph transitioning smoothly to the next. Check for a clear introduction, body, and conclusion. Each body paragraph should have a single main idea, supported by evidence, and contribute to the overall argument.

Example Feedback: "The structure of your essay is generally strong, with clear transitions between paragraphs. However, the second paragraph introduces a counterargument without first establishing your main points. Rearranging this to follow the initial argument would strengthen the flow."

Argument Development

Assess how well the writer develops their argument. This includes the use of evidence, examples, and reasoning to support their thesis. Strong arguments are built on relevant and credible evidence that directly supports the writer's position.

Example Feedback: "Your argument is compelling and supported by relevant examples, particularly the case study on Germany's renewable energy policies. To enhance your argument further, consider providing additional data or statistics to back up your points about the economic benefits of renewable energy."

Addressing Counterarguments

A critical component of a strong argumentative essay is the ability to address and refute counterarguments. This demonstrates the writer's understanding of the topic and their ability to engage with opposing viewpoints.

Example Feedback: "You effectively acknowledge and refute the counterargument about the reliability of fossil fuels. This strengthens your essay by showing you have considered multiple perspectives. However, the rebuttal could be more detailed, perhaps by including more evidence on advancements in renewable energy technology."

Style and Tone

Review the style and tone of the essay. The writing should be formal and academic, avoiding colloquial language. The tone should be confident but not aggressive, and the language should be precise and concise.

Example Feedback: "Your writing style is appropriate for an academic essay, and you maintain a formal tone throughout. Be mindful of overly complex sentences, which can obscure your argument. Simplifying some of these will enhance readability."

Grammar and Syntax

Finally, check for grammatical errors, punctuation mistakes, and syntactical issues. These can distract from the content and undermine the writer's credibility.

Example Feedback: "There are a few grammatical errors, particularly with subject-verb agreement in the second paragraph. Proofreading for these mistakes will help improve the overall quality of your essay."

Overall Evaluation

Summarize the overall strengths and areas for improvement in the essay. Highlight what the writer did well and provide specific suggestions for improvement.

Example Feedback: "Overall, your essay presents a well-structured and persuasive argument for prioritizing renewable energy. Your use of evidence is strong, and you effectively address counterarguments. Focus on maintaining clarity and conciseness, and watch out for minor grammatical errors. With these adjustments, your essay will be even more compelling."

Providing detailed feedback and critique involves a balance of praise and constructive criticism. By focusing on clarity, structure, argument development, counterarguments, style, tone, and grammar, you can offer comprehensive guidance that helps writers improve their skills and prepare effectively for the LSAT's argumentative writing section.

CHAPTER 5: Creating an Effective Study Plan

Assessing your starting point: taking a diagnostic test

Creating an effective study plan for the LSAT begins with accurately assessing your current skill level. The best way to do this is by taking a diagnostic test. This initial step is crucial as it provides a clear baseline of your strengths and weaknesses, allowing you to tailor your study plan to your specific needs.

When you take a diagnostic test, it's important to simulate actual test conditions as closely as possible. This means setting aside a quiet space, allotting the full time for each section, and minimizing interruptions. Treat this test seriously, as if it were the real exam. The goal is to gauge your performance under conditions similar to those you'll face on test day.

Upon completing the diagnostic test, review your results thoroughly. Look beyond the overall score to see how you performed in each section. This breakdown will highlight which areas require the most attention. For instance, if you scored well in logical reasoning but poorly in reading comprehension, your study plan should allocate more time to improving your reading comprehension skills.

Analyzing your performance in each section involves more than just noting your raw scores. Examine the types of questions you missed and try to identify patterns. Are you consistently missing inference questions in the logical reasoning section? Do specific types of passages in the reading comprehension section trip you up? Understanding these patterns can provide deeper insights into the areas you need to focus on.

In addition to reviewing incorrect answers, take time to analyze the questions you got right. Understanding why you chose the correct answers can reinforce effective strategies and help you replicate your success in future practice. This dual approach of analyzing both strengths and weaknesses will provide a comprehensive understanding of your current abilities.

It's also beneficial to assess your test-taking strategies during the diagnostic test. Did you manage your time effectively? Were there sections where you felt rushed or sections where you had extra time? Effective time management is a critical component of success on the LSAT, and identifying issues early allows you to address them in your study plan.

After you've analyzed your diagnostic test, set specific, measurable goals for improvement. These goals should be realistic and achievable, based on your initial performance. For example, if you scored a 150 on your diagnostic test, setting a goal to achieve a 160 after three months of study might be a realistic target. Breaking down these goals into smaller milestones can also help track your progress and keep you motivated.

Incorporate a variety of study materials and methods in your plan. Use LSAT prep books, online resources, and practice questions to address your weak areas. Regularly timed practice tests will help you monitor your progress and adjust your study plan as needed. Remember to review each practice test thoroughly, just as you did with your diagnostic test.

Finally, consider seeking additional help if needed. This could include joining a study group, hiring a tutor, or enrolling in an LSAT prep course. These resources can provide structured guidance and additional strategies to help you improve.

Taking a diagnostic test is the first crucial step in creating an effective LSAT study plan. It provides a baseline from which to measure progress and identifies specific areas that need improvement. By thoroughly analyzing your performance, setting realistic goals, and using a variety of study methods, you can develop a tailored study plan that maximizes your chances of success on the LSAT.

Analyzing your initial score

This process involves a detailed review of your performance to identify strengths, weaknesses and areas needing improvement. By understanding your initial score, you can tailor your preparation to address specific gaps and enhance your overall performance.

Start by breaking down your score into its component parts. The LSAT comprises multiple sections, each assessing different skills: logical reasoning, reading comprehension, and, starting August 2024, argumentative writing. Review your performance in each section individually. Note the raw score and percentile rank for each, as this will give you a clear picture of where you stand relative to other test-takers.

Pay particular attention to the logical reasoning sections, as they now constitute a significant portion of the exam. These sections test your ability to analyze and evaluate arguments, a critical skill for law school. Look at the types of questions you struggled with the most. Were they questions about identifying assumptions, drawing inferences, or evaluating the validity of arguments? Understanding the specific challenges, you faced can help you focus your study efforts on these areas.

For the reading comprehension section, evaluate your ability to understand and analyze complex texts. Note which passages were more challenging. Was it the scientific texts, legal arguments, or humanities-based passages? Determine if your difficulties were due to the content of the passages or the types of questions asked, such as main idea, inference, or detail questions. This will help you develop strategies to improve your comprehension and analysis skills.

With the new argumentative writing section, assess how well you constructed your essay. Review the clarity and coherence of your argument, the strength of your evidence, and your ability to address counterarguments. This section tests your ability to write persuasively, so consider how effectively you communicated your position and supported it with logical reasoning.

In addition to reviewing your scores and question types, analyze your test-taking strategies. Reflect on your time management. Did you feel rushed in certain sections? Did you spend too much time on difficult questions at the expense of easier ones? Effective time management is crucial for maximizing your score, so identify areas where you can improve your pacing.

Consider the psychological aspects of your performance as well. Were there moments when anxiety or stress impacted your ability to concentrate? Developing techniques to manage test anxiety, such as mindfulness or breathing exercises, can be beneficial for maintaining focus during the exam.

Based on your analysis, set specific, achievable goals for improvement. If you scored lower in logical reasoning, aim to increase your accuracy in this section by a certain percentage. If reading comprehension was a weak point, set a goal to improve your understanding and analysis of complex texts. For the writing section, focus on enhancing your ability to construct clear and persuasive arguments.

Incorporate a variety of study materials and methods into your plan. Use LSAT prep books, online resources, and practice questions to target your weak areas. Regularly timed practice tests will help you monitor your progress and adjust your study plan as needed. Reviewing each practice test thoroughly, as you did with your diagnostic test, is crucial for continuous improvement.

Finally, seek additional help if necessary. Join a study group, hire a tutor, or enroll in an LSAT prep course to gain structured guidance and additional strategies. These resources can provide valuable insights and support to help you achieve your goals.

By thoroughly analyzing your initial score, you can develop a focused and effective study plan that addresses your specific needs, ultimately enhancing your performance on the LSAT and increasing your chances of success in law school admissions.

Setting realistic short-term and long-term goals

Goals help maintain focus, measure progress, and stay motivated throughout the study process. To set these goals effectively, it's important to understand what you aim to achieve and how to balance ambition with practicality.

Begin by establishing your long-term goal. This is typically your target LSAT score, which should align with the admission requirements of your preferred law schools. Research the median LSAT scores of these institutions to set a realistic and achievable target. For instance, if the median score for your top-choice school is 165, aim slightly above that to increase your competitiveness. This long-term goal provides a clear endpoint and helps shape your overall study plan.

Once the long-term goal is clear, break it down into manageable short-term goals. These smaller, incremental objectives act as stepping stones toward your ultimate target and make the preparation process less overwhelming. Short-term goals could include improving your score on individual sections, mastering specific question types, or consistently meeting practice test benchmarks.

A practical approach to setting short-term goals is to start with a diagnostic test to assess your current level. Based on this initial score, create a timeline that outlines gradual improvements. For example, if your diagnostic score is 150 and your target is 165, aim to increase your score by 3-5 points every month. This gradual progression helps maintain steady improvement without causing burnout or frustration.

Incorporate specific, measurable actions into your short-term goals. Instead of vaguely aiming to "study more," set concrete tasks such as completing a certain number of practice questions daily, reviewing a specific number of logical reasoning passages weekly, or writing and critiquing an argumentative essay bi-weekly. These specific tasks help track your progress and ensure that each study session is productive.

Balancing study with other commitments is crucial. Many LSAT candidates juggle work, school, or family responsibilities. Therefore, it's essential to set realistic goals that fit into your daily schedule. Allocate consistent, dedicated study time each day, even if it's just an hour or two. Consistency is key to gradual improvement.

Flexibility is also important when setting goals. While having a structured plan is beneficial, it's equally important to adapt if you find certain areas more challenging than expected. For instance, if you struggle with reading comprehension more than anticipated, adjust your goals to allocate additional time and resources to this section. Regularly reviewing and adjusting your goals ensures they remain aligned with your progress and needs.

Moreover, incorporate a mix of study activities to keep the preparation process engaging. Alternate between practice tests, individual question drills, and review sessions. This variety helps maintain interest and addresses different aspects of your test-taking skills.

In addition to academic goals, consider setting personal goals to manage stress and maintain a healthy balance. Regular exercise, adequate sleep, and relaxation techniques are vital for sustaining long-term study efforts. Goals related to physical and mental well-being can enhance your overall performance and resilience.

Tracking progress is another vital component. Maintain a study journal or use digital tools to record your achievements, note areas needing improvement, and reflect on your study habits. Regular progress reviews help identify patterns and adjust strategies accordingly.

Finally, celebrate your achievements, no matter how small. Recognizing and rewarding your progress boosts motivation and reinforces positive study habits. Whether it's achieving a new personal best on a practice test or mastering a challenging question type, these milestones deserve acknowledgment.

Setting realistic short-term and long-term goals involves understanding your target score, breaking down the preparation process into manageable tasks, balancing study with other commitments, remaining flexible, and regularly tracking progress. By doing so, you create a structured yet adaptable study plan that can lead to success on the LSAT and beyond.

Tracking progress

Tracking progress is a crucial element in preparing for the LSAT. It ensures that your study efforts are effective and that you are steadily moving toward your goals. By systematically monitoring your progress, you can identify areas of strength and weakness, adjust your study plan as needed, and maintain motivation throughout the preparation period.

One effective method of tracking progress is through regular practice tests. Taking these tests at consistent intervals allows you to measure improvements in your score and identify specific sections or question types that require more focus. After each practice test, analyze your performance thoroughly. Look beyond the overall score to examine how you performed in each section. Identify patterns in the types of mistakes you are making. Are there certain question types that consistently trip you up? Are you running out of time on specific sections? This detailed analysis helps in pinpointing exact areas that need improvement.

Maintaining a study journal is another valuable tool for tracking progress. In your journal, record your daily study activities, noting what you studied, for how long, and how you felt about your understanding of the material. Include reflections on what strategies worked well and which ones didn't. Over time, this journal becomes a rich resource for understanding your study habits and their impact on your performance. It also provides a sense of accomplishment as you see the accumulation of your efforts.

Using digital tools and apps designed for study tracking can enhance this process. There are various apps available that allow you to log study hours, track completed tasks, and even provide analytics on your progress. These tools can offer visual representations of your progress through charts and graphs, making it easier to see trends over time. Some apps also offer reminders and goal-setting features, helping you stay organized and on track.

Regularly reviewing your progress with a mentor, tutor, or study group can provide additional insights. External perspectives can highlight areas you might overlook and offer new strategies for tackling difficult sections. Scheduled check-ins with a mentor or tutor can keep you accountable and motivated. They can also help you adjust your study plan based on your progress and any challenges you encounter.

Flexibility is key when tracking progress. Your initial study plan is a guide, not a strict schedule. As you monitor your progress, be prepared to adjust your plan. If you notice that certain sections are improving faster than others, reallocate your study time to focus more on weaker areas. Similarly, if you find that certain study methods are not effective, don't hesitate to try new approaches. Regularly updating your study plan ensures that it remains aligned with your evolving needs and goals.

Celebrating milestones and achievements is an important aspect of tracking progress. Recognize and reward yourself for reaching short-term goals, such as improving your score on a practice test or mastering a difficult question type. These small victories keep you motivated and reinforce positive study habits. They remind you that your hard work is paying off and bring a sense of accomplishment.

Finally, maintaining a positive mindset is essential throughout this process. Progress can sometimes be slow, and setbacks are inevitable. Instead of viewing them as failures, see them as opportunities to learn and grow. Stay patient and persistent, focusing on the incremental improvements rather than the final goal.

Tracking progress involves regular practice tests, maintaining a study journal, using digital tools, seeking external feedback, being flexible with your study plan, celebrating milestones, and maintaining a positive mindset. By systematically monitoring and adjusting your approach, you can ensure steady progress toward achieving your target LSAT score and ultimately, gaining admission to your desired law school.

Building your study schedule: allocating time for each section

Building an effective study schedule for LSAT preparation involves careful allocation of time to each section of the test, ensuring a balanced approach that addresses all areas of the exam. The goal is to create a schedule that maximizes efficiency, covers all necessary material, and adapts to your personal strengths and weaknesses.

Begin by assessing the total amount of time available until your test date. This gives you a clear framework within which to plan your study sessions. If you have several months, you can afford to take a more measured pace, whereas a shorter timeframe necessitates more intensive study periods. Knowing your availability will help you set realistic and achievable goals.

Next, divide your available study time into manageable blocks, dedicating specific periods to each section of the test: Logical Reasoning, Reading Comprehension, and Argumentative Writing. The two Logical Reasoning sections, given their weight, should receive a significant portion of your study time. Reading Comprehension, while singular in number, is equally crucial and should not be neglected. Allocate time based on your initial diagnostic test results, focusing more on weaker areas while still maintaining regular practice in stronger sections to ensure continued proficiency.

A typical weekly study plan might look something like this: spend three days focusing on Logical Reasoning, two days on Reading Comprehension, and one day on Argumentative Writing, leaving one day for a full-length practice test and review. Within each day, break down your study sessions into smaller segments, typically 1-2 hours each, with breaks in between to avoid burnout and maintain focus.

Logical Reasoning requires consistent practice. Spend your dedicated days working through various question types, from assumption to inference questions. Begin each session with a brief review of strategies, followed by timed practice to simulate test conditions. After completing a set of questions, review your answers thoroughly, analyzing mistakes to understand where you went wrong and how to correct it in the future. This iterative process helps solidify understanding and improve accuracy and speed over time.

For Reading Comprehension, focus on building your ability to quickly and effectively comprehend complex texts. Practice skimming and scanning techniques to identify main ideas and supporting details swiftly. Work on a variety of passage types to build versatility, and regularly practice annotating passages to highlight key points and structure. Reviewing your answers should involve analyzing why certain choices are correct and others are not, which deepens your comprehension skills and test-taking strategies.

Argumentative Writing, though less frequent in practice, requires a clear and methodical approach. Spend time analyzing prompts, outlining responses, and writing timed essays. Focus on clarity, coherence, and addressing counterarguments effectively. Peer reviews or professional feedback can provide valuable insights into improving your essays.

Incorporate full-length practice tests into your schedule regularly, ideally once a week. These tests are essential for building stamina and getting a realistic sense of your timing and performance under exam conditions. After each test, review your results comprehensively, identifying patterns in your mistakes and areas that need further improvement. Adjust your study schedule based on these insights, allocating more time to sections or question types where you continue to struggle.

Maintaining flexibility in your study schedule is crucial. Life can be unpredictable, and sticking rigidly to a plan without room for adjustments can lead to unnecessary stress. Regularly assess your progress and be willing to shift your focus as needed. If you find a particular section consistently challenging, increase the time dedicated to it. Conversely, if you notice significant improvement in one area, you can reduce its focus slightly to balance your efforts elsewhere.

Ultimately, building a study schedule for LSAT preparation is about creating a structured yet adaptable plan that prioritizes consistent practice and thorough review. By dedicating specific time blocks to each section, regularly assessing your progress, and remaining flexible, you can ensure comprehensive preparation that maximizes your chances of success on test day.

Balancing study with other commitments

Balancing study with other commitments is a critical aspect of effective LSAT preparation. Many test-takers juggle a myriad of responsibilities, including work, family, and social obligations, making it essential to develop strategies that integrate studying into a busy schedule without compromising other important aspects of life.

Firstly, it's important to recognize the value of planning and time management. Begin by conducting a thorough assessment of your weekly commitments. Identify blocks of time that can be dedicated to study sessions. This might involve early mornings, lunch breaks, evenings, or weekends. The key is to find consistent times that can be reserved solely for LSAT prep, ensuring that it becomes a regular part of your routine.

Creating a realistic and flexible study schedule is crucial. Allocate study time based on your availability and the demands of the other commitments. For instance, if you work full-time, it might be more feasible to have shorter, focused study sessions on weekdays and longer sessions on weekends. Flexibility is essential because unexpected events can disrupt even the best-laid plans. Build buffer time into your schedule to accommodate these disruptions without falling behind on your study goals.

Prioritization is another vital component. Determine which commitments are non-negotiable and which can be adjusted or temporarily minimized. For example, social activities might be scaled back during your intensive study period. Communicate your goals and schedule with family and friends, explaining the importance of your LSAT preparation. This transparency can foster support and understanding, allowing you to create an environment conducive to focused study.

Utilizing time efficiently is also important. Incorporate study methods that maximize your learning during short periods. Techniques like active reading, summarizing key points, and practicing questions in timed conditions can enhance your efficiency. Additionally, leveraging technology can be beneficial. LSAT prep apps, online resources, and digital flashcards can make it easier to study during commutes or breaks at work.

Self-care should not be neglected. Balancing study with other commitments can be stressful, and maintaining physical and mental well-being is crucial for effective preparation. Ensure you get adequate sleep, eat nutritious meals, and incorporate regular physical activity into your routine. Short breaks during study sessions can prevent burnout and help maintain focus. Mindfulness practices, such as meditation or deep-breathing exercises, can also be useful in managing stress.

Setting realistic and achievable goals is essential for maintaining motivation and tracking progress. Break down your study plan into manageable tasks and milestones. Celebrate small victories along the way to stay encouraged. Regularly reviewing and adjusting your goals based on your progress can help keep you on track and prevent feelings of overwhelm.

Finally, seek support when needed. Whether it's joining a study group, finding a study partner, or enlisting the help of a tutor, having a support system can provide motivation and accountability. Discussing challenges and sharing strategies with others who are also preparing for the LSAT can offer valuable insights and moral support.

Balancing the study with other commitments requires careful planning, prioritization, and flexibility. By creating a realistic schedule, utilizing time efficiently, and maintaining self-care, you can effectively integrate LSAT preparation into your busy life. Remember, it's about finding a balance that allows you to achieve your study goals while still fulfilling other responsibilities. With the right approach, you can manage both successfully and position yourself for success on the LSAT.

CHAPTER 6: Practice tests and review

Practice Test 1: Logical Reasoning section

1. Two things are true of all good deeds. First, they are accompanied by feelings of satisfaction. Second, if they are publicly known, they elicit general approval.

If all of the above statements are true, then which of the following cannot also be true?

    A. Good deeds are good solely because they are accompanied by feelings of satisfaction.
    B. Even if they frequently elicit general approval when known publicly, some deeds that are accompanied by feelings of satisfaction are not good deeds.
    C. Every publicly known act that is accompanied by feelings of satisfaction is a good deed.
    D. Some publicly known deeds that elicit general approval are not accompanied by feelings of satisfaction.
    E. Some good deeds that are not publicly known are not accompanied by feelings of satisfaction.

2. Many home renters buy their first homes believing that it is clearly more profitable to make mortgage payments than to pay rent. Other costs, such as maintenance, property taxes, and insurance must be factored in, however. All housing expenses together total at least 40% of most homeowners' income. It is not financially reasonable to spend any more than 30% of income on housing expenses.

If the information is correct, which of the following cannot be true?

    A. A majority of renters pay an unreasonable amount for housing expenses
    B. A majority of homeowners have unreasonable housing expenses
    C. A minority of homeowners have reasonable housing expenses
    D. The combination of property taxes, insurance, and home maintenance costs is greater than mortgage payments for a minority of homeowners
    E. A minority of homeowners have unreasonable housing expenses

3. Most successful professional football players began playing football as youths, though a significant number learned the sport later in life. No professional football player who ignored the advice of his coaches, however, has ever become successful.

If the above statements are true, which of the following must also be true?

    A. The most successful professional football players played the sport as youths.
    B. All unsuccessful professional football players have ignored the advice of coaches.
    C. No professional football player who learned the sport later in life will ignore his coaches' advice.
    D. Not all professional football players who played the sport as youths ignored the advice of coaches.
    E. The more attentive a professional football player is to his coaches' advice, the more likely he is to be successful.

4. A growing world population has caused growing concerns about increasing famine. The population in 2000 was 6 billion. Ten years later the population was 7 billion. There were also more people affected by famines in 2010 than in 2000. Furthermore, in each year from 2000 to 2010, when the world's population increased, so did the number of those affected by famine.

Based on the information given, which of the following is true?

    A. The population increased in every year between 2000 to 2010
    B. If the population increased in 2005, then more people were affected by famine in 2005 than in 2004
    C. There was greater concern about famine in 2010 than in 2000
    D. If the population decreased in a particular year between 2000 and 2010, the number of those affected by famine also decreased in that year
    E. From 2000 to 2010, when the world's population increased, the percentage of the population affected by famine also increased

5. Most movie critics dislike Hollywood blockbusters. If someone dislikes Hollywood blockbusters they are a snob. Most people who are over the age of fifty dislike Hollywood blockbusters. Some people who dislike Hollywood blockbusters are huge fans of theater. If someone does not dislike Hollywood blockbusters they like large explosions.

Each of the following must be true EXCEPT:

    A. Most movie critics are snobs.
    B. Some people who dislike Hollywood blockbusters are over the age of fifty.
    C. If someone is not a snob, they like large explosions.
    D. Some movie critics are huge fans of theater.
    E. Most people over the age of fifty are snobs.

6. If the bookstore does not respond to modern trends, it will not stay in business. And if the bookstore does not offer electronic books in a popular format, it will not respond to modern trends. Furthermore, no electronic book format is popular unless it can be used on each of the top three e-book readers.

If the statements above are true, which one of the following must be true?

A. It is significantly more likely that the bookstore will stay in business if it responds to modern trends than if it does not respond to them.
B. If the bookstore stays in business, it will offer electronic books in a format which can be used on the top three e-book readers.
C. Popular electronic book formats generate more business for the bookstore than unpopular formats.
D. The bookstore will probably stay in business if it offers electronic books in a popular format.
E. If the bookstore offers electronic books in a format which can be used on each of the top three e-book readers, it will stay in business.

7. Frank: I'm tired of hearing people talk about ghosts and disembodied spirits nowadays. Everyone knows that thousands of years ago these supernatural forces were given as explanations for phenomena which we could not explain. Now that we have a scientific explanation for these occurrences, there's no reason to go back to the old myths.

Annie: These old myths, while they might not sound as logical as you'd like them to, are vital to the continuing development of both religion and literature in many cultures. Besides, who is to say that ghosts don't exist? Just because something can be explained scientifically doesn't rule out the possibility of supernatural intervention that happens to utilize natural laws.

Annie's statement that the "old myths" spoken of by Frank were vital to the development of religion and literature in many cultures serves to:

A. refute Frank's assertion that supernatural forces cannot explain certain phenomena
B. illustrate a point which is further developed in the remainder of Annie's argument
C. merely change the topic of discussion rather than address Frank's argument
D. challenge Frank's conclusion by providing an example of usefulness outside a scientific context
E. provide an emotional argument to challenge Frank's logical one

8. A small shop has a policy that in order to sell fruit at the front of the store, it must be both organic and locally grown. Recently, a producer who has farmland slightly more than a quarter of a mile away wanted to have his persimmons sold at the store and showcased in the store's large wooden display case. Upon receiving his request, the storeowners did a background check and determined that the farmer's produce was in fact organic. Therefore, the storeowners allowed the farmer's persimmons to be sold as he had requested.

The argument's conclusion follows logically if which of the following is assumed to be true?

A. In order for produce to be deemed organic, it is necessary to conduct a background check on the farming practices.
B. It can reasonably be inferred that if the farmer's land is a little more than a quarter of a mile away from the store that he would qualify as a local farmer.
C. If the farmer did not use organic farming practices, he would not have been allowed to sell his produce in the store.
D. Customers tend to buy organic and locally grown produce much more frequently than other produce that is not labeled as such.
E. Only fruit that would be allowed in the front of the store can be showcased in the store's large wooden display case.

9. Publisher: It is usually not a good idea for a first-time author to begin with a novel which the author intends to become part of a series. Most series novels are not published, but publishing companies are more likely to make series deals with authors who have previously published at least one stand-alone novel. If the stand-alone novel is a success, it is a good possibility that a subsequent series by that author will also be successful.

Which one of the following most accurately describes the role played in the publisher's argument by the statement that most series novels are not published?

A. It is a claim that is used to introduce another claim which supports the argument's main conclusion.
B. It is one of the argument's conclusions, but not its main conclusion.
C. It is an unsupported statement which serves only to weaken the argument.
D. It identifies a condition which, if not met, is fatal to the argument's main conclusion.
E. It is the argument's only conclusion.

10. Beth: We should stop spending so much time and money on climate change research. From the studies I've read, even if it is an issue, it will not significantly affect our lifestyle for thousands of years. With the pressing problems we face today, we cannot afford to expend our resources in such a way. Besides, it's politically divisive.

Stan: So you'd rather we just turn a blind eye and ignore climate change? It's not just future generations that will be affected by these issues. Having environmental awareness right now will help to solve our energy and waste problems, not to mention the impact on health. You have to look at the bigger picture.

Stan's response to Beth's argument is most vulnerable to criticism on which of the following grounds?

A. It presupposes what it seeks to establish, and ignores potential counterevidence.
B. It appeals to evidence which has not been properly supported.
C. It attempts to refute a distorted version of an opposing position.
D. It cites irrelevant data in support of its conclusion.
E. It fails to recognize the importance of planning for one's future.

11. Market analyst: Physical media, like DVDs and CDs, will not be sold for much longer. In the past five years, digital movie downloads have increased by 60%, and digital music downloads have increased by 70%. These trends are likely to continue, especially when one considers the fact that digital media content providers are not hampered by the manufacturing and labor costs of physical media.

The reasoning in the argument is most vulnerable to criticism on the grounds that the argument

   A. presumes, without providing justification, that an increase in sales of one type of media necessarily leads to a decrease in sales of another type
   B. presumes that the rights to most movies and music will be given to digital media content providers
   C. fails to provide a source for its claim that digital download trends are likely to continue
   D. fails to take into account the possibility that some digital movies and music are illegally downloaded
   E. fails to define the terms "manufacturing" and "labor"

12. Cook: Often times when I cook, I find that I can become over-ambitious and prepare multiple dishes at once. As a result, I don't always pay enough attention to everything that I am preparing and tend to overcook some of my creations. I have heard about a new type of cookware that is designed to prevent overcooking, and am thinking of investing in it so that I can prepare better food.

The cook's reasoning is flawed because he is:

   A. Assuming that a condition precedent has already occurred.
   B. Relying on a sample size that is too narrow.
   C. Relying on information that does not have a credible source.
   D. Confusing cause and effect.
   E. Mistaking correlation for causation.

13. Art history books are always written using elaborate language. Economics books are always written using unsophisticated language. Amanda's professor wrote a book about the economics of art history. Therefore, the book uses moderately elaborate language.

Which answer choice uses the same flawed reasoning that is used in this example?

   A. Women who shop at department stores always wear expensive clothing. Women who shop at thrift stores always wear inexpensive clothing. Therefore, women who shop at both department stores and thrift stores wear both expensive and inexpensive clothing.
   B. Email is delivered more quickly than post mail. Post mail is more personal than email. Arnold scanned a letter that he received as post mail and then delivered it to his father

using email. Therefore, the email that Arnold sent is both personal and was delivered quickly.

C. People who go fishing always live along the coast. People who go hunting always live in rural areas. John has property both along the coast and in a rural area. Therefore, John both goes fishing and hunting.

D. Chihuahuas are dogs that always have high-strung personalities. Corgis are dogs that always have mellow dispositions. Taylor has a dog that is a mix between a Chihuahua and a corgi. Therefore, Taylor's dog has a moderately high-strung personality.

E. Dresses that are made from cotton are always comfortable. Dresses made from nylon are usually uncomfortable. Andrea bought a dress that is mostly made from cotton, but includes some nylon. Therefore, the dress is mostly comfortable.

14. All English Springer Spaniels have long hair. All Rottweilers have short hair. Each of Tina's dogs is a cross between an English Springer Spaniel and a Rottweiler. Therefore, Tina's dogs have medium-length hair.

Which one of the following uses flawed reasoning that most closely resembles the flawed reasoning used in the argument above?

A. All halogen gases are toxic to humans. All non-radioactive noble gases are non-toxic to humans. "Nobagen" gas is a mixture of a halogen gas and a noble gas. Therefore, "nobagen" gas is moderately toxic to humans.

B. All economists know linear algebra. All physicists know relativistic mechanics. Wilma is both an economist and a physicist. Therefore, Wilma knows both linear algebra and relativistic mechanics.

C. All cars made by Chord are very well made. All cars made by Fysler are very poorly made. Half of the cars on Jim's lot are very well made and the other half are very poorly made. Therefore, half of the cars on Jim's lot are Chords and half are Fyslers.

D. All players on the Wildcats have brown hair. All players on the Razorbacks have red hair. Members of the Moye family are on both the Wildcats and the Razorbacks. Therefore, some members of the Moye family have brown hair and others have red hair.

E. All typists who practice at least one hour per day can type one hundred words per minute. But some typists who do not practice can also type one hundred words per minute. Mike, a typist, practices thirty minutes per day. Therefore, Mike types fifty words per minute.

15. A high school football coach has made public comments criticizing the decision by the football coaching staff of the local university to not play their star quarterback. However, we should not listen to the high school coach's criticism. His high school football team has not won a game in several seasons.

The flawed reasoning above most closely resembles which of the following arguments?

A. It is likely that the scholar plagiarized this paper because she has been known to plagiarize in the past.

B. We should not listen to this art critic's negative comments because it is well known that the art critic is a mediocre artist.

C. We should not listen to the neurobiologist's predictions about the future state of the economy because he has no formal training in economics.

D. We should not listen to the car salesperson because she has an incentive to ignore negative features of the car in order to make commission off of a sale.

E. We should not heed the weather channel's warnings. They have failed to correctly predict the past twenty rainy days.

16. While there are certain dog-training techniques that generally tend to be effective for most dogs, it is important to keep in mind that each dog will respond particularly well to certain techniques that other dogs might not be receptive to. Therefore, the best practice is to keep general principles in mind when training dogs, while tailoring their educations to their particular traits.

Which of the following propositions does this reasoning above most closely conform to?

A. Although dogs are different, they are similar enough that a basic set of training principles can be applied to them universally, with slight room for variation.

B. Unique individuals and unique circumstances call for specialized training to meet their needs.

C. It is dangerous to apply a broad set of principles to a set of unique individuals because they will react to the same set of circumstances differently.

D. While a general set of principles exist for accomplishing a goal, it is important to acknowledge the unique circumstances or qualities that may exist, and to take them into consideration.

E. Even though general principles are broad enough to encompass most individuals or circumstances, there will always be outliers that require special attention.

17. All limes are green. Therefore, any fruit that is green is a lime. If a person sees a fruit that is green, that person may assume that the fruit is a lime.

Which of the following most closely parallels the flawed reasoning above?

A. Immigration courts tend to adopt more liberal views. Therefore, if a person encounters a conservative view, it is unlikely that the view was expressed in an immigration court.

B. Liberal views are expressed in immigration courts. Therefore, immigration courts are liberal. If a person encounters a liberal view, that person can assume that the view was expressed in an immigration court.

C. Liberal views are often expressed in immigration courts. Therefore, if a person encounters a liberal view, it is likely that the view was expressed in an immigration court.

D. Immigration courts adopt more liberal views. Therefore, any court that adopts a more liberal view is an immigration court. If a person encounters a court that has a more liberal view, that person may assume that the court is an immigration court.

E. Immigration courts have more liberal views. Therefore, liberal views are only expressed by immigration courts. Therefore, if a person encounters an immigration court, that person can assume that the court will have a liberal view.

18. Smoking cigarettes continues to be a common practice despite countless studies demonstrating that the habit causes deadly diseases. The government has attempted to reduce the number of smokers with advertising campaigns that explain the consequences of smoking, but the campaigns have been ineffective because the habit continues to be as prevalent as it was previous to the campaigns. The government should try one or more of the many alternatives to advertising. For instance, the government could raise the tax on cigarettes to the extent that smoking is prohibitively expensive.

Which of the following, if true, most weakens the argument?

A. At the time when most cigarette smokers began smoking, the effects of smoking were unknown
B. There are various, prevalent habits that cause deadly diseases
C. When taxes on products increase, people are often willing to pay the increased cost to maintain a habit
D. Advertising campaigns are generally successful only many years after being implemented; the government's campaign has been in effect for one year
E. The vast majority of government advertising campaigns are effective

19. Recent polls of admissions officers at colleges have shown that when evaluating student applications, volunteering is valued less than taking on leadership roles in student organizations. However, despite having this information, some high school counselors encourage students to spend time volunteering over taking on leadership roles in student organizations.

Which of the following, if true, resolves this discrepancy?

A. Admissions officers consider many different types of criteria when they evaluate student applications.
B. Roles in student leadership are limited, and so not every student can obtain such a position. Volunteer work, however, can be completed by anyone.
C. Some high school counselors believe that the personal development that can result form volunteering is more important than the competitive edge that a leadership role can earn a student applying for college.
D. Volunteer work is something that a person can engage in at any stage of life, while leadership positions in student organizations are isolated to a particular place and time.
E. High school counselors tend to disagree with the admissions criteria at colleges.

20. Under the modern model for music distribution, musicians sell the right to broadcast their music to companies who give listeners affordable access to large quantities of music. Some musicians who have been selling their music for many years are displeased with the new

model and have seen decreased revenue. Yet, musicians as a whole are making more money under the new model than they were previously.

Which of the following, if true, would most help to reconcile the apparent conflict?

A. Some musicians want to make more money than they made under the old model
B. The old model could be used now and would generate more revenue than the new model
C. A greater number of musicians sell music now than under the old model
D. The new model is not generating as much revenue as it could be generating
E. Music producers charge higher fees now, leaving less revenue for musicians

Answer sheet with explanation

1. **Correct Answer:** E. Some good deeds that are not publicly known are not accompanied by feelings of satisfaction.

Explanation: According to sentences 1 and 2 of the passage, all good deeds are accompanied by feelings of satisfaction. Therefore, the correct answer has to be false. That is, no good deed, whether or not publicly known, comes without satisfaction.

2. **Correct Answer:** E. A minority of homeowners have unreasonable housing expenses

Explanation: We know from the information given that most homeowners have housing expenses that are at least 40% of their incomes. If housing expenses of more than 30% of a homeowner's income is unreasonable, then at least a majority of homeowners have unreasonable housing expenses.

3. **Correct Answer:** D. Not all professional football players who played the sport as youths ignored the advice of coaches.

Explanation: According to the second sentence of the passage, a necessary condition for being a successful professional football player is not ignoring the advice of coaches. So all of the successful professional football players mentioned in the passage's first sentence, including those who played the sport as youths, do not ignore the advice of coaches. That's what the correct answer states.

4. **Correct Answer:** B. If the population increased in 2005, then more people were affected by famine in 2005 than in 2004

Explanation: The number affected by famine always increases with the population. Therefore, if the population increased in 2005, then the number of those affected by famine also increased. If there was an increase in 2005, there must have been more people affected in that year than the previous year of 2004. The available information does not allow us to draw any of the other inferences.

The number of those affected by famine could increase without a corresponding percentage of the population increase. Neither can we draw inferences about any particular year between 2000 and 2010.

5. **Correct Answer:** D. Some movie critics are huge fans of theater.

Explanation: We cannot assume that some movie critics are huge fans of theater because the only connection between both is two "some" statements. The rest of the answers must be true based on inferences we can make from the stimulus.

6. **Correct Answer:** B. If the bookstore stays in business, it will offer electronic books in a format which can be used on the top three e-book readers.

Explanation: The correct answer choice correctly notes that the bookstore will not stay in business unless it offers electronic books in a popular format as defined. Therefore, if the bookstore does stay in business, it must offer electronic books in such a format. The other answer choices employ incorrect information and/or probability reasoning unsupported by the argument. Remember: we do not know the conditions under which the bookstore will stay in business; we only know for certain what will cause the bookstore to not stay in business.

7. **Correct Answer:** D. challenge Frank's conclusion by providing an example of usefulness outside a scientific context

Explanation: Frank concludes that these "old myths" are antiquated, and implies that they are useless in light of modern scientific explanations. Annie's statement does not dispute the scientific usefulness of the old myths, but rather provides an example of their usefulness on different grounds.

8. **Correct Answer:** E. Only fruit that would be allowed in the front of the store can be showcased in the store's large wooden display case.

Explanation: The passage explains that the farmer's persimmons are organic, and a reasonable inference can be made that they are also locally grown. Given that the passage states that "...therefore" the farmer may sell the persimmons in the shop, the argument will only logically flow if it is required that the farmer's persimmons be both organic and locally grown. Given that these are the same prerequisites for selling the fruit at the front of the store, "Only fruit that would be allowed in the front of the store can be showcased in the store's large wooden display case" is the correct answer. None of the other answer choices make it clear that it is required for the persimmons to be both organic and locally grown.

9. **Correct Answer:** A. It is a claim that is used to introduce another claim which supports the argument's main conclusion.

Explanation: While not vital to the argument, the claim that most series novels are not published is used to lead to the argument's main premise, which is that publishing a stand-alone novel gives authors a better chance of later publishing a series. The statement does not weaken the argument, but rather puts it in context.

10. **Correct Answer:** C. It attempts to refute a distorted version of an opposing position.

Explanation: Stan's response focuses on awareness of climate change, whereas Beth's argument was about spending time and funding on climate change research. Therefore, Stan distorts Beth's position and attempts to argue against the distorted position. The other answer choices, to the extent that they are valid at all, are not nearly as fundamental to Stan's reasoning.

11. **Correct Answer:** A. Presumes, without providing justification, that an increase in sales of one type of media necessarily leads to a decrease in sales of another type

Explanation: The argument provides no data indicating that sales of physical media are decreasing, nor does it explain any connection between increased digital media sales and physical media sales. Without additional information, one could assume that both types of media are increasing in sales. The incorrect answer choices do not attack the argument's reasoning, but focus on other factors which do not necessarily affect the conclusion.

12. **Correct Answer:** E. mistaking correlation for causation.

Explanation: The cookware is correlated to reduced overcooking. However, the chef thinks that the cookware will cause his food to no longer be overcooked, when the cause of such overcooking appears to be his inability to focus on a single dish because of his excessive multitasking. Therefore, the chef mistakes the cookware that he is using as being the cause of his food being overcooked.
The correct answer identifies the cause correlation error that the chef has made.

13. **Correct Answer:** D. Chihuahuas are dogs that always have high-strung personalities. Corgis are dogs that always have mellow dispositions. Taylor has a dog that is a mix between a Chihuahua and a corgi. Therefore, Taylor's dog has a moderately high-strung personality.

Explanation: The flawed reasoning follows the pattern that if "A" always has quality "X" and if "B" always has the opposite of quality "X," then something that is a mix of "A" and "B" will have a moderate amount of quality X.
In the example, "art history books" (A) always has the quality of "using elaborate language" (=X) However, "economics books" (=B) do not. Therefore, a mix of art history books and economics books (A + B) would use a moderate amount of (X), elaborate language.
In the correct answer, this same reasoning is followed.
Chihuahuas = A
Corgis = B
High-strung personalities = X

14. **Correct Answer:** A. All halogen gases are toxic to humans. All non-radioactive noble gases are non-toxic to humans. "Nobagen" gas is a mixture of a halogen gas and a noble gas. Therefore, "nobagen" gas is moderately toxic to humans.

Explanation: The flawed reasoning used in the passage is that a combination of two "parent" items with different attributes necessarily yields a "child" product having attributes that are averages of its parents' attributes. The correct answer uses parallel reasoning inasmuch as the argument uses the fact that halogen and noble gases differ with respect to toxicity to conclude that a combination of such gases would yield a gas having toxicity that is the average of the toxicity of its "parent" gases.

15. **Correct Answer:** B. We should not listen to this art critic's negative comments because it is well known that the art critic is a mediocre artist.

Explanation: The stimulus holds that an opinion is false on the basis that the person with that opinion has made past mistakes in the same area. The correct answer is similar because it follows the same pattern of critiquing a position based on the person with the opinion not the opinion itself.

16. **Correct Answer:** D. While a general set of principles exist for accomplishing a goal, it is important to acknowledge the unique circumstances or qualities that may exist, and to take them into consideration.

Explanation: The correct answer most closely conforms with the excerpt.
The incorrect answers are wrong for the following reasons:
1. Saying that dogs should be treated the same with "slight room for variation" emphasizes continuity over individualization, and therefore is wrong.
2. The statement "It is dangerous to apply a broad set of principles... " is not stated in the excerpt.
3. "Unique individuals and unique circumstances call for specialized training to meet their needs" exaggerates the need for individualization.
4. The concept of "outliers" is not present in the excerpt, a red flag that this is an incorrect answer choice.

17. **Correct Answer:** D. Immigration courts adopt more liberal views. Therefore, any court that adopts a more liberal view is an immigration court. If a person encounters a court that has a more liberal view, that person may assume that the court is an immigration court.

Explanation: The flawed reasoning in the text is as follows:
X has trait Y. Therefore, anything with trait Y must be X. If a person encounters something with trait Y, then it must be X.
The correct answer properly reflects this reasoning. All the other answer choices do not properly follow this pattern: they may leave out a link of the causal reasoning or misconstruction it.

18. **Correct Answer:** D. Advertising campaigns are generally successful only many years after being implemented; the government's campaign has been in effect for one year

Explanation: A key premise of the argument is that the government's advertising campaign has been unsuccessful because smoking is as prevalent as it was prior to the campaign. The campaign may still be successful, however, if campaigns are generally successful only after many years. The new information would undermine a fundamental premise of the argument.

19. **Correct Answer:** C. Some high school counselors believe that the personal development that can result form volunteering is more important than the competitive edge that a leadership role can earn a student applying for college.

Explanation: The correct answer is:
Some high school counselors believe that the personal development that can result form volunteering is more important than the competitive edge that a leadership role can earn a student applying for college.
In order to justify why a high school counselor might favor volunteering over student leadership roles, it is important to show that there is an incentive more powerful than helping a student gain an edge for getting into college. This is the only answer choice that provides such an incentive. Therefore, it is the correct choice.

20. **Correct Answer:** C. A greater number of musicians sell music now than under the old model

Explanation: The paradox in the passage is that some musicians generate less revenue now than they did under the old model while, on the whole, musicians earn more revenue than previously. If there are more musicians than under the old model, revenues could increase for the industry as a whole while decreasing for certain musicians. This is not the only information that could explain the paradox, but it does so better than any of the other answers given here.

Practice Test 2: Reading Comprehension section

This section assesses a candidate's ability to read, understand and analyze complex texts; Includes 26-28 questions.

Passage:

When we study law, we are not studying a mystery but a well-known profession. We are studying what we shall want in order to appear before judges, or to advise people in such a way as to keep them out of court. The reason why it is a profession, why people will pay lawyers to argue for them or to advise them, is that in societies like ours the command of the public force is intrusted to the judges in certain cases, and the whole power of the state will be put forth, if necessary, to carry out their judgments and decrees. People want to know under what circumstances and how far they will run the risk of coming against what is so much stronger than themselves, and hence it becomes a business to find out when this danger is to be feared. The object of our study, then, is prediction, the prediction of the incidence of the public force through the instrumentality of the courts.

The means of the study are a body of reports, of treatises, and of statutes, in this country and in England, extending back for six hundred years, and now increasing annually by hundreds. In these sibylline leaves are gathered the scattered prophecies of the past upon the cases in which the axe will fall. These are what properly have been called the oracles of the law. Far the most important and pretty nearly the whole meaning of every new effort of legal thought is to make these prophecies more precise, and to generalize them into a thoroughly connected system. The process is one, from a lawyer's statement of a case, eliminating as it does all the dramatic elements with which his client's story has clothed it, and retaining only the facts of legal import, up to the final analyses and abstract universals of theoretic jurisprudence. The reason why a lawyer does not mention that his client wore a white hat when he made a contract, while Mrs. Quickly would be sure to dwell upon it along with the parcel gilt goblet and the sea-coal fire, is that he foresees that the public force will act in the same way whatever his client had upon his head. It is to make the prophecies easier to be remembered and to be understood that the teachings of the decisions of the past are put into general propositions and gathered into textbooks, or that statutes are passed in a general form. The primary rights and duties with which jurisprudence busies itself again are nothing but prophecies. One of the many evil effects of the confusion between legal and moral ideas, about which I shall have something to say in a moment, is that theory is apt to get the cart before the horse, and consider the right or the duty as something existing apart from and independent of the consequences of its breach, to which certain sanctions are added afterward. But, as I shall try to show, a legal duty so called is nothing but a prediction that if a man does or omits certain things he will be made to suffer in this or that way by judgment of the court; and so of a legal right.

The number of our predictions when generalized and reduced to a system is not unmanageably large. They present themselves as a finite body of dogma which may be mastered within a reasonable time. It is a great mistake to be frightened by the ever-increasing number of reports. The reports of a given jurisdiction in the course of a generation take up pretty much the whole body of the law, and restate it from the present point of view. We could reconstruct the corpus from them if all that went before were burned.

Questions:

1. Which of the following most closely resembles proper theoretic jurisprudence as it is described by the author?

    A. A philosopher starting with certain assumed truths and common sense principles, then combining them and teasing out their implications to deduce what must be done to resolve ethical dilemmas

    B. A philosopher conducting thought experiments to test the soundness of a theory under extreme cases, documenting where the theory produced counterintuitive or paradoxical results

    C. A biologist noticing trends in a set of collected data, accounting and controlling for extranious variables, and creating a general model that can be applied to other relevant instances

D. An anthropologist conducting interviews and listening to the oral traditions of several different cultures, then constructing a theory that describes the development of cultural values in human societies

E. A physicist working with mathematical models to construct a theory, then testing this theory by conducting experiments

2. With which of the following positions would the author of this passage most likely disagree?

A. Legal principles are mainly aids to help guess how a law case will turn out.
B. While one can never learn every fact of the law, such learning is unnecessary to mastering the law.
C. In practicing law, one can only make predictions on how a particular case might turn out, and never certain ones.
D. There is nothing irrelevant to the practice of law.
E. While there may be a relationship between morality and law, the law is not simply a codification and enforcement of ethical principles.

3. Which of the following views is most nearly opposed to the main thesis of the author?

A. The proper subject of the study of law itself, as opposed to individual laws, is to derrive and deduce legal principles from first principles.
B. The law considers no detail irrelevant, no piece of evidence too small, in making its decisions; the most weighty matters are sometimes decided on what seem to be the most trivial of details.
C. Nobody can escape the "long arm of the law," and all fear it; thus, they seek the advice of attornies and counselors to avoid crossing those well-defined lines that are poorly known to the layman in which the law must act.
D. The law is often obscure, and open to interpretation; thus, the best lawyer is the one who can work in these "penumbras of the law," fashioning the best interpretation of it in the open spaces between certain cases.
E. The past dictates the present, and what has come before what comes now—indeed, what is to come. Thus, the student of law who knows the greatest part of the body of past law will have the best chance of predicting the outcome of present and future cases.

4. Which of the following best captures the primary point of the final paragraph?

A. New cases merely rehash and go over old issues in ways an experienced practicioner will have seen before. As such, one need not study old decisions and principles, as newer ones present them in exactly the same way.
B. It is not necessary to learn every single court decision, statute, or legal determination that has been issued in the last 600 years, as the relevent issues are recapitulated and reinterpreted regularly.
C. As laws are valid only in particular jurisdictions, and legal principles are derrived from these laws, it therefore follows that legal principles are valid only in certain jurisdictions;

thus, while the body of law worldwide might seem overwhelming, one need only learn the laws of the jurisdictions in which one practices, and likewise only the principles that can be deduced from them.

D. The body of law, in its statutes, principles, and decisions, is increasing at such a rate that anyone who would hope to master it must constantly "run to stay in place;" by the time a practicioner has digested some part of the legal corpus, new decisions and statutes have supplanted what was learned.

E. The body of law is ever-increasing, with courts adding to it by the moment; as such, it is impossible to ever truly learn the whole of the law in the course of a single lifetime.

Passage:

To present a general view of the Common Law, other tools are needed besides logic. It is something to show that the consistency of a system requires a particular result, but it is not all. The life of the law has not been logic: it has been experience. The felt necessities of the time, the prevalent moral and political theories, intuitions of public policy, avowed or unconscious, even the prejudices which judges share with their fellow-men, have had a good deal more to do than the syllogism in determining the rules by which men should be governed. The law embodies the story of a nation's development through many centuries, and it cannot be dealt with as if it contained only the axioms and corollaries of a book of mathematics. In order to know what it is, we must know what it has been, and what it tends to become. We must alternately consult history and existing theories of legislation. But the most difficult labor will be to understand the combination of the two into new products at every stage. The substance of the law at any given time pretty nearly corresponds, so far as it goes, with what is then understood to be convenient; but its form and machinery, and the degree to which it is able to work out desired results, depend very much upon its past.

In Massachusetts today, while, on the one hand, there are a great many rules which are quite sufficiently accounted for by their manifest good sense, on the other, there are some which can only be understood by reference to the infancy of procedure among the German tribes, or to the social condition of Rome under the Decemvirs.

I shall use the history of our law so far as it is necessary to explain a conception or to interpret a rule, but no further. In doing so there are two errors equally to be avoided both by writer and reader. One is that of supposing, because an idea seems very familiar and natural to us, that it has always been so. Many things which we take for granted have had to be laboriously fought out or thought out in past times. The other mistake is the opposite one of asking too much of history. We start with man full grown. It may be assumed that the earliest barbarian whose practices are to be considered, had a good many of the same feelings and passions as ourselves.

Questions:

5. Which of the following statements would the author of this passage be most likely to agree with?

A. "Rights and responsibilities flow from past decisions and so count as legal, not just when they are explicit in these decisions but also when they follow from the principles of personal and political morality the explicit decisions presuppose by way of justification."
B. "Justice is what the judge had for breakfast."
C. "We must always stand by past decisions, and not disturb the undisturbed."
D. "We must beware of the pitfall of antiquarianism, and must remember that for our purposes our only interest in the past is for the light it throws upon the present."
E. "Law aims to lay principle over practice to show the best route to a better future, keeping the right faith with the past."

6. Which of the following statements would the author of the passage be most likely to disagree with most strongly?

A. There is, strictly speaking, no law apart from society; what is found in the one is found in the other.
B. The story of law is seen in its history, a history that includes the present day and even the future.
C. Human nature does not change, but the circumstances in which men live do; thus, some laws of great antiquity ought to still be followed, but others have outlived their use.
D. The law is itself lawful, and the one who understands its first principles can reason to its conclusions.
E. In studying the paths of the law, we can discern certain principles that appear time and again, and, inasmuch as they are useful for the present, ought to learn them.

7. Each of the following can be inferred from the passage EXCEPT _____.

A. laws generally reflect the societies in which they were enacted
B. there are some contemporary laws based in ancient Roman law
C. there is no role for systematic logic in the interpretation of laws
D. human nature has generally been the same throughout history
E. many laws of ancient origin that have little relevance to contemporary society were once relevant to an older social order

8. Which of the following best describes the purpose of the underlined paragraph in the passage?

A. A specific example used as evidence to bolster a premise in an earlier argument
B. A set of examples used to illustrate an assertion earlier in the passage
C. An example illustrating the effects of applying procedures advocated for earlier
D. A rhetorical contrast between good sense and adherance to ancient tradition
E. A contrast between two approaches to understanding a single body of law

Passage:

The first thought that men had concerning the heavenly bodies was an obvious one: they were lights. There was a greater light to rule the day, a lesser light to rule the night, and there were the stars also.

In those days there seemed an immense difference between the earth upon which men stood and the bright objects that shone down upon it from the heavens above. The earth seemed to be vast, dark, and motionless; the celestial lights seemed to be small, and moved and shone. The earth was then regarded as the fixed center of the universe, but the Copernican theory has since deprived it of this pride of place. Yet from another point of view, the new conception of its position involves a promotion, since the earth itself is now regarded as a heavenly body of the same order as some of those that shine down upon us. It is amongst them, and it too moves and shines—shines, as some of them do, by reflecting the light of the sun. Could we transport ourselves to a neighboring world, the earth would seem a star, not distinguishable in kind from the rest.

But as men realized this, they began to ask, "Since this world from a distant standpoint must appear as a star, would not a star, if we could get near enough to it, show itself also as a world? This world teems with life; above all, it is the home of human life. Men and women, gifted with feeling, intelligence, and character, look upward from its surface and watch the shining members of the heavenly host. Are none of these the home of beings gifted with like powers, who watch in their turn the movements of that shining point that is our world?"

This is the meaning of the controversy on the Plurality of Worlds which excited so much interest some sixty years ago, and has been with us more or less ever since. It is the desire to recognize the presence in the orbs around us of beings like ourselves, possessed of personality and intelligence, lodged in an organic body.

This is what is meant when we speak of a world being "inhabited." It would not, for example, at all content us if we could ascertain that Jupiter was covered by a shoreless ocean, rich in every variety of fish, or that the hard rocks of the Moon were delicately veiled by lichens. Just as no richness of vegetation and no fullness and complexity of animal life would justify an explorer in describing some land that he had discovered as being "inhabited" if no men were there, so we cannot rightly speak of any other world as being "inhabited" if it is not the home of intelligent life.

On the other hand, of necessity we are precluded from extending our inquiry to the case of disembodied intelligences, if such be conceived possible. All created existences must be conditioned, but if we have no knowledge of what those conditions may be, or means for attaining such knowledge, we cannot discuss them. Nothing can be affirmed, nothing denied, concerning the possibility of intelligences existing on the Moon or even in the Sun if we are unable to ascertain under what limitations those particular intelligences subsist.

The only beings, then, the presence of which would justify us in regarding another world as "inhabited" are such as would justify us in applying that term to a part of our own world. They must possess intelligence and consciousness on the one hand; on the other, they must likewise have corporeal form. True, the form might be imagined as different from that we possess, but, as with ourselves, the intelligent spirit must be lodged in and expressed by a living material body. <u>Our inquiry is thus rendered a physical one; it is the necessities of the living body that must guide us in it; a world unsuited for living organisms is not, in the sense of this enquiry, a "habitable" world.</u>

Questions:

9. Which of the following statements does the passage most strongly suggest that the author would agree with?

    A. Science could possibly discover the truth about anything that could possibly exist.
    B. The work of Copernicus was a necessary step for people to be able to think of other worlds as possibly inhabited.
    C. There are some worlds that are home to beings without bodies, even though we cannot study these beings.
    D. The controversy of the plurality of worlds is settled.
    E. Every star is a world like our own.

10. Which of the following CANNOT be inferred from the passage?

    A. No uninhabited world is the home of intelligent beings.
    B. Some uninhabited world could be the home of intelligent beings.
    C. Some inhabited world could be the home of non-intelligent beings.
    D. Some uninhabited world could be the home of non-intelligent beings.
    E. Every inhabited world is the home of intelligent beings.

11. Which of the following best describes the primary purpose of the underlined final sentence of the passage?

    A. A key assumption assumed by earlier arguments that, if true, would validate them
    B. An additional, secondary conclusion that can be derived from the primary conclusion of the passage
    C. The primary conclusion of the passage, supported by an earlier subordinate conclusion
    D. A question raised by the conclusion of the passage that will be investigated later
    E. An empirical observation that must guide the theoretical model under consideration

12. Which of the following best describes the tone of the first three paragraphs?

    A. Witty and ironic
    B. Objective and serious
    C. Formal and didactic
    D. Reflective and philosophical
    E. Elegiac and wistful

13. Which of the following most accurately describes the main idea of the passage?

    A. In order for a world to be considered inhabited, it must have intelligent life with material bodies.
    B. The inhabitants of other worlds could have very different bodies than those of humans.
    C. As science has progressed, people have wondered if there are other worlds that might be inhabited by creatures like ourselves.
    D. Advances in science have allowed us to contemplate whether other worlds are inhabited.
    E. The presence of non-intelligent life, like lichens or oysters, is not sufficient to make another world inhabited.

14. Which of the following best describes the structure of the passage?

    A. Giving the history of the development of a theory; mentioning a consequence of this development; describing necessary conditions for a state of affairs; drawing conclusions from these conditions
    B. Describing a scientific problem; laying out some possible solutions to that problem; describing a new theory that addresses some of the common problems in previous models; addressing the limits of how this new theory can be applied
    C. Explaining the history of a scientific discipline; making deductions from the progress of this discipline; describing sufficient conditions for further progress in a particular area; laying out avenues for future investigation
    D. Describing the results of empirical investigations; conducting a thought experiment based on these results; describing further observations that fit both the initial investigation and the thought experiment; creating a new theoretical model
    E. Describing the development of a theoretical model; explaining how this model influenced more recent observations; describing a new application for the kinds of observations influenced by this model; mentioning how a different model could also account for these observations

15. What is the primary purpose of the fourth paragraph?

    A. To introduce a premise that will be used to support a conclusion in the final paragraph
    B. To transition between the historical and metaphysical survey of the opening paragraphs and the logical arguments of the following ones
    C. To provide an introduction and historical context for the controversy of the plurality of worlds
    D. To reach a secondary conclusion important to the main argument of the overall passage
    E. To present evidence that will be used to counter an opposing argument

Passage:

When we try to ascertain the motives which have led men to the investigation of philosophical questions, we find that, broadly speaking, they can be divided into two groups, often antagonistic, and leading to very divergent systems. These two groups of motives are, on the one hand, those derived from religion and ethics, and, on the other hand, those derived from science. Plato, Spinoza, and Hegel may be taken as typical of the philosophers whose interests are mainly religious and ethical, while Leibniz, Locke, and Hume may be taken as representatives of the scientific wing. In Aristotle, Descartes, Berkeley, and Kant we find both groups of motives strongly present.

Herbert Spencer, in whose honor we are assembled today, would naturally be classed among scientific philosophers; it was mainly from science that he drew his data, his formulation of problems, and his conception of method. But his strong religious sense is obvious in much of his writing, and his ethical preoccupations are what make him value the conception of evolution—that conception in which, as a whole generation has believed, science and morals are to be united in fruitful and indissoluble marriage.

It is my belief that the ethical and religious motives, in spite of the splendidly imaginative systems to which they have given rise, have been, on the whole, a hindrance to the progress of philosophy, and ought now to be consciously thrust aside by those who wish to discover philosophical truth. Science, originally, was entangled in similar motives, and was thereby hindered in its advances. It is, I maintain, from science, rather than from ethics and religion, that philosophy should draw its inspiration.

But there are two different ways in which a philosophy may seek to base itself upon science. It may emphasize the most general results of science, and seek to give even greater generality and unity to these results. Or it may study the methods of science, and seek to apply these methods, with the necessary adaptations, to its own peculiar province. Much philosophy inspired by science has gone astray through preoccupation with the results momentarily supposed to have been achieved. It is not results, but methods that can be transferred with profit from the sphere of the special sciences to the sphere of philosophy. What I wish to bring to your notice is the possibility and importance of applying to philosophical problems certain broad principles of method which have been found successful in the study of scientific questions.

The opposition between a philosophy guided by scientific method and a philosophy dominated by religious and ethical ideas may be illustrated by two notions which are very prevalent in the works of philosophers, namely the notion of the universe, and the notion of good and evil. A philosopher is expected to tell us something about the nature of the universe as a whole, and to give grounds for either optimism or pessimism. Both these expectations seem to me mistaken. I believe the conception of "the universe" to be, as its etymology indicates, a mere relic of pre-Copernican astronomy, and I believe the question of optimism and pessimism to be one which the philosopher will regard as outside his scope, except, possibly, to the extent of maintaining that it is insoluble.

Questions:

16. With which of these statements would the author of this argument be most likely to disagree?

   A. Scientific inquiry has flourished in Twentieth and Twenty First Centuries due to an increasing neglect of religious motivations.
   B. The monasteries of Medieval Europe were centers of scientific learning because of their ability to merge religious and scientific inquiry cohesively.
   C. None of these; the author would agree with all these statements.
   D. Organized religion has had a profoundly negative impact on the development of scientific thought and inquiry.
   E. Philosophers' motivations may be classed as either scientific or as religious and ethical, or as drawing from both areas.

17.

The author of this passage would argue that determining the nature of the universe is

_____.

   A. fundamental to the field
   B. impossible
   C. pointless
   D. suspicious
   E. highly important, but challenging

18. Which of the following philosophers would the author be most likely to agree with and sympathize with?

   A. Plato
   B. Descartes
   C. Hegel
   D. Hume
   E. Kant

19. Based on the passage, which of the following is true?

   A. Only scientific philosophers are expected to tell us something about the nature of the universe.
   B. Scientific results are remarkably useful when applied to the sphere of philosophy.
   C. Science has experienced the same sort of setbacks in recent years as religion has during the past.
   D. While many believe that evolution represents a successful combination of science and ethics, the author would likely disagree with this view.
   E. A number of philosophers cannot be classed as either being motivated by science or as being motivated by ethics and religion.

20. The author's attitude towards religion is primarily _____.

    A. critical and intolerant
    B. bellicose and frustrated
    C. disparaging and mocking
    D. apathetic and cautious
    E. dismissive and haughty

21. The author of this essay would most likely describe the relationship between scientific philosophy and religious philosophy as _____.

    A. Wanton and pointless
    B. Supplementary and positive
    C. Hostile and non-complementary
    D. Puzzling and oppositional
    E. Surprising and overwhelming

22. This essay could best be titled _____.

    A. "On the Importance of Religious Philosophical Inquiry"
    B. "On Results-Based and Method-Based Scientific Philosophical Inquiry"
    C. "In Praise of Herbert Spencer"
    D. "On the Positive Applications of Scientific Method to Philosophy"
    E. "In Defense of Scientific Inquiry and Exploration"

23. What does the author believe has long hindered the progress of science?

    A. The general disdain for scientific investigation among the general population
    B. The overriding influence of religious institutions
    C. The inattention to detail among leading scientific figures
    D. Ignorance of the scientific method among leading scientific figures
    E. Its entanglement with religious and ethical motivations

Passage:

The spectator who casts a mournful view over the ruins of ancient Rome, is tempted to accuse the memory of the Goths and Vandals, for the mischief which they had neither leisure, nor power, nor perhaps inclination, to perpetrate. The tempest of war might strike some lofty turrets to the ground; but the destruction which undermined the foundations of those massy fabrics was prosecuted, slowly and silently, during a period of ten centuries; and the motives of interest, that afterwards operated without shame or control, were severely checked by the taste and spirit of the emperor Majorian. The decay of the city had gradually impaired the value of the public works. The circus and theaters might still excite, but they seldom gratified, the desires of the people: the temples, which had escaped the zeal of the Christians, were no longer inhabited, either by gods or men; the diminished crowds of the Romans were lost in the immense space of their baths and porticos; and the stately libraries and halls of justice became useless to an indolent generation, whose repose was seldom disturbed, either by study or business. The monuments of consular, or Imperial, greatness were no longer revered, as the immortal glory of the capital: they were only esteemed as an inexhaustible mine of materials, cheaper, and more convenient than the distant quarry. Specious petitions were continually addressed to the easy magistrates of Rome, which stated the want of stones or bricks, for some necessary service: the fairest forms of architecture were rudely defaced, for the sake of some paltry, or pretended, repairs; and the degenerate Romans, who converted the spoil to their own emolument, demolished, with sacrilegious hands, the labors of their ancestors. Majorian, who had often sighed over the desolation of the city, applied a severe remedy to the growing evil.

He reserved to the prince and senate the sole cognizance of the extreme cases which might justify the destruction of an ancient edifice; imposed a fine of fifty pounds of gold (two thousand pounds sterling) on every magistrate who should presume to grant such illegal and scandalous license, and threatened to chastise the criminal obedience of their subordinate officers, by a severe whipping, and the amputation of both their hands. In the last instance, the legislator might seem to forget the proportion of guilt and punishment; but his zeal arose from a generous principle, and Majorian was anxious to protect the monuments of those ages, in which he would have desired and deserved to live. The emperor conceived that it was his interest to increase the number of his subjects; and that it was his duty to guard the purity of the marriage-bed: but the means which he employed to accomplish these salutary purposes are of an ambiguous, and perhaps exceptionable, kind. The pious maids, who consecrated their virginity to Christ, were restrained from taking the veil till they had reached their fortieth year. Widows under that age were compelled to form a second alliance within the term of five years, by the forfeiture of half their wealth to their nearest relations, or to the state. Unequal marriages were condemned or annulled. The punishment of confiscation and exile was deemed so inadequate to the guilt of adultery, that, if the criminal returned to Italy, he might, by the express declaration of Majorian, be slain with impunity.

Questions:

24. The way in which the author describes the barbarians is analogous to _____.

    A. a man talking about his brother
    B. a person in a debate reassessing a misconceived subject
    C. an apologist talking about a taboo topic
    D. a doctor describing a malignant and highly feared illness
    E. a professor talking about rudimentary facts in a room full of experts

25. The passage provides evidence to suggest that the author would be most likely to assent to which one of the following proposals?

    A. There should have been allowances made for adultery.

B. Majorian was too harsh towards the magistrates.
C. The Romans displayed values and principles when they chose to demolish older buildings and monuments
D. Majorian should have been more lax in trying to increase the numbers of his citizens.
E. People had no right to utilize the decaying buildings for building materials.

26. The argument made suggests that the author believes _____.

A. The Roman civilization is comparable to more modern civilizations.
B. The Vandals were equal to the Goths and the Romans in culpability.
C. Great buildings go towards making and defining a great culture.
D. The enforcement of repopulation was a mistake, as it detracted from the number of nuns.
E. We can learn from Majorian's mistakes.

27. Which of the following statements, if shown to be true, would most detract from the author's conclusions about the destruction of buildings and monuments?

A. The city's plumbing was in some ways better than that of the modern world during the years in question.
B. The amount of people visiting the temples at the time was actually quite high.
C. A poll of the city from the dates in question revealed the popular opinion to be that the most important buildings were in fact the temples, monuments, and consular buildings.
D. During the period in question the quarries sold more stone than in the previous century.
E. Several of the ministers for architecture had plans to reinvigorate the city.

28. The author most likely lists some of Majorian's population control methods primarily to _____.

A. criticize the policy
B. honor the decisiveness of such a controversial set of rules, which by modern methods would be considered extreme
C. bring the subjects of religion and marriage into the argument
D. show that Majorian was striving, beyond reasonable morals, to reinstate Rome's greatness
E. describe at length the procedures used as an example

Answer sheet with explanation

1. **Correct Answer:** A biologist noticing trends in a set of collected data, accounting and controlling for extraneous variables, and creating a general model that can be applied to other relevant instances

Explanation: The form of theoretic jurisprudence, according to the author, is one that very closely resembles an empirical science-that is, it draws conclusions based on trends noted from relevant data, with extraneous or distracting factors accounted for or removed, used to create models that predict future results. As such, the most closely analogous case would be the one that follows this pattern, especially the necessary condition that the model be useful for predicting future cases.

2. **Correct Answer:** There is nothing irrelevant to the practice of law.

Explanation: The author states ("The reason why a lawyer does not mention that his client wore a white hat when he made a contract") that there are some details that are irrelevant in making legal arguments. Other responses can be supported by specific statements in the passage (e.g., "It is to make the prophecies easier to be remembered and to be understood that the teachings of the decisions of the past are put into general propositions and gathered into textbooks" and its surrounding context supporting the notion that legal principles are guides to helping predict the outcome of a case).

3. **Correct Answer:** The proper subject of the study of law itself, as opposed to individual laws, is to derive and deduce legal principles from first principles.

Explanation: While it is unlikely that the author would agree with any of the responses, as they either have no relevance to the passage or contradict details of it, the credited response is the one that most nearly contradicts the main idea of the passage: that jurisprudence is concerned not with deriving legal principles from eternal first principles of morality, but with predicting how courts will act in certain situations given past cases and statutes.

4. **Correct Answer:** It is not necessary to learn every single court decision, statute, or legal determination that has been issued in the last 600 years, as the relevent issues are recapitulated and reinterpreted regularly.

Explanation: The final paragraph claims that, while the already overwhelming body of law in its statutes and decisions is growing by the moment at a rate nobody could ever hope to keep up with, mastering every single detail of the centuries-old corpus is not necessary as the main issues are reinterpreted in ways relevent to contemporary society in every generation. The credited response most closely matches this point in its details, capturing not only the overwhelming size of the legal corpus and its inexorable increase, but also the nature of how it is recapitulated in every generation and the practical consequences for legal practice.

5. **Correct Answer:** "We must beware of the pitfall of antiquarianism, and must remember that for our purposes our only interest in the past is for the light it throws upon the present."

Explanation: The author's attitude towards past legal decisions and statutes is one in which this history has its uses for understanding the present, but there are certain limits to its use; as soon as a historical approach ceases to be useful in "explaining a conception or interpreting a rule," it is to be abandoned. Thus, while an understanding of legal history is useful to a degree, it is not to be used to the exclusion of other methods. The credited response is the one that best shows this limited approach to the use of legal history. While some other responses mention history, and, indeed, how present practice can flow from the past, they do not mention the limits that ought to be placed on deference to the past; indeed, the requirement in one response that legal reasoning "follow from the principles of personal and political morality" of past legislators contradicts Holmes's assertion that there are strict limits to the use of history.

6. **Correct Answer:** The law is itself lawful, and the one who understands its first principles can reason to its conclusions.

Explanation: The credited response most closely matches the idea, rejected by the author, that law can be conducted as if by syllogism, proceeding from known premises always and truly via logic to certain conclusions. The picture painted by the author is one in which many factors—history, ethics, society and its changes, and "what is then considered to be convenient"-combine and meld to form the body of law, a sometimes disorderly and not strictly logical body. The other responses, while perhaps not always strictly in agreement with all of the author's nuances and ideas, do not so directly contradict the central thesis of the passage.

7. **Correct Answer:** there is no role for systematic logic in the interpretation of laws

Explanation: While the author does spend the first paragraph attacking the idea that law is a strictly logical discipline, he never says that it is not one in which logical procedures and operations are not to be used-just that their use must be subordinated to experience. Other responses can be validly extrapolated from specific citations in the text (e.g., "The felt necessities of the time ... should be governed" supporting the idea that laws reflect the societies in which they were enacted), while the idea that there is nothing formally logical in the practice of law cannot.

8. **Correct Answer:** A set of examples used to illustrate an assertion earlier in the passage

Explanation: The passage makes an allusion to a body of examples - the laws of Massachusetts - in order to show through an example how a certain assertion made in the previous paragraph - that law reflects what is convenient at a certain place and time and its present form reflects its past - might be justified; however, it cannot be called a specific example (no particular law of the Commonwealth is referred to, much less how that law is indebted to ancient Europe), nor one that bolsters a premise in an earlier argument. The paragraph does not illustrate procedures being applied, as no specific procedures are being discussed here; nor does it contrast two approaches to the study of any subject, but rather the reasons behind the form and functioning of laws; nor does it make a merely rhetorical contrast.

9. **Correct Answer:** The work of Copernicus was a necessary step for people to be able to think of other worlds as possibly inhabited.

Explanation: The author implies that the Copernican revolution was a necessary first step to people thinking of the Earth as one celestial body among many ("the new [Copernican] conception of [the Earth's] position involves a promotion, since the earth itself is now regarded as a heavenly body of the same order as some of those that shine down upon us"), which was itself a necessary step for people to also think of other celestial bodies as possibly being inhabited. Thus, without the Copernican revolution, it would not have been possible to consider other worlds as potentially being inhabited if the author's assumptions are true.

10. **Correct Answer:** No uninhabited world is the home of intelligent beings.

Explanation: The presence of intelligent beings is a necessary, but not sufficient, condition for a world to be inhabited; however, the passage also implies that the presence of intelligent beings on an inhabited world does not necessarily imply a lack of unintelligent ones as well. While this is most strongly suggested by the description of terrestrial explorers needing to find human beings in addition to plant and animal life, it is not precluded by the logical structure of the argument. The presence of intelligent life does not necessarily exclude the presence of non-intelligent life (A does not imply not-B), even if there is nothing in the passage that suggests that intelligent life requires non-intelligent life.

11. **Correct Answer:** An additional, secondary conclusion that can be derived from the primary conclusion of the passage

Explanation: The final sentence is a secondary conclusion based on one of the implications of the main conclusion of the section. As the primary conclusion states that all inhabited planets must have intelligent life with physical bodies, one may draw the subsequent conclusion that any inhabited planets must, as a necessary condition for these beings, meet certain conditions required by the bodies of living beings. This point is not so much the primary conclusion of the passage as it is an inference drawn from analyzing an assumption implicit in the necessary conditions for supporting certain kinds of life.

12. **Correct Answer:** Reflective and philosophical

Explanation: The author, who spends his first few paragraphs reflecting on the development of humanity's conception of the cosmos, adopts a philosophical point of view, examining the implications of these developments primarily from a metaphysical standpoint. While his tone is not especially emotional or passionate (ruling out many of the more extreme or emotionally charged options, like "witty" or "elegiac"), it is not overly detached and dry, like one would expect from "formal," "didactic," "objective," or "serious" writing.

The balanced, moderate, and reflective tone leads to choosing descriptors that are themselves neither overly intense nor overly removed in describing passion and emotion.

13. **Correct Answer:** As science has progressed, people have wondered if there are other worlds that might be inhabited by creatures like ourselves.

Explanation: The credited response is the only one that addresses the thesis of the passage as a whole, rather than the points of individual paragraphs or sections. While the other responses are supported by the passage, they do not capture the overall aim of the passage as a whole, which is what this particular type of question asks about. There are several parts and subsidiary ideas in this passage to look for in determining the credited response: the advancement of science, the conditions needed for a world to be considered inhabited, and how like human beings the inhabitants of other worlds must be. All of these are present in the correct response.

14. **Correct Answer:** Giving the history of the development of a theory; mentioning a consequence of this development; describing necessary conditions for a state of affairs; drawing conclusions from these conditions

Explanation: The credited response is the only one that describes the rhetorical and logical structure of the passage. The passage begins with a historical overview, before describing the scientific and philosophical consequences of the developments described in that overview. It then lays out the necessary conditions needed for a world to be considered inhabited before extrapolating conclusions from the consequences of these conditions. There is no mention of empirical scientific investigation based on observations, nor are there discussions of theoretical models, eliminating all responses that mention them.

15. **Correct Answer:** To transition between the historical and metaphysical survey of the opening paragraphs and the logical arguments of the following ones

Explanation: This paragraph is primarily a transition between the first and second sections of the passage. It attempts to connect the historical development of a contemporary problem—the controversy over the plurality of worlds—with some logical arguments that relate to that controversy, which is discussed in later paragraphs. By foreshadowing the eventual conclusion that will be argued for in the next paragraphs (inhabited worlds must contain intelligent creatures with physical bodies), the paragraph shows where the passage will eventually be heading. By mentioning the then-contemporary controversy of the plurality of worlds, it brings the historical sketch into the present, where it may be concluded, and by uniting the history of the first part of the passage and the logical arguments of the second part of the passage, it unites the two modes used in their respective sections and transitions from the one to the other.

16. **Correct Answer:** The monasteries of Medieval Europe were centers of scientific learning because of their ability to merge religious and scientific inquiry cohesively.

Explanation: Answering this question requires a good deal of inference on your part. Let us tackle this question by eliminating one answer choice at a time. The author's discussions of different philosophers' motivations in the first paragraph suggest that he would certainly agree that "Philosophers' motivations may be classed as either scientific or religious and ethical, or as drawing from both areas." Additionally, although he makes no mention of "organized" religion, we can assume he would be as dismissive of it as he is of religion in general. Similarly, although the author is writing at the beginning of the twentieth century, we can infer from his arguments that he would believe a great deal of the scientific achievement of the last century is down to mankind's increasing neglect for religious motivations. That leaves either "None of these" or "The monasteries of Medieval Europe were centers of scientific learning because of their ability to merge religious and scientific inquiry cohesively." Based on the author's general disdain for the influence of religion on science, it is reasonable to assume he would argue that the monasteries of Medieval Europe achieved their success in science "in spite" of their preoccupation with religion, rather than because of their ability to merge science and religion cohesively.

17. **Correct Answer:** Impossible

Explanation: This question can be answered quite easily, either through an understanding of context or by understanding the definition of the word "insoluble." In context, the author discusses how philosophers are expected to determine the nature of the universe, and give cause for optimism or pessimism, and how this expectation is misplaced. One could reasonably infer that he believes determining the nature of the universe is "impossible." Also, the author states plainly, "I believe the conception of 'the universe' to be, as its etymology indicates, a mere relic of pre-Copernican astronomy, and I believe the question of optimism and pessimism to be one which the philosopher will regard as outside his scope, except, possibly, to the extent of maintaining that it is insoluble." "Insoluble" means not achievable, or impossible to solve.

18. **Correct Answer:** Hume

Explanation: In the opening paragraph, the author details the different types of philosophical inquiry, and throughout the essay he argues that philosophy grounded in science is significantly more useful than philosophy grounded in religion. He states, "These two groups of motives are, on the one hand, those derived from religion and ethics, and, on the other hand, those derived from science. Plato, Spinoza, and Hegel may be taken as typical of the philosophers whose interests are mainly religious and ethical, while Leibniz, Locke, and Hume may be taken as representatives of the scientific wing. In Aristotle, Descartes, Berkeley, and Kant we find both groups of motives strongly present." In answering this question, we must identify a philosopher who is in the same camp as the author; this is plainly Hume, who is "representative of the scientific wing."

19. **Correct Answer:** While many believe that evolution represents a successful combination of science and ethics, the author would likely disagree with this view.

Explanation: We can figure out the correct answer by considering each answer choice carefully. "Only scientific philosophers are expected to tell us something about the nature of the universe" is incorrect because the passage says, "A philosopher is expected to tell us something about the nature of the universe as a whole," and does not differentiate between scientifically-motivated and religiously-motivated philosophers in describing this expectation. "Scientific results are remarkably useful when applied to the sphere of philosophy" is incorrect because in the fourth paragraph, the author argues that "Much philosophy inspired by science has gone astray through preoccupation with the results momentarily supposed to have been achieved." "A number of philosophers cannot be classed as either being motivated by science or as being motivated by ethics and religion" is incorrect because in the first paragraph, the author claims that "broadly speaking, [philosophers] can be divided into two groups... those derived from religion and ethics, and ... those derived from science." While the author continues by mentioning that certain philosophers fall into both of these groups, no mention is made of a significant number of philosophers falling outside these two groups entirely. "Science has experienced the same sort of setbacks in recent years as religion has during the past" is entirely unsupported by the passage, as at no point does the author compare setbacks experienced by science to setbacks experienced by religion; he blames the first on religious influence and urges the second.

Eliminating all of these answer choices leaves us with the correct answer, "While many believe that evolution represents a successful combination of science and ethics, the author would likely disagree with this view." This answer is supported by the last sentence of paragraph two, "[Herbert Spencer's] ethical preoccupations are what make him value the conception of evolution-that conception in which, as a whole generation has believed, science and morals are to be united in fruitful and indissoluble marriage." We can infer based on the author's view as explained in the rest of the passage that he would not agree that science and morals can be successfully united, as he sees religious and moral influences as hindering scientific philosophical enquiry and the proponents of each camp as "often antagonistic."

20. **Correct Answer:** critical and intolerant

Explanation: Throughout the text, the author rallies against the influence of religion and ethics on science and on philosophical inquiry.

Consider this excerpt: "It is my belief that the ethical and religious motives in spite of the splendidly imaginative systems to which they have given rise have been on the whole a hindrance to the progress of philosophy, and ought now to be consciously thrust aside by those who wish to discover philosophical truth. Science, originally, was entangled in similar motives, and was thereby hindered in its advances." From this quotation, we may determine that the author views religion and its influence negatively.

However, he is never arrogant or mocking in his dismissal; rather, it is more accurate to say he is "critical and intolerant." When determining tone and attitude of an author, be wary of selecting an answer that is overly strong without sufficient evidence to support this conclusion. Authors of well-known essays are rarely completely one-sided or brazen in their attacks, for this generally weakens academic writing.

21. **Correct Answer:** Hostile and non-complementary

Explanation: This question might be answered from an understanding of the whole text, but then there are a couple of different answers that might be reasonably selected, such as "Puzzling and oppositional," "Wanton and pointless," and "Hostile and non-complementary." Instead, it is better to look for a piece of specific evidence to give the best possible answer. Luckily, such a piece of evidence appears early in the introduction when the author states, "When we try to ascertain the motives which have led men to the investigation of philosophical questions, we find that, broadly speaking, they can be divided into two groups, often antagonistic, and leading to very divergent systems. These two groups of motives are, on the one hand, those derived from religion and ethics, and, on the other hand, those derived from science." The author states that the two groups are "antagonistic, and leading to very divergent systems." From "antagonistic" we may derive "hostile," and from "divergent" we may derive "non-complementary."

22. **Correct Answer:** "On the Positive Applications of Scientific Method to Philosophy"

Explanation: When asked to determine the best title for an essay, you are mostly being asked if you understand the primary motivation and thesis of the passage. Many of these answer choices are part of the argument, but only one represents an accurate portrayal of the thesis. The following answer choices are deficient: "On Results-Based and Method-Based Scientific Philosophical Inquiry" is incorrect because it does not convey the author's support of method-based scientific philosophical inquiry whereas another the correct answer does; "In Praise of Herbert Spencer" is incorrect because the author only mentions Spencer in passing, and indeed is as much critical (although in a veiled manner) as he is effusive with praise; "In Defense of Scientific Inquiry and Exploration" is incorrect because it covers only part of the argument and does not transcend the whole of the essay; and "On the Overwhelming Influence of Religion on the Development of Philosophical Thought" is incorrect because this is discussed only in passing to reinforce part of the author's argument against religious motivations. The best answer choice is "On the Positive Applications of Scientific Method to Philosophy" because it captures the primary motivation of the author, to urge his audience to embrace scientific method in their pursuit of philosophical truth.

23. **Correct Answer:** Its entanglement with religious and ethical motivations

Explanation: Answering this question requires paying close attention to detail.
In the third paragraph, the author states, "It is my belief that the ethical and religious motives in spite of the splendidly imaginative systems to which they have given rise have been on the whole a hindrance to the progress of philosophy... Science, originally, was entangled in similar motives, and was thereby hindered in its advances." Based on this quotation, we can ascertain quite plainly that science's entanglement with religious and ethical motives has long hindered its progress, in the author's opinion.

24. **Correct Answer:** a person in a debate reassessing a misconceived subject

Explanation: Of these five choices, the best is "a person in a debate reassessing a misconceived subject." The author is supposedly presenting facts, but they are more opinions than facts as he does not go into any great detail to prove them. He does reassess the general opinion of the barbarians as those who destroyed Rome, so he is initially dealing with a misconceived subject. The analogy of the doctor would be correct if the word "malignant" was replaced with "benign."

25. **Correct Answer:** Majorian should have been laxer in trying to increase the numbers of his citizens.

Explanation: When addressing Majorian's rules concerning repopulation, the author states that "the means which he employed to accomplish these salutary purposes are of an ambiguous, and perhaps exceptionable, kind." He goes on to list some of the harsh rules instated during Majorian's rule. Perhaps if Majorian had been more lax or easygoing in his rules, the author would be more likely to assent to them. The other answers can be proven false by searching the text. The answer concerning "virtues and principles" is made false by the phrase "the degenerate Romans."

26. **Correct Answer:** Great buildings go towards making and defining a great culture.

Explanation: The passage argues a great deal about architecture and the city slowly falling into ruin and would suggest that a great culture is defined by its buildings more than its people. The people who destroyed the city are seen as lesser than those who tried to save it. The author does not mention functional buildings, only those we would consider magnificent. The author draws a parallel between building and culture in Majorian, who he cites as a man of "taste and spirit" who seems to be alone in the author's description of those who worked to save the city.

27. **Correct Answer:** During the period in question the quarries sold more stone than in the previous century.

Explanation: The author states quite emphatically that "the monuments of consular, or Imperial, greatness were no longer revered, as the immortal glory of the capital: they were only esteemed as an inexhaustible mine of materials, cheaper, and more convenient than the distant quarry." Whilst some of the other statements would conflict with the author's argument, the one which would be most harmful to the author's conclusions would be that the quarries actually prospered during this time. If the quarries had prospered, then it would suggest that building occurred more often and demolishing to recycle cheap materials did not occur as much.

28. **Correct Answer:** Show that Majorian was striving, beyond reasonable morals, to reinstate Rome's greatness

Explanation: The author quite clearly respects Majorian yet disagrees with the brutality of some of his methods, as he switches between the apologetic tone found in the line "Majorian was anxious to protect the monuments of those ages, in which he would have desired and deserved to live," and the questioning tone of the line "the means which he employed to accomplish these salutary purposes are of an ambiguous, and perhaps exceptionable, kind." So we can only really say that the author is stating the methods with which Majorian was trying to reinstate Rome's greatness and how they were questionable measures from a modern perspective.

Practice Test 3: Argumentative Writing section

The Argumentative Writing section of the LSAT evaluates your ability to construct a well-reasoned argument. You will be presented with a prompt that outlines a controversial issue. Your task is to take a position on the issue, support your stance with logical reasoning and evidence, and address potential counterarguments.

Prompt: The city council of Rivertown is considering implementing a congestion charge in the downtown area to reduce traffic and pollution. The charge would require drivers to pay a fee to enter the city center during peak hours. Proponents argue that the congestion charge will lead to decreased traffic, lower pollution levels, and encourage the use of public transportation. Opponents claim that the charge will disproportionately affect low-income residents, increase the cost of living, and hurt local businesses.

Assignment: Write an essay in which you argue for or against the implementation of the congestion charge in Rivertown. In your essay, you should:

1. Clearly state your position on the issue.
2. Provide reasons and evidence to support your position.
3. Address at least one counterargument to your position.
4. Conclude by summarizing your argument and reinforcing your stance.

Example Essay Outline

1. Introduction

   - Briefly introduce the issue of the congestion charge.
   - State your thesis clearly, indicating your position on the matter.

2. Supporting Argument 1

   - Present your first reason supporting your position.
   - Provide evidence or examples to back up this reason.

3. Supporting Argument 2

   - Present your second reason supporting your position.
   - Provide evidence or examples to back up this reason.

4. Counterargument

   - Address a counterargument to your position.
   - Refute the counterargument with reasoning and evidence.

5. Conclusion

   - Summarize your main points.
   - Restate your thesis and reinforce your argument.

Answer sheet with explanation

Sample Essay Answer

Introduction:
The proposal to implement a congestion charge in Rivertown's downtown area has sparked considerable debate. While the measure aims to alleviate traffic and reduce pollution, its potential socioeconomic impacts cannot be overlooked. I argue against the implementation of the congestion charge because it disproportionately affects low-income residents and poses a risk to local businesses.

Explanation:
The introduction clearly states the writer's position against the congestion charge and introduces the main reasons for their stance, setting up the structure for the essay.

Supporting Argument 1:
Firstly, the congestion charge unfairly burdens low-income residents. Many individuals who rely on their vehicles for commuting to work or accessing essential services may find the additional fee financially straining. Unlike more affluent residents who can easily absorb the extra cost or shift to alternative transportation, low-income individuals may have limited options, thereby exacerbating economic inequality.

Explanation:
This paragraph provides a clear reason supported by an explanation of how the congestion charge affects low-income residents. It highlights the financial strain and limited options for these individuals.

Supporting Argument 2:
Secondly, the introduction of a congestion charge could hurt local businesses. Many small businesses in the downtown area depend on regular customer traffic. An additional fee for entering the city center might deter shoppers, resulting in reduced sales and potential closures. The long-term economic health of Rivertown hinges on the vitality of its local businesses, which could be jeopardized by the congestion charge.

Explanation:
The second supporting argument focuses on the negative impact on local businesses. It explains how the fee might reduce customer traffic and hurt the economic health of the community.

Counterargument:
Proponents of the congestion charge argue that it will lead to decreased traffic and pollution, benefiting the environment and overall quality of life. While these goals are commendable, there are alternative approaches to achieving them without imposing financial hardships. For example, improving public transportation infrastructure and offering incentives for using eco-friendly vehicles can address traffic and pollution issues more equitably.

Explanation:
This paragraph addresses a counterargument by acknowledging the benefits of the congestion charge but proposing alternative solutions that do not impose financial hardships.

Conclusion:
In conclusion, while the congestion charge in Rivertown aims to tackle significant urban challenges, it poses serious risks to low-income residents and local businesses. Alternative solutions should be explored to achieve the desired environmental benefits without compromising economic fairness and community welfare. Therefore, I oppose the implementation of the congestion charge as it stands.

Explanation:
The conclusion summarizes the main points of the essay and restates the writer's position, reinforcing the argument against the congestion charge.

Key Points and Explanations:

- Position Statement: The writer clearly states their opposition to the congestion charge in the introduction.
- Supporting Arguments: The essay provides two well-explained reasons: the financial burden on low-income residents and the potential negative impact on local businesses.
- Counterargument: The writer acknowledges the opposing view and offers alternative solutions, demonstrating critical thinking.
- Conclusion: The essay concludes by summarizing the arguments and restating the position, ensuring a coherent and persuasive argument.

This sample essay serves as a model for structuring an argumentative essay, showcasing how to effectively present and support a position while addressing counterarguments.

Practice Test 4: Full-length simulated exam practice tests

LOGICAL REASONING SECTION

1. After replacing her old air conditioner with a new, energy-efficient unit, Paula's electric bills increased.

Each of the following, if true, contributes to an explanation of the increase mentioned above EXCEPT:
   A. Paula's electricity costs increased by 15 cents per kilowatt hour after she replaced her air conditioner.
   B. Following the installation of her new air conditioner, Paula's neighborhood experienced a prolonged and severe heat wave, requiring heavy use of the new unit.
   C. Paula installed an electricity-intensive indoor tanning bed after she replaced her air conditioning unit.
   D. Soon after the new air conditioner was installed, Paula adopted a child, doubling the size of her household.
   E. The new air conditioner uses a smaller share of the electricity used by Paula's home than did the old unit.

2. Roger: The only reason diesel cars are not commonly used in the United States is that people believe they are more costly to fuel and maintain than gasoline cars. Fueling diesel cars is less expensive than fueling gasoline cars because they get many more miles per gallon. Diesel cars also last many more years. While other countries transition to diesel, the United States follows a myth.

Tamara: Many people in the United states do not even know that purchasing a diesel car is an option. Others may choose to purchase a gasoline car because they overemphasize the purchase price difference.

Roger and Tamara most likely disagree about which of the following?

   A. Diesel cars last many more years than gasoline cars
   B. There is a purchase price difference between diesel and gasoline cars
   C. Diesel cars are more costly than gasoline cars
   D. Diesel cars are not commonly used in the United States because people believe they are more costly to operate than gasoline cars
   E. Diesel cars should be used more often than they are

3. Paul: The U.S. should prohibit deer hunting for at least ten years. If the deer population continues to decrease, other species will be affected, which would harm industries in various parts of the country.

Lisa: While I believe that hunting is cruel, the only way to protect drivers from deer is to hunt them. Humans should be valued above deer and industries.

Paul and Lisa are most likely to agree that

 A. Deer hunting should be permitted only if there is no other available means of protecting drivers
 B. Hunting should be prohibited in order to protect various species
 C. Deer hunting harms U.S. industry
 D. Hunting deer is cruel
 E. Deer pose an unacceptable danger to drivers

4. Employee 1: I am considering resigning and obtaining other available work. I do not have any disputes with my employers and enjoy my coworkers, but the benefits are less than they were, the hours are longer, and the work has become tedious. Many of my friends are satisfied with their jobs and employment openings are advertised everywhere.

Employee 2: I have also considered resigning. I stay because I am risk averse. Sure, this job has downsides, but our benefits here are above average and I might resign only to ask for my job again because other jobs are unavailable.

The employees are most likely to disagree about whether:

 A. Other jobs are available
 B. Their current benefits are above average
 C. It is preferable to be risk averse
 D. They have disputes with their employers
 E. Employment opportunities are advertised everywhere

5. The spiritual basketball coach encourages his players to practice Zen meditation techniques only when facing difficult opponents. These meditation techniques are a more highly disciplined form of the ritual meditation that the coach has his players practice on a regular basis prior to games and involves unique practices such as chanting and fasting.

Which one of the statements below does NOT follow logically from the passage above?

 A. The coach believes that mediation benefits his players.
 B. The coach has his players meditate in preparation for facing their opponents.
 C. The ritual daily meditation that the players practice is largely undisciplined.
 D. Some meditation practices are less disciplined than Zen meditation.
 E. The ritual daily meditation does not involve chanting and fasting.

6. We all have an obligation to do our part to protect nature. Only those who do are environmentally responsible. No people who insist on using incandescent light bulbs do their part to protect nature.

Which of the following conclusions follows:

A. All those who do not insist on using incandescent light bulbs are environmentally responsible
B. Incandescent light bulbs are only used by those who are environmentally irresponsible
C. People who insist on using incandescent light bulbs are not environmentally responsible
D. Environmentally responsible people have an obligation to discourage others from using incandescent light bulbs
E. Incandescent light bulbs cause harm to nature

7. When describing weather, people describe only sunny days as "nice" days. Why should this be? The meaning of "nice" in other contexts depends on the subjective preferences of the speaker. For instance, a person would only describe a car as being "nice" if the person personally preferred it, and one person might describe a particular car as "nice" while another would not. A person who prefers rain to sun, however, would likely still describe a sunny day as a "nice" day, but would not describe a rainy day the same way.

Which of the following most accurately describes the main point of the argument?

A. The precise meaning of words depends on the context in which they are used
B. People generally use the word "nice" more subjectively when describing cars than when describing weather
C. In the context of describing weather, the word "nice" has a different, less subjective meaning than in other contexts
D. The meaning of the word "nice" varies substantially from one context to another
E. Some people prefer rainy days to sunny days

8. Public transportation plays less of a role in commuting within cities than it once did, which is unfortunate because the benefits for cities and residents are substantial. Public transportation leads to less traffic congestion, more parking for those who do drive, less stress, less expense, and better air quality. Legitimate downsides to taking public transportation include safety concerns and lengthened commutes. Addressing these concerns would take effort but would also produce tremendous benefits.

Which of the following conclusions best follows from the argument?

A. If public transportation were used more widely, traffic in cities would run more smoothly and there would be other benefits as well
B. Public transportation is used less often in cities now than it once was because of safety concerns and longer commutes

C. It is difficult to explain why fewer people use public transportation than once did because the benefits are substantial for cities and city residents

D. While there are significant benefits to public transportation in cities, the substantial downsides explain why it is used less than it once was

E. While there are downsides to public transportation, they could be addressed and public transportation has benefits for both cities and residents

9. Although most people occasionally bring their cars to an automated car wash, few really ensure that their cars are thoroughly cleaned–probably because most people care only that their cars have a generally clean appearance. An automated car wash will generally accomplish that goal, but a car wash should accomplish more. An automated car wash will not thoroughly clean a car, and a car that is not thoroughly cleaned will quickly rust.

Which of the following best expresses the main point of the passage?

A. Automated car washes provide some protection against rust, but alone are not sufficient protection

B. Cars are generally not washed often enough to be protected from rust

C. Cars that are only cleaned at automated car washes will quickly rust

D. Most cars are not thoroughly cleaned

E. Most people are overly concerned about their cars having a generally clean appearance

10. The general contractor working on the new bridge should use caution before hiring subcontractors because many subcontractors defraud general contractors who do not take appropriate caution. When general contractors take appropriate caution, however, they always avoid being defrauded. The general contractor working on the new bridge will not be defrauded because he has formal contracts with his subcontractors.

Which of the following assumptions, if true, allows the conclusion to be properly drawn?

A. General contractors are only sometimes defrauded

B. Obtaining a formal contract is appropriate caution

C. Some general contractors take appropriate caution without obtaining formal contracts

D. Some contractors who take appropriate caution also obtain formal contracts

E. Some general contractors who obtain formal contracts are defrauded

11. A paleontologist found a dinosaur tibia and fibula bone group that was too large to be placed into a stabilized storage chest. Luckily, an assistant discovered a way to safely separate the tibia and fibula bones. These bones could be reassembled later without a noticeable change in either bone. Now the bones can be placed in two stabilized storage chests.

The argument above depends on which of the following assumptions?

A. The procedure for using two chests does not cost more money than using just one vault.
B. The optimal conditions for preservation of the bones are found in the stabilized storage chest.
C. Placing the bones into the chest does not alter the accuracy of a later carbon-14 dating.
D. Neither the tibia or fibula bone is too large to fit into the chest.
E. The tibia and fibula bone group can be separated into two equal sized parts.

12. At this school, there are no ballet dancers who are also salsa dancers. However, all ballroom dancers are also salsa dancers. Therefore, no ballroom dancers will be competing in the upcoming competition.

The conclusion above follows logically if which one of the following is assumed?

A. Some salsa dancers will compete in the upcoming competition.
B. No ballet dancers are also ballroom dancers.
C. Everyone who will compete in the upcoming competition is not a ballet dancer.
D. Everyone who will compete in the upcoming competition is a salsa dancer.
E. Everyone who will compete in the upcoming competition is a ballet dancer.

13. Soccer players are faster than baseball players because soccer players use more strenuous training programs. Baseball players should use the same training programs as soccer players to become more athletic. More athletic players will be more successful.

Which of the following, if assumed, would allow the conclusion above to be properly drawn?

A. Fast baseball players sometimes also play soccer
B. Baseball players do not train very often during the season
C. Players who become faster become more athletic
D. Baseball requires different skills than soccer
E. Speed is important to success in baseball

14. Standard sheets of printer paper do not vary in the amount of wood pulp that they contain. Twenty-five percent of the wood pulp contained in a certain class of sheets of standard printer paper (Class B) was recycled from used sheets of standard printer paper of a different class (Class A). Since all Class A sheets were recycled into Class B sheets and since the amount of material other than wood pulp in a sheet of standard printer paper is negligible, it follows that Class B contains 4 times as many sheets of paper as Class A.

The conclusion of the argument follows logically if which one of the following is assumed?

A. Unrecycled wood pulp is of better quality than recycled wood pulp.
B. All of the paper in Class A had been made from recycled wood pulp.
C. Class B sheets of paper cannot be recycled further.

D. When a sheet of standard printer paper is a recycled, all of its wood pulp is recovered.
E. The percentage of wood pulp in a sheet of standard printer paper that can be recovered during recycling varies depending on how such paper was used.

15. A medical degree is necessary for appointment to the hospital's board of directors. Further, no one having more than a five-percent equity stake in a pharmaceutical company can be appointed to the board of directors. Consequently, Dell, a practicing physician with a PhD in bioethics, cannot be appointed the hospital's treasurer, since he owns fifteen percent of PillCo, a pharmaceutical company.

The argument's conclusion follows logically if which one of the following is assumed?

A. Only those eligible for appointment to the hospital's board of directors can be appointed as the hospital's treasurer.
B. A PhD is not necessary for appointment to the position of treasurer.
C. Anyone with a medical degree who does not hold more than a five-percent stake in any pharmaceutical company is eligible for appointment to the hospital's board of directors.
D. PillCo is one of the hospital's pharmaceutical vendors.
E. If Dell sold his stake in PillCo, he would be appointed treasurer.

16. Academics in theology departments generally agree that there are fewer religious people today than fifty years ago. There are two primary critiques of that view, however. First, the conclusion depends on a definition that is highly subject to debate. If "religion" is defined as a strongly held conviction about the purpose of the world, for instance, the academics may be incorrect. On the other hand, the conclusion would be justified if "religion" is defined as a belief in a supernatural god. Second, the academics base their conclusion almost exclusively on data collected from the western hemisphere.

Which of the following, if assumed, strengthens the conclusion of the academics?

A. The conclusion applied only to the western hemisphere
B. The definition of "religion" was as highly subject to debate fifty years ago as it is today
C. Fewer people believe in a supernatural god today than fifty years ago
D. Academics often draw conclusions based on evidence based almost exclusively on data from the western hemisphere
E. Most people believe "religion" should be defined as a belief in a supernatural god

17. When car manufacturers place a high priority on generating large profits, they neglect their responsibility to make safe cars. Those manufacturers with the highest profits also make the most unsafe cars. Car manufacturers should be less concerned with generating large profits in order to improve car safety.

Which of the following, if true, most strengthens the argument?

A. All car manufacturers expend approximately the same resources on car safety

B. When car manufacturers reduce their priority on generating large profits, their profits actually increase
C. Car manufacturers that make the safest cars also give large amounts of money to charities
D. The car manufacturers with the highest profits also place a high priority on generating large profits
E. Car safety can be improved with little effort on the part of car manufacturers

18. Some arguments for expanding U.S. oil production are misguided. Vehicles that do not burn gasoline will be readily available within fifty years, and vehicles that do not burn gasoline do not require oil production. Furthermore, any job creation benefits from increased oil production would be offset by the negative economic effects of producing a product that will not be in demand. Alternatively, jobs can also be created by increased development of oil alternatives.

The argument is strengthened by all of the following, if true, except:

A. Current oil production will meet the demand for oil over the next fifty years
B. When vehicles that do not burn gasoline are readily available, they will be used exclusively
C. Oil will not be used for any purpose after 50 years
D. Oil consumption causes substantial environmental harms
E. Production of alternatives to oil will create as many jobs as the increased production of oil

19. I saw John running through the rain to get to his next class. Even though he forgot his umbrella today, he accomplished nothing by running instead of walking. People get just as wet running in the rain as they do walking, even though they may arrive at their destinations more quickly.

Which of the following, if true, most weakens the argument?

A. John runs more quickly than most people
B. John was using an umbrella
C. John did not have to run very far to get to class
D. John ran to class in order to get there more quickly
E. John arrived at class more quickly than if he had walked

20. Professor: A British scholar criticized a recent publication on John Milton's Paradise Lost, written by a colleague of mine. Specifically, the British scholar lambasted the thesis, calling it a "publicity stunt," formulated simply to generate attention, and said that it was not a scholarly product. However, you should know that the British scholar and my colleague have personal distaste towards one another. Given that the British scholar's criticism of my colleague is based on mere personal bias, my colleague's thesis is clearly a product of scholarship.

The reasoning in the professor's argument is most vulnerable to criticism on the grounds that

   A. The professor himself is biased because he seems to be defending his colleague based solely on their personal relationship.
   B. The professor falsely implies that "scholarly product" and "product of scholarship" mean the same thing.
   C. The professor assumes that because there are personal tensions between the British scholar and his colleague, that the colleague's thesis must be based on scholarly merit, when in fact it may have been a publicity stunt.
   D. The professor did not discuss the content of the thesis at all, and is simply offering his own opinion as evidence as to the character of his colleague's thesis.
   E. The professor frames a "publicity stunt" and "product of scholarship" as being opposite when they are not.

READING COMPREHENSION SECTION

Passage:

Some twenty-one years ago I heard the first great anarchist speaker—the inimitable John Most. It seemed to me then, and for many years after, that the spoken word hurled forth among the masses with such wonderful eloquence, such enthusiasm and fire, could never be erased from the human mind and soul. How could any one of all the multitudes who flocked to Most's meetings escape his prophetic voice! Surely they had but to hear him to throw off their old beliefs, and see the truth and beauty of anarchism!

My one great longing then was to be able to speak with the tongue of John Most, that I, too, might thus reach the masses. Oh, for the naivety of youth's enthusiasm! It is the time when the hardest thing seems but child's play. It is the only period in life worthwhile. Alas! This period is but of short duration. Like spring, the Sturm und Drang period of the propagandist brings forth growth, frail and delicate, to be matured or killed according to its powers of resistance against a thousand vicissitudes.

My great faith in the wonder-worker, the spoken word, is no more. I have realized its inadequacy to awaken thought, or even emotion. Gradually, and with no small struggle against this realization, I came to see that oral propaganda is at best but a means of shaking people from their lethargy: it leaves no lasting impression. The very fact that most people attend meetings only if aroused by newspaper sensations, or because they expect to be amused, is proof that they really have no inner urge to learn.

It is altogether different with the written mode of human expression. No one, unless intensely interested in progressive ideas, will bother with serious books. That leads me to another discovery made after many years of public activity. It is this: all claims of education notwithstanding, the pupil will accept only that which his mind craves. Already this truth is recognized by most modern educators in relation to the immature mind. I think it is equally true regarding the adult. Anarchists or revolutionists can no more be made than musicians. All that can be done is to plant the seeds of thought. Whether something vital will develop depends largely on the fertility of the human soil, though the quality of the intellectual seed must not be overlooked.

In meetings the audience is distracted by a thousand non-essentials. The speaker, though ever so eloquent, cannot escape the restlessness of the crowd, with the inevitable result that he will fail to strike root. In all probability he will not even do justice to himself.

The relation between the writer and the reader is more intimate. True, books are only what we want them to be; rather, what we read into them. That we can do so demonstrates the importance of written as against oral expression. It is this certainty that has induced me to gather in one volume my ideas on various topics of individual and social importance. They represent the mental and soul struggles of twenty-one years—the conclusions derived after many changes and inner revisions.

Questions:

1. The author of this passage would be most likely to disagree with which of the following?

    A. An argument that youthful enthusiasm and certainty is often misplaced.
    B. A dissertation on the difficulties of impacting individuals through oration and spoken propaganda.
    C. An essay explaining the inherent value of the anarchist movement.
    D. A statement that the relationship between the reader and writer is as detached as the relationship between speaker and listener.
    E. A biographic exposition that praises the impact of John Most on the anarchist movement.

2. What does the author believe is the best-case scenario that can result from oral propaganda?

    A. The listener will be awoken from his or her apathy.
    B. The audience will be collectively inspired to act.
    C. The individual will be forced to reconsider his or her opinions and may even join the movement.
    D. None of these answers; the author believes that almost nothing good can come from oral propaganda to the extent that it is essentially pointless.
    E. The individual will seek to further advance his or her knowledge on the subject.

3. Which of these bests restates the meaning of the underlined sentence, "Like Spring, the STURM UND DRANG period of the propagandist brings forth growth, frail and delicate, to be matured or killed according to its powers of resistance against a thousand vicissitudes"?

A. In the face of widespread criticism, the opinions of the propagandist are likely to be severely tested during the early periods of his or her activism; they require constant nurturing to preserve them.
B. The propagandist is a weak and easily swayed individual who requires constant nurturing during the early periods of his or her life; otherwise he or she will quickly abandon the cause in favor of something more universally agreeable.
C. During the early period of an activist's life his or her opinions usually become set in stone and are only subject to change if the resistance of the individual is too weak to resist the impositions and criticisms of others.
D. The early period of an activist's life is crucial to the formation of his or her ideas; it is best that those ideas be heavily questioned by the individual in order to ensure they are what he or she truly believes.
E. The turbulent and emotional young period of an activist's life changes how they approach their work; it can lead to a maturity or abandonment of values depending on the will of the individual to resist change or complete alteration.

4. This essay is most likely _____.

A. the conclusion to a piece about the author's changes from youthful optimism to mature realism
B. the conclusion to a piece about the value of the written word when compared to oral propaganda
C. an introduction to a series of essays written by a group of authors about anarchism
D. an introduction to a series of essays written by one author
E. a stand-alone exposition about the author's changing emphasis on oral propaganda over the written word

5. What function does the third paragraph serve in the formation of the author's overall argument?

A. It introduces the author's argument that oral propaganda cannot function on its own, but requires written exposition and encouragement.
B. It allows for consideration of the opposite side of the author's argument to provide balance and insure the author against accusations of bias.
C. It negates the argument made earlier by the author that the written word is limited in how much it can affect the mindset of the individual.
D. It discusses the relationship between the reader and the writer and how this can be manipulated by a skilled author.
E. It acts as a transition from a discussion of the author's youthful and naïve faith in the power of the oral propaganda to a more lasting belief in the power of the written word.

6. The primary purpose of this essay is _____.

A. to lament the loss of oration as an art form and suggest that the written word, when argued convincingly, is the only recourse left to a would-be anarchist trying to bring others into the fold.
B. to compare the benefits of the written and spoken word
C. to demonstrate why orators have such difficulty in convincing an audience to change its opinions
D. to argue in favor of political anarchism
E. to explain the author's transition into writing her arguments, as opposed to offering her opinions in the form of oration

7. The author's point of view in this passage is primarily that _____.

A. When trying to influence people's perspectives and opinions the written word is a much more powerful tool than oral expression.
B. The power of oral propaganda is on the decline as people become more and more resistant against the opinions of others.
C. John Most is an exemplary figure in the propagandist movement, one whose influence the author cannot hope to match.
D. Neither the written word nor oral propaganda can function independently of one another.
E. It is naïve to place one's faith in the power of oral propaganda when people are so apt to ignore what they hear.

8. The author's attitude towards oral propaganda could best be described as _____.

A. disparaging
B. disenchanted
C. supportive
D. uneasy
E. nostalgic

Passage:

Municipal law, thus understood, is properly defined to be "a rule of civil conduct prescribed by the supreme power in a state, commanding what is right and prohibiting what is wrong." Let us endeavor to explain its several properties as they arise out of this definition.

And, first, it is a rule; not a transient sudden order from a superior to or concerning a particular person; but something permanent, uniform, and universal. Therefore, a particular act of the legislature to confiscate the goods of Titius or to attaint him of high treason does not enter into the idea of a municipal law: for the operation of this act is spent upon Titius only and has no relation to the community in general. But an act to declare that the crime of which Titius is accused shall be deemed high treason; this has permanency, uniformity, and universality, and therefore is properly a rule. It is also called a rule to distinguish it from advice or counsel, which we are at liberty to follow or not, as we see proper, and to judge upon the reasonableness or unreasonableness of the thing advised. Whereas our obedience to the law depends not upon our approbation, but upon the maker's will. Counsel is only matter of persuasion, law is matter of injunction; counsel acts only upon the willing, law upon the unwilling also.

It is also called a rule to distinguish it from a compact or agreement; for a compact is a promise proceeding from us, and law is a command directed to us. The language of a compact is, "I will, or will not, do this"; that of a law is, "Thou shalt, or shalt not, do it." It is true there is an obligation that a compact carries with it, equal in point of conscience to that of a law; but then the original of the obligation is different. In compacts, we ourselves determine and promise what shall be done, before we are obliged to do it; in laws, we are obliged to act, without ourselves determining or promising anything at all. Upon these accounts law is defined to be "a rule."

It is likewise "a rule prescribed," because a bare resolution, confined in the breast of the legislator, without manifesting itself by some external sign, can never be properly a law. It is requisite that this resolution be notified to the people who are to obey it. But the manner in which this notification is to be made is matter of very great indifference. It may be notified by universal tradition and long practice, which supposes a previous publication, and is the case of the common law of England. It may be notified, viva voce, by officers appointed for that purpose, as is done with regard to proclamations, and such acts of parliament as are appointed to be publicly read in churches and other assemblies. It may lastly be notified by writing, printing, or the like; which is the general course taken with all our acts of parliament.

Yet, whatever way is made use of, it is incumbent on the promulgators to do it in the most public and perspicuous manner; not like Caligula, who wrote his laws in a very small character, and hung them up upon high pillars, the more effectually to ensnare the people. There is still a more unreasonable method than this, which is called making of laws ex post facto; when after an action is committed, the legislator then for the first time declares it to have been a crime, and inflicts a punishment upon the person who has committed it. Here it is impossible that the party could foresee that an action, innocent when it was done, should be afterwards converted to guilt by a subsequent law; he had therefore no cause to abstain from it, and all punishment for not abstaining must of consequence be cruel and unjust. But when this rule is in the usual manner notified, or prescribed, it is then the subject's business to be thoroughly acquainted therewith; for if ignorance, of what he might know, were admitted as a legitimate excuse, the laws would be of no effect, but might always be eluded with impunity.

Questions:

9. Which of the following would most WEAKEN the author's assertions regarding the nature of law?

- A. New technologies used to communicate legislative acts in novel ways
- B. Developments in political theory and practice in which the governed and the governors became one and the same
- C. Laws specifying the mode and form in which new laws were to be promulgated

D. Historians of law showing that the particular origins of most of what is considered part of common law is obscure, lost to history, and may not have been properly promulgated according to modern standards

E. The passing of a law to ban future recurrence of some particular previous act that had once been legal

10. Which of the following is most analogous with the author's conception of a law as explained in the passage?

A. A government agency issues a set of guidelines that clarify and explain a new regulation.
B. An international judicial body decides that certain actions that took place during a war violated common principles of ethics and morality, and codify procedures under which the perpetrators can be tried.
C. A president declares a certain day a national day of mourning following a catastrophe and orders that all government offices be closed on that day.
D. An attorney drafts a contract between two parties, both of whom agree to follow its terms.
E. A local school board approves a set of teacher-hiring standards during a public meeting.

11. Which of the following is most analogous to "universal tradition and long practice, which supposes a previous publication," as is mentioned in the bolded and underlined selection in the fourth paragraph?

A. As proclaimed by the UN General Assembly, each 10 December is Human Rights Day throughout the world.
B. While it used to be the custom at a certain college, for reasons that are lost to history, to have a torchlit procession with a dead duck around the quad, this custom is today all but extinct and known to only a few historians.
C. In England, a trail or bridleway that has been used at least once in the last year may not be obstructed by the landowner whose property it crosses, as was established in a royal decree from the Norman era.
D. A certain ancient diocese celebrates its patron saint's day on 25 June every year, despite there being no record of a proclamation or edict establishing this.
E. It is generally considered a breech of social protocol for a man of whatever station to wear a hat, except as a vestment, inside a church.

12. Which of the following statements would the author of the passage be most likely to support?

A. Ignorance of the law is never an excuse for breaking the law.
B. Only those who are affected by a law have any need to know about that law.
C. Custom gains the force of law when it is written and codified by a legislator.

D. Unwritten customs, even if they have the force of rules, are not properly laws, but ethical norms.

E. The people ruled by a law ought to be notified of it before it enters force.

13. The passage does NOT support which of the following as being essential to law?

A. That there are certain standards according to which an enacted rule may be considered promulgated

B. That there shall be no ex post facto law

C. That it be generally applicable, rather than applicable to particular cases

D. That disobedience of the law is punished

E. That it be obeyed willingly or not

14. The primary purpose of the passage is _____.

A. to lay out some of the sufficient conditions for a certain phenomenon

B. to describe the historical and cultural development of a phenomenon from Classical Rome to the author's own era

C. to advocate for a certain precise definition of a philosophical term over other rival definitions

D. to lay out some of the necessary conditions for a certain phenomenon

E. to explain sub concepts and define terms that must first be understood before attempting to work with a larger, more general concept

15. What is the purpose of the bolded and underlined section in the final paragraph of the passage?

A. An injunction to observe the letter, as well as the spirit, of a principle

B. A historical example that illustrates the general principle being discussed in the passage

C. A concrete example demonstrating a seeming exception to a rule

D. A moral fable drawn from history, illustrating the methods of the unjust

E. An example of a minimum standard necessary for something to be considered promulgated

16. Which of the following is closest in meaning to the bolded and underlined word "attaint" as it is used in the second paragraph?

A. deprive

B. corrupt

C. stain

D. sentence

E. mark

Passage:

The many slight differences which appear in the offspring from the same parents, or which it may be presumed have thus arisen, from being observed in the individuals of the same species inhabiting the same confined locality, may be called individual differences. No one supposes that all the individuals of the same species are cast in the same actual mold. These individual differences are of the highest importance for us, for they are often inherited, as must be familiar to every one; and they thus afford materials for natural selection to act on and accumulate, in the same manner as man accumulates in any given direction individual differences in his domesticated productions. These individual differences generally affect what naturalists consider unimportant parts; but I could show, by a long catalogue of facts, that parts which must be called important, whether viewed under a physiological or classificatory point of view, sometimes vary in the individuals of the same species. I am convinced that the most experienced naturalist would be surprised at the number of the cases of variability, even in important parts of structure, which he could collect on good authority, as I have collected, during a course of years. It should be remembered that systematists are far from being pleased at finding variability in important characters, and that there are not many men who will laboriously examine internal and important organs, and compare them in many specimens of the same species. It would never have been expected that the branching of the main nerves close to the great central ganglion of an insect would have been variable in the same species; it might have been thought that changes of this nature could have been effected only by slow degrees; yet Sir J. Lubbock has shown a degree of variability in these main nerves in Coccus, which may almost be compared to the irregular branching of the stem of a tree. This philosophical naturalist, I may add, has also shown that the muscles in the larvæ of certain insects are far from uniform. Authors sometimes argue in a circle when they state that important organs never vary; for these same authors practically rank those parts as important (as some few naturalists have honestly confessed) which do not vary; and, under this point of view, no instance will ever be found of an important part varying; but under any other point of view many instances assuredly can be given.

Questions:

17. From the passage, it can be inferred that many scientists believe that _____.

   A. Sir J. Lubbock is the most important scientist of his age
   B. variation happens across all individuals in all species
   C. variations among individuals only occur in key animal features
   D. important organs do not vary within species
   E. individual differences do not exist among siblings in nature

18. It can be inferred from the passage that "Sir J. Lubbock" is which of the following?

   A. A well-respected member of the House of Lords
   B. A prominent opponent of the author in scientific circles
   C. A well-known researcher whose work has touched on the variability of animal organs

D. A noted professor of science at an eminent university
E. The author's lifelong friend and partner

19. Which of the following statements, if true, would most seriously weaken the author's argument?

    A. Variation in species have been studied by a number of different scientists, with differing conclusions.
    B. Certain species have no variabilities from individual to individual among their major organs.
    C. Individuals of the same species are mostly similar to each other with only minor differences.
    D. Individual variations make little difference in the health or longevity among members of the same species.
    E. Species are distinguished from each other by only the smallest of variable differences.

20. Which of the following best describes the primary purpose of the passage?

    A. An explanation of why certain body parts shows no differences between individuals of the same species
    B. An effort to argue against rival scientists who believe animal organs are immutable
    C. An outline of the arguments against the assertion that there are high degrees of variability between different individuals of the same species
    D. An attempt to outline the nature of variability between individuals in a species
    E. A detailing of one specific example of variability between species

21. The author references the muscles in larvae of certain insects for which of the following reasons?

    A. The research on larvae muscles has been used to challenge many of the author's fundamental claims
    B. To show that larvae muscle research is severely limited in its applications
    C. To prove that larvae are the only living organisms that show a wide amount of variation
    D. To provide a clear example of variation among individuals in a species
    E. The research supports the author's own, previously mentioned, independent research into larvae muscles

22. Which of the following statements best summarizes the author's main idea in the passage?

    A. Individual differences among members of a species are usually inconsequential.
    B. The idea that every essential organ is immutable is not scientifically accurate.
    C. Immutable characteristics are the chief element which unite all species.
    D. Each species has immutable characteristics that distinguish it from other species.

E. Every individual of every species has important variations that are unique.

Passage:

It seems beyond doubt that in the aboriginal society the husband exercised almost complete authority over his wife; she was entirely in his hands and he might ill-treat her, provided he did not kill her. Out of our thirty statements, in six cases (Kurnai, Bangerang, Lower Murray tribes, according to Bonney, Geawe-Gal, Port Jackson tribes, North-west Central Queenslanders) the absolute authority of the husband is explicitly affirmed. We read in them either the bare statement that the husband had an absolute power over his family; or, in the better of them, we are more exactly informed that he had only to abstain from inflicting death on his wife. It was the latter's kinsman who would avenge her (Kurnai, Bangerang, North-west Central Queenslanders). It is difficult to ascertain in what form society would interfere with the husband if he transgressed the limits of his legal authority, i. e. killed his wife. Curr informs us that the woman's relatives would avenge her death. Howitt says that there would ensue a blood feud, which comes nearly to the same. It is very probable that the woman's kin retained some rights of protection. The remaining statements implicitly declare that the husband's authority was very extensive. (Encounter Bay tribes according to Meyer; New South Wales tribes according to Hodgson; Port Stephens tribes according to R. Dawson; Arunta; Herbert River tribes; Queenslanders according to Palmer; Moreton Bay tribes according to J. D. Lang; South-Western tribes according to Salvado; West Australians according to Grey.) It is clear that wherever we read of excessive harshness and bad treatment, wounds, blows inflicted on women, the husband must possess the authority to do it; in other words, he does not find any social barrier preventing him from ill-treatment. Especially as, in these statements, such ill-treatment is mentioned to be the rule and not an exception. In two statements we can gather no information on this point. According to the statement of J. Dawson on the West Victoria tribes, the husband's authority appears strictly limited by the potential intervention of the chief, who could even divorce the woman if she complained. But Curr warns us against Dawson's information concerning the chief and his power. Curr's arguments appear to be very conclusive. Too much weight cannot be attached, therefore, to
Dawson's exceptional statement. Discarding it, we see that we have on this point fairly clear information. We may assume that society interfered but seldom with the husband, in fact, only in the extreme case of his killing his wife. Six statements are directly, and the remainder indirectly, in favor of this view, and the only one contradictory is not very trustworthy.

Questions:

23. It can be inferred from the passage that the author views Australian aboriginal marriage practices as _____.

    A. a model of behavior in marriages
    B. culturally underdeveloped
    C. morally questionable
    D. worthy of respect and inquiry
    E. in need of some changes

24. If information were presented that showed some aboriginal societies gave women a large amount of authority, the effect on the passage would be to _____.

A. cause the author to view Australian aboriginal marriage practices in a less favorable light
B. make it easier to compare Australian aboriginal marriage practices with other types of marriage practices
C. reinforce the point made in "Dawson's exceptional statement."
D. show a different form of authority in marriage than the one presented by the author
E. further help the author's portrayal of the nature of authority in Australian aboriginal society

25. Which of the following statements best summarizes the author's purpose in writing this passage?

A. To compare the marriage practices of Australian aboriginals to those of other indigenous societies
B. To outline the nature of authority in marriages among Australian aboriginal societies
C. To promote Western marriage values over those of Australian aboriginal societies
D. To argue with other academics who have studied the marriage practices of societies around the world
E. To belittle and mock the marriage practices of Australian aboriginal societies

26. Why does the author cite so many other authorities in his passage?

A. To belittle his fellow academics
B. To show the many agreements between various academics
C. To support the claims, he makes and confirm the facts of his argument
D. To cover for not having any of his own research
E. To show the number of people who dismiss Australian aboriginal marriages as suspect

27. The underlined and bolded phrase "transgressed the limits" as used in the passage most nearly refers to _____.

A. creating new kinds of legal protections
B. overstepping normal boundaries
C. working on various methods of asserting authority
D. creating new kinds of marriage arrangements
E. moving between different kinds of authority

28. The author dismisses the argument by Dawson largely because _____.

A. the author has used enough sources before he considers Duncan's argument

B. Dawson discusses a different issue than the one the author does
C. another academic has largely rebutted Duncan's claims
D. Dawson's argument largely does not add anything to the author's argument
E. the author has a personal problem with Duncan

ARGUMENTATIVE WRITING SECTION

Prompt:

A university is considering whether to require all undergraduate students to participate in community service as part of their graduation requirements. Proponents argue that mandatory community service will enhance students' civic responsibility and provide valuable life experiences. Critics, however, contend that making community service mandatory could lead to resentment and diminish the quality of volunteer efforts, as students may participate only to fulfill a requirement rather than out of genuine interest.

Assignment:

Write an essay in which you argue for or against the university's proposed requirement for mandatory community service. In your essay, discuss the potential benefits and drawbacks of such a policy, taking into account its impact on students' personal development, academic workload, and community engagement.

Answer sheet with explanation

LOGICAL REASONING SECTION

1. **Correct Answer:** E. The new air conditioner uses a smaller share of the electricity used by Paula's home than did the old unit.

Explanation: The correct answer here is the one that does not explain the apparent paradox. That the new unit uses a smaller share of total electricity is consistent with its being more energy efficient. It does not explain how her electric bills could have gone up despite her installation of the more efficient unit; all other answers provide possible resolutions of such apparent paradox.

2. **Correct Answer:** D. Diesel cars are not commonly used in the United States because people believe they are more costly to operate than gasoline cars

Explanation: Roger asserts that incorrect beliefs are the only reason people do not drive diesel cars. Tamara directly counters that assertion by presenting several alternative reasons for why diesel cars are not used.

3. **Correct Answer:** C. Deer hunting harms U.S. industry

Explanation: Both people have different reasons for objecting to hunting deer. They also disagree about whether deer hunting should be prohibited. Both, however, agree that deer hunting may harm industry.

4. **Correct Answer:** A. Other jobs are available

Explanation: Employee 1 implicitly asserts that jobs would be available by claiming that jobs are advertised everywhere. Employee 2 expressly challenges the assertion that jobs would be available but not the claim that employment opportunities are advertised everywhere. Note, also, the employees do not disagree about benefits because the first asserts only that they are less than they once were.

5. **Correct Answer:** C. The ritual daily meditation that the players practice is largely undisciplined.

Explanation: The author states that there are differences between Zen meditation and the meditation that the coach has his players practice on a regular basis. This question asks for the answer choice that cannot be inferred or is not stated in the passage. The only answer choice that does not logically flow and is not a valid inference is: "The ritual daily mediation that the players practice is largely undisciplined." The author only implies that the daily meditation is less disciplined than Zen meditation; and not necessarily an undisciplined practice.

6. **Correct Answer:** C. People who insist on using incandescent light bulbs are not environmentally responsible

Explanation: Only people who do their part to protect nature are environmentally responsible. Those who insist on using incandescent light bulbs do not do their part to protect the environment. It follows that those who insist on using incandescent light bulbs are not environmentally responsible.

7. **Correct Answer:** C. In the context of describing weather, the word "nice" has a different, less subjective meaning than in other contexts

Explanation: The key to this question is to not construe the purpose of the passage too narrowly or too broadly. The passage indicates that the discussion of cars serves only as an example and is not the primary point. Conversely, the purpose of the passage is not so broad as to apply beyond a discussion of the unique use of "nice" in the context of weather.

8. **Correct Answer:** E. While there are downsides to public transportation, they could be addressed and public transportation has benefits for both cities and residents

Explanation: While the argument recognizes benefits of public transportation, it does not directly endorse its use, instead, recognizing legitimate downsides as well. On the other hand, the passage is clear that public transportation has real, positive implications for modern cities. Finally, the point of the argument is not to compare the present and past.

9. **Correct Answer:** C. Cars that are only cleaned at automated car washes will quickly rust

Explanation: The purpose of the passage is to establish that cars cleaned only at automated car washes will quickly rust. The other claims in the passage are intended only as support for that primary assertion.
The passage makes no claim about how often a car should be washed or about whether automated car washes offer at least some protection from rust.

10. **Correct Answer:** B. Obtaining a formal contract is appropriate caution

Explanation: We know that if there is appropriate caution, general contractors are not defrauded. We also know that the general contractor in this case obtained formal contracts. If obtaining formal contracts is appropriate caution, then the contractor here has taken appropriate caution and will not be defrauded.

11. **Correct Answer:** D. Neither the tibia or fibula bone is too large to fit into the chest.

Explanation: Here, size offered the only barrier to putting the tibia and fibula bone group into the chest. Since the separated bones can now fit into their own separate chests, the author assumes that each bone can fit into a chest. Thus, the correct choice is: "Neither the tibia or fibula bone is too large to fit into the chest."

12. **Correct Answer:** E. Everyone who will compete in the upcoming competition is a ballet dancer.

Explanation: We already know from the premises that ballroom dancers and ballet dancers are mutually exclusive. The only question that remains is who will compete in the upcoming competition. If only ballet dancers will compete, ballroom dancers are excluded (as well as salsa dancers), and the conclusion must logically follow.

13. **Correct Answer:** C. Players who become faster become more athletic

Explanation: The argument asserts that different training programs cause soccer players to be faster than baseball players. The next assertion is that baseball players would become more athletic if they used training programs of soccer players. This only follows if becoming faster necessarily makes one more athletic.

14. **Correct Answer:** D. When a sheet of standard printer paper is a recycled, all of its wood pulp is recovered.

Explanation: Since 25 percent of wood pulp in the Class B sheets comes from recycled Class A sheets, the maximum number of Class B sheets is 4 times the number of Class A sheets. However, the correct answer correctly notices that the maximum number of Class B sheets can be produced only if all pulp from the Class A sheets can be recovered through recycling; if less than all of the pulp can be recovered, the actual number of Class B sheets produced will fall short of the maximum. For example, if there were 100 Class A sheets recycled, but only 25 percent of pulp could be recovered through recycling, only 100 Class B sheets could be produced.

15. **Correct Answer:** A. Only those eligible for appointment to the hospital's board of directors can be appointed as the hospital's treasurer.

Explanation: To answer this question, it is necessary to recognize that while appointment criteria are set forth for the board of directors, they are applied to the position of Treasurer. We are never told that a Treasurer is a member of the board of directors. Thus, the conclusion is only warranted if eligibility for appointment to the board is a necessary condition for appointment to the position of Treasurer.

16. **Correct Answer:** A. The conclusion applied only to the western hemisphere

Explanation: None of the answers responds to both objections. If the academics' conclusion applied only to the western hemisphere, however, then the second objection would be defeated and the academics' conclusion would be strengthened. At first glance, the answer that "most people believe 'religion' should be defined as a belief in a supernatural god," seems like an equally correct answer; but this does not directly refute the claim that the definition is
"subject to debate."

17. **Correct Answer:** D. The car manufacturers with the highest profits also place a high priority on generating large profits

Explanation: The argument states that manufacturers with the highest profits also make the most unsafe cars. This is only supporting evidence, however, if manufacturers with the highest profits also place the highest priority on profits.

18. **Correct Answer:** D. Oil consumption causes substantial environmental harms

Explanation: The passage only claims that some arguments for increasing oil production are misguided. It does not indicate that any environmental arguments are misguided.

19. **Correct Answer:** D. John ran to class in order to get there more quickly

Explanation: The argument claims that John accomplished nothing by running, but assumes that his objective was to avoid getting wet.
If John's goal was to get to class more quickly, then he accomplished something despite getting

20. **Correct Answer:** C. The professor assumes that because there are personal tensions between the British scholar and his colleague, that the colleague's thesis must be based on scholarly merit, when in fact it may have been a publicity stunt.

Explanation: The problem with the professor's reasoning is that he assumes a fact (that the work was a scholarly product) based on the circumstance that his colleague and the British scholar had personal tensions. There is not a causal relationship between these two circumstances. Therefore, the professor made an error in his causal reasoning. The correct answer conveys this most effectively.

READING COMPREHENSION SECTION

1. **Correct Answer:** A statement that the relationship between the reader and writer is as detached as the relationship between speaker and listener.

Explanation: The author states quite plainly that "[t]he relation between the writer and the reader is more intimate," with the comparison being made between writer and reader and speaker and listener.
So, we know that author would be most likely to disagree that the relationship between reader and writer is as detached as the relationship between speaker and listener. You could also attempt to disprove all the incorrect answers. The author laments her own youthful naiveté, so we can assume she would agree with an argument that youthful enthusiasm and certainty is often misplaced. Additionally, the author clearly is in favor of the anarchist movement and praises John Most heavily in the introduction, so we can infer that she would agree with the two statements relating to his subject matter. Finally, the author discusses at length the difficulty faced by an individual who attempts to impact others through spoken word, so we can also infer that she would agree with this statement.

2. **Correct Answer:** The listener will be awoken from his or her apathy.

Explanation: This question simply requires reading in detail and understanding that the word "lethargy" means something very similar to
"apathy." The author states, "I came to see that oral propaganda is at best but a means of shaking people from their lethargy: it leaves no lasting impression."

3. **Correct Answer:** The turbulent and emotional young period of an activist's life changes how they approach their work; it can lead to a maturity or abandonment of values depending on the will of the individual to resist change or complete alteration.

Explanation: The German phrase "Sturm und Drang" means something like turbulent, youthful, and emotional period, but you do not need to know this information to answer the question. The specified quotation appears immediately following the author's exclamation, "Oh, for the naivety of youth's enthusiasm! It is the time when the hardest thing seems but child's play. It is the only period in life worthwhile. Alas! This period is but of short duration." This provides the context with which the quotation can be analyzed and inferred to have a similar meaning. The author is saying that in the turbulent period of youth a propagandist (or activist) will undergo changes in opinion and perspective, and that these opinions are subject to maturity or abandonment depending on the individual's ability to resist "vicissitudes." "Vicissitudes" are unwelcome changes.

4. **Correct Answer:** an introduction to a series of essays written by one author

Explanation: The manner in which the author concludes this essay suggests that it is intended to function as an introduction to a larger body of works written by this author, probably on the topic of anarchism. The author states, "It is this certainty that has induced me to gather in one volume my ideas on various topics of individual and social importance. They represent the mental and soul struggles of twenty-one years-the conclusions derived after many changes and inner revisions."

5. **Correct Answer:** It acts as a transition from a discussion of the author's youthful and naïve faith in the power of the oral propaganda to a more lasting belief in the power of the written word.

Explanation: In the first two paragraphs, the author discusses her early experiences with oration as a convincing means of conveying a message to a large group of people; however, from her tone and expressions, we can tell that she believes this faith to be misguided and attributes it distinctly to youthful naiveté. The author begins the third paragraph by stating, "My great faith in the wonder-worker, the spoken word, is no more. I have realized its inadequacy to awaken thought, or even emotion." This seems to demonstrate a renunciation of her previous faith. She continues in the fourth paragraph to state how "[i]t is altogether different with the written mode of human expression." Collectively, this information suggests that the third paragraph functions as a transition.

6. **Correct Answer:** to explain the author's transition into writing her arguments, as opposed to offering her opinions in the form of oration

Explanation: It is true that based on the evidence in this passage, the author would be likely to argue in favor of anarchism. It is also true that the author discusses why orators have such difficulty in convincing an audience to change its opinions, and finally, it is true that the author compares the benefits of the written word to those of the spoken word; however, the primary purpose of this essay is to reveal the reasons and motivations behind the author's own transition from a belief in oration to an emphasis on the written word. Evidence for this can be found most noticeably in the conclusion when the author summarizes her purpose for writing the passage: "The relation between the writer and the reader is more intimate. True, books are only what we want them to be; rather, what we read into them. That we can do so demonstrates the importance of written as against oral expression. It is this certainty which has induced me to gather in one volume my ideas on various topics of individual and social importance."

7. **Correct Answer:** When trying to influence people's perspectives and opinions the written word is a much more powerful tool than oral expression.

Explanation: This question is primarily aimed at determining whether you understand the author's attitude, intentions, and thesis. Two of the answer choices have no evidence whatsoever to support them in the text; these are: "The power of oral propaganda is on the decline as people become more and more resistant against the opinions of others" and "Neither the written word nor oral propaganda can function independently of one another. " Two of the answer choices summarize only a part of the author's point of view and do not capture the primary thesis and intention of the text; these are: "It is naïve to place one's faith in the power of oral propaganda when people are so apt to ignore what they hear" and "John Most is an exemplary figure in the propagandist movement, one whose influence the author cannot hope to match." The only answer choice that matches the thesis, the author's attitude, and her intentions is "When trying to influence people's perspectives and opinions the written word is a much more powerful tool than oral expression." In answering questions about the author's "primary point of view," be careful not to pick an answer that only summarizes the author's secondary or partial opinions.

8. **Correct Answer:** disenchanted

Explanation: From the author's description in the first two paragraphs, it is clear that she once placed great faith and optimism in the power of oral propaganda; however, from the context of the remainder of the essay, it is clear that that faith has evaporated as the author has matured. Therefore, her attitude could best be described as "disenchanted." She certainly could not be described as "supportive," as she spends much of the essay arguing against the power of oral propaganda. "Nostalgic" functions to an extent, as the author is reflecting on past events and thoughts, but "nostalgia" suggests at a positive reflection and this is clearly negative. "Disparaging" is too strong of a word in this instance to accurately convey the whole of the author's attitude, and "uneasy" is too weak of a word, as it suggests merely limited confidence, as opposed to "disenchanted," which suggests a loss of confidence.

9. **Correct Answer:** Developments in political theory and practice in which the governed and the governors became one and the same

Explanation: A point that would weaken the author's point would be one that would undermine one of the necessary conditions he outlines.
While all of the noncredited responses fit with the author's points about the necessary conditions of law—or, at the very least, do not contradict them—a legal theory that identified the governors with the governed would reduce law to a compact or social contract, rather than an edict from a superior to an inferior. In this case, the lawgiver would not be superior to those governed, nor the one obligated to follow the laws inferior to the one issuing them; thus, the necessary condition that a legal rule be issued by a superior and obliged by an inferior would collapse.

10. **Correct Answer:** A local school board approves a set of teacher-hiring standards during a public meeting.

Explanation: The author lays out several necessary features of laws: that they be given from a superior to an inferior; that they be sufficiently promulgated; that they apply generally, rather than to particular instances and cases; and that they oblige, rather than council or advise. The credited response is the only one that does not violate one of these necessary conditions.

11. **Correct Answer:** A certain ancient diocese celebrates its patron saint's day on 25 June every year, despite there being no record of a proclamation or edict establishing this.

Explanation: The sense of the highlighted passage suggests that, while the law or principle that is now followed throughout its jurisdiction as a binding law must have been at some time promulgated in the (presumably) distant past, the original edict of promulgation, if there ever was one (e.g., assuming the law was not promulgated verbally), has been lost. Thus, the necessary conditions for the credited response are that the rule be a legal rule, binding and compelling; that it be recognized as law in its jurisdiction; and that, if there ever was a document by which it was first promulgated, that document be lost to time. The credited response is the one that most closely fits these necessary conditions.

12. **Correct Answer:** The people ruled by a law ought to be notified of it before it enters force.

Explanation: While the credited response can be directly supported by the text of the passage (e.g., "a bare resolution, confined in the breast of the legislator, without manifesting itself by some external sign, can never be properly a law"), the other responses, while sometimes close to statements made in the passage, either require unwarranted extrapolations (e.g., one might be ignorant of a law that was deceitfully or improperly promulgated, and thus cannot morally be held responsible for breaking that law, according to the author) or are not properly supported by the passage.

13. **Correct Answer:** That disobedience of the law is punished

Explanation: While the passage does lay out several necessary conditions for some edict to be considered a law-some of which are outlined in the non-credited responses-nowhere does the author explicitly discuss punishment as a necessary feature of law.

14. **Correct Answer:** to lay out some of the necessary conditions for a certain phenomenon

Explanation: The author gives a definition of law, then proceeds to describe and explain certain necessary conditions that must be met by any kind of law; however, the author never mentions sufficient conditions, nor does he explicitly mention alternative theories of law. While legal history is drawn from for examples and sub concepts are described and defined, neither legal history nor defining sub concepts are the author's primary purpose.

15. **Correct Answer:** A concrete example demonstrating a seeming exception to a rule

Explanation: While it might seem at first glance as if the lack of a requirement for laws to be promulgated in any specific way would allow for a great many abuses and injustices-promulgation only within the mind of the legislator, or only after someone unknowingly broke a law, or promulgated in such a way as to remain unknown to those governed by it—the author goes on to rule out these forms of insufficient or unjust promulgation. The example of Caligula is a specific example that illustrates this specific subpoint, albeit not as a minimum standard or moral example.

16. **Correct Answer:** sentence

Explanation: While all the meanings of "attaint" given are possible correct meanings in other contexts, in this particular instance, the passage indicates that a word is needed that somehow conveys a sense of judicial punishment. While "deprive" might seem to be a reasonable synonym for "attaint" in this case, as one who is attainted would be deprived of their goods and titles, it does not also convey the sense of being part of a legal proceeding that
"sentence" does. By analogy, while "kill" and "execute" might seem to have similar meanings, only the latter conveys the important sense of legal punishment that specifically distinguishes executions from the generic killing.

17. **Correct Answer:** important organs do not vary within species

Explanation: There are two important elements in this passage that would aid an attempt to assess the beliefs of others: the author is making an argument against most scientists and the author only brings up the beliefs with which he disagrees. The only idea that the author insinuates almost every scientist believes is that variations never exist in organs which are "important," although this is an idea that the author mocks. The passing reference to "Sir J. Lubbock" references just one finding, and does not cover Lubbock's theories or conclusions stemming from those empirical findings, nor does it mention his status within the scientific community. Given the tone of most of the passage it is easiest to infer that most scientists disagree with the author and believe that major organs do not significantly vary within species.

18. **Correct Answer:** A well-known researcher whose work has touched on the variability of animal organs

Explanation: The reference to "Sir J. Lubbock" is made only passing, but is used to support the author's overall claims about the variability of organs within species. Lubbock has found variation in the nerves of "Coccus." Without any other information, the only thing that can be inferred is that Lubbock has done scientific research which is both in league with the author's argument and, from the casual reference, somewhat widely read. There is no specific mention of Lubbock's position at a university, nor to his personal or professional relationship to the author.

19. **Correct Answer:** Certain species have no variabilities from individual to individual among their major organs.

Explanation: The author's main argument is that all species feature variations among individual members of the same species. The amount of variation or the significance of that variety is not as important to the author as the fact that variation exists consistently among species. If a species was proven to have no variation, it would undermine the very heart of the author's argument by countering the fundamental claim of the argument, upon which most other claims and assertions made in the passage are based. Several of the answers would somewhat undermine the author's argument, but the straightforward refutation of the author's major claim would most significantly weaken the author's argument.

20. **Correct Answer:** An attempt to outline the nature of variability between individuals in a species

Explanation: The author addresses the significant degrees of variability found in every individual species, making a point to show how widespread variability is in individual biological organisms. While this is presented as one side of an argument, the author is stating his point as, essentially, the bare facts of the situation. The author's purpose is more of an outline of his views than any detailed arguments or examples.

21. **Correct Answer:** To provide a clear example of variation among individuals in a species

Explanation: The author's main argument in the passage is that variations are not only present in organisms, but that studying and understanding these variations is key to understanding the organisms themselves. As the author does not rely on his own research, the information about larvae muscles is a key piece of evidence for his argument.

22. **Correct Answer:** Every individual of every species has important variations that are unique.

Explanation: The author's main theme in this passage is the nature of differences between individuals among a particular species. For the author, the most important aspect of the variability between individuals is just how many there are, as well as the sheer number of variabilities being the most consistent feature of species. In this way, the author argues that variability is, in fact, the most consistent presence in the studies and experiences of a naturalist. An "immutable characteristic" is an aspect of something that is unchanged or unchanging over time. Given the emphasis the author places on diversity and variablity, it seems unlikely that the main idea would be concerned with the unchanging nature of anything (especially anything in under the purview of "naturalist" study).

23. **Correct Answer:** worthy of respect and inquiry

Explanation: The overall tone of the passage is extremely balanced and fair, as the author is essentially providing a detailed account of what is found in aboriginal Australian marriages. This means that the author never takes an extremely strong stand on aboriginal Australian society; however, the fact that the author does write in such detail about Australian aboriginal marriage practices indicates he is certainly interested in them and finds them worthy of study.

24. **Correct Answer:** show a different form of authority in marriage than the one presented by the author

Explanation: The passage neatly outlines how authority is vested in husbands in Australian aboriginal marriages. A piece of information that highlights women's authority would contradict the main information presented in the passage; however, since the author portrays the information in a calm manner, it would have simply presented a new piece of evidence for the author.

25. **Correct Answer:** To outline the nature of authority in marriages among Australian aboriginal societies

Explanation: The author is extremely detailed, factual, and sourced, discussing the issue of authority in Australian aboriginal marriages as completely as possible. Notably, though, the author essentially never takes a stand on the values or quality of Australian aboriginal marriages. This means that his main purpose is simply to detail the nature of authority in Australian aboriginal marriages.

26. **Correct Answer:** To support the claims he makes and confirm the facts of his argument

Explanation: The author calmly lays out all of the details of the nature of authority in Australian aboriginal marriages, while referencing many other authorities who have studied the same issue. The even tone of the author's writing means that he references other academics in order to support claims and confirm facts.

27. **Correct Answer:** overstepping normal boundaries

Explanation: The author discusses a husband who has "transgressed the limits of his legal authority" in the context of a husband who has killed his wife, one thing no husband can legally do in aboriginal society.
This means that the author uses the phrase to indicate the husband has done something that goes past what is an acceptable boundary.

28. **Correct Answer:** another academic has largely rebutted Duncan's claims

Explanation: The author specifically cites Dawson's argument about the authority of the chief in aboriginal Australian societies as one that cannot be trusted. Citing another author's better-reasoned and better-sourced statement, the author does not give credence to Dawson's position.

ARGUMENTATIVE WRITING SECTION

Prompt Recap:
A university is considering whether to require all undergraduate students to participate in community service as part of their graduation requirements. Argue for or against this policy, focusing on the impact on students' personal development, academic workload, and community engagement.

Introduction:
Community service plays a vital role in personal growth and societal contribution, offering students the opportunity to develop essential life skills and foster a sense of civic responsibility. However, mandating such service as a graduation requirement poses several challenges. While the intention behind the policy is noble, the compulsory nature of the requirement may undermine its effectiveness, leading to negative outcomes such as diminished intrinsic motivation and increased academic stress. Therefore, I argue against making community service a mandatory component of university education.

Body Paragraph 1:
Voluntary community service allows students to engage more deeply and meaningfully, as their participation is driven by personal interest and a genuine desire to contribute. This intrinsic motivation is crucial for the development of empathy, leadership, and problem-solving skills, which are best cultivated when students are genuinely invested in their service activities. When students choose to volunteer, they are more likely to reflect on their experiences, leading to greater personal growth and a stronger commitment to community engagement. Research shows that students who voluntarily engage in community service experience higher levels of satisfaction and learning, as they are able to connect their service experiences to their personal values and academic goals.

Body Paragraph 2:
On the other hand, making community service a graduation requirement could result in a "check-the-box" mentality, where students participate solely to fulfill an obligation rather than out of a genuine desire to help others. This compulsory approach risks reducing the overall effectiveness of community service programs, as students may become disengaged and view their service as just another task to complete. Furthermore, the added pressure of meeting service requirements could exacerbate the already demanding academic workload faced by students, leading to increased stress and burnout. In such cases, the potential benefits of community service are overshadowed by the negative impact on students' mental health and well-being.

Body Paragraph 3:
Proponents of mandatory community service argue that it ensures all students contribute to society, thereby fostering a sense of civic duty and social responsibility. However, this argument overlooks the importance of voluntary engagement in cultivating a meaningful

connection to community service. Rather than imposing a blanket requirement, universities should focus on creating incentives that encourage voluntary participation, such as offering academic credit, recognition programs, or opportunities for leadership development. These alternatives can achieve the same goals as mandatory service, without the drawbacks associated with compulsion.

Conclusion:
In conclusion, while the goal of promoting community service among university students is commendable, making it a mandatory graduation requirement is not the most effective approach. Voluntary engagement, supported by appropriate incentives, allows students to derive greater personal and academic benefits from their service experiences. By fostering a culture of voluntary participation, universities can ensure that community service remains a meaningful and rewarding aspect of student life, contributing to the development of well-rounded, socially responsible graduates.

Practice Test 5: Full-length simulated exam practice tests

LOGICAL REASONING SECTION

1. Because the native salmon in Lake Clearwater had nearly disappeared, sockeye salmon were introduced in 1940. After being introduced, this genetically uniform group of sockeyes split into two distinct populations that do not interbreed, one inhabiting deep areas of the lake and the other inhabiting shallow areas. Since the two populations now differ genetically, some researchers hypothesize that each has adapted genetically to its distinct habitat.

Which of the following, if true, most strongly supports the researchers' hypothesis?

A. Neither of the two populations of sockeyes has interbred with the native salmon.
B. When the native salmon in Lake Clearwater were numerous, they comprised two distinct populations that did not interbreed.
C. Most types of salmon that inhabit lakes spend part of the time in shallow water and part in deeper water.
D. One of the populations of sockeyes is virtually identical genetically to the sockeyes originally introduced in 1940.
E. The total number of sockeye salmon in the lake is not as large as the number of native salmons had been many years ago.

2. Clinician: Patients with immune system disorders are usually treated with a class of drugs that, unfortunately, increase the patient's risk of developing osteoporosis, a bone-loss disease. So these patients take another drug that helps to preserve existing bone. Since a

drug that enhances the growth of new bone cells has now become available, these patients should take this new drug in addition to the drug that helps to preserve existing bone.

Which one of the following would be most useful to know in order to evaluate the clinician's argument?

A. How large is the class of drugs that increase the risk of developing osteoporosis?
B. Why are immune system disorders treated with drugs that increase the risk of developing osteoporosis?
C. Is the new drug more expensive than the drug that helps to preserve existing bone?
D. How long has the drug that helps to preserve existing bone been in use?
E. To what extent does the new drug retain its efficacy when used in combination with the other drugs?

3. After replacing his old gas water heater with a new, pilotless, gas water heater that is rated as highly efficient, Jimmy's gas bills increased.

Each of the following, if true, contributes to an explanation of the increase mentioned above EXCEPT:

A. The new water heater uses a smaller percentage of the gas used by Jimmy's household than did the old one.
B. Shortly after the new water heater was installed, Jimmy's uncle came to live with him, doubling the size of the household.
C. After having done his laundry at a laundromat, Jimmy bought and started using a gas dryer when he replaced his water heater.
D. Jimmy's utility company raised the rates for gas consumption following installation of the new water heater.
E. Unusually cold weather following installation of the new water heater resulted in heavy gas usage.

4. The chairperson should not have released the Election Commission's report to the public, for the chairperson did not consult any other members of the commission about releasing the report before having it released.

The argument's conclusion can be properly inferred if which one of the following is assumed?

A. It would have been permissible for the chairperson to release the commission's report to the public only if most other members of the commission had first given their consent.
B. All of the members of the commission had signed the report prior to its release.
C. The chairperson would not have been justified in releasing the commission's report if any members of the commission had serious reservations about the report's content.
D. The chairperson would have been justified in releasing the report only if each of the commission's members would have agreed to its being released had they been consulted.

E. Some members of the commission would have preferred that the report not be released to the public.

5. Ethicist: On average, animals raised on grain must be fed sixteen pounds of grain to produce one pound of meat. A pound of meat is more nutritious for humans than a pound of grain, but sixteen pounds of grain could feed many more people than could a pound of meat. With grain yields leveling off, large areas of farmland going out of production each year, and the population rapidly expanding, we must accept the fact that consumption of meat will soon be morally unacceptable.

Which one of the following, if true, would most weaken the ethicist's argument?

A. Even though it has been established that a vegetarian diet can be healthy, many people prefer to eat meat and are willing to pay for it.
B. Often, cattle or sheep can be raised to maturity on grass from pastureland that is unsuitable for any other kind of farming.
C. If a grain diet is supplemented with protein derived from non-animal sources, it can have nutritional value equivalent to that of a diet containing meat.
D. Although prime farmland near metropolitan areas is being lost rapidly to suburban development, we could reverse this trend by choosing to live in areas that are already urban.
E. Nutritionists agree that a diet composed solely of grain products is not adequate for human health.

6. Antonio: One can live a life of moderation by never deviating from the middle course. But then one loses the joy of spontaneity and misses the opportunities that come to those who are occasionally willing to take great chances, or to go too far.

Marla: But one who, in the interests of moderation, never risks going too far is actually failing to live a life of moderation: one must be moderate even in one's moderation.

Antonio and Marla disagree over

A. whether it is desirable for people occasionally to take great chances in life
B. what a life of moderation requires of a person
C. whether it is possible for a person to embrace other virtues along with moderation
D. how often a person ought to deviate from the middle course in life
E. whether it is desirable for people to be moderately spontaneous

7. So far this summer there has been no rain in the valley. But usually a few inches of rain fall there each summer. Since only one week of summer is left, it will probably rain in the valley within the next week.

The flawed pattern of reasoning in the argument above is most similar to that in which one of the following arguments?

A. Aisha has finished proofreading all but the last two pages of an issue of the journal Periodos and has encountered no errors. However, there are sometimes a few errors in an issue of the journal Periodos. So there may be errors in the pages that Aisha has not yet checked.

B. There are generally few errors in an issue of the journal Periodos. Aisha has finished proofreading all but the last two pages of an issue of this journal but has encountered no errors. Hence, there are probably no errors in the pages that Aisha has not yet checked in this issue of the journal.

C. On average, there are a few errors in an issue of the journal Periodos. Aisha has finished proofreading all but the last two pages of an issue of this journal but has encountered no errors. So there are probably errors in the pages she has not yet checked in this issue of the journal.

D. Aisha has proofread several issues of the journal Periodos and has encountered no errors. But there are seldom any errors in an issue of this journal. So there will probably be no errors in the next issue of the journal Periodos that she proofreads.

E. There usually are errors in each issue of the journal Periodos. Since Aisha has finished proofreading the latest issue of this journal and has detected no errors, Aisha has probably made a mistake in her proofreading.

8. If Suarez is not the most qualified of the candidates for sheriff, then Anderson is. Thus, if the most qualified candidate is elected and Suarez is not elected, then Anderson will be.

The reasoning in which one of the following is most similar to the reasoning in the argument above?

A. If the excavation contract does not go to the lowest bidder, then it will go to Caldwell. So if Qiu gets the contract and Caldwell does not, then the contract will have been awarded to the lowest bidder.

B. If the lowest bidder on the sanitation contract is not Dillon, then it is Ramsey. So if the contract goes to the lowest bidder and it does not go to Dillon, then it will go to Ramsey.

C. If Kapshaw is not awarded the landscaping contract, then Johnson will be. So if the contract goes to the lowest bidder and it does not go to Johnson, then it will go to Kapshaw.

D. If Holihan did not submit the lowest bid on the maintenance contract, then neither did Easton. So if the contract goes to the lowest bidder and it does not go to Easton, then it will not go to Holihan either.

E. If Perez is not the lowest bidder on the catering contract, then Sullivan is. So if Sullivan does not get the contract and Perez does not get it either, then it will not be awarded to the lowest bidder.

9. Inez: Space exploration programs pay for themselves many times over, since such programs result in technological advances with every day, practical applications. Space exploration is more than the search for knowledge for its own sake; investment in space

exploration is such a productive investment in developing widely useful technology that we can't afford not to invest in space exploration.

Winona: It is absurd to try to justify funding for space exploration merely by pointing out that such programs will lead to technological advances. If technology with practical applications is all that is desired, then it should be funded directly.

Winona responds to Inez by:

A. showing that there is no evidence that the outcome Inez anticipates will in fact be realized
B. suggesting that Inez has overlooked evidence that directly argues against the programs Inez supports
C. demonstrating that the pieces of evidence that Inez cites contradict each other
D. providing evidence that the beneficial effects that Inez desires can be achieved only at great expense
E. claiming that a goal that Inez mentions could be pursued without the programs Inez endorses

10. It is now a common complaint that the electronic media have corroded the intellectual skills required and fostered by the literary media. But several centuries ago the complaint was that certain intellectual skills, such as the powerful memory and extemporaneous eloquence that were intrinsic to oral culture, were being destroyed by the spread of literacy. So, what awaits us is probably a mere alteration of the human mind rather than its devolution.

The reference to the complaint of several centuries ago that powerful memory and extemporaneous eloquence were being destroyed plays which one of the following roles in the argument?

A. evidence supporting the claim that the intellectual skills fostered by the literary media are being destroyed by the electronic media
B. an illustration of the general hypothesis being advanced that intellectual abilities are inseparable from the means by which people communicate
C. an example of a cultural change that did not necessarily have a detrimental effect on the human mind overall
D. evidence that the claim that the intellectual skills required and fostered by the literary media are being lost is unwarranted
E. possible evidence, mentioned and then dismissed, that might be cited by supporters of the hypothesis being criticized

11. Hospital executive: At a recent conference on nonprofit management, several computer experts maintained that the most significant threat faced by large institutions such as universities and hospitals is unauthorized access to confidential data. In light of this testimony, we should make the protection of our clients' confidentiality our highest priority.

The hospital executive's argument is most vulnerable to which one of the following objections?

    A. The argument confuses the causes of a problem with the appropriate solutions to that problem.
    B. The argument relies on the testimony of experts whose expertise is not shown to be sufficiently broad to support their general claim.
    C. The argument assumes that a correlation between two phenomena is evidence that one is the cause of the other.
    D. The argument draws a general conclusion about a group based on data about an unrepresentative sample of that group.
    E. The argument infers that a property belonging to large institutions belongs to all institutions.

12. When exercising the muscles in one's back, it is important, in order to maintain a healthy back, to exercise the muscles on opposite sides of the spine equally. After all, balanced muscle development is needed to maintain a healthy back, since the muscles on opposite sides of the spine must pull equally in opposing directions to keep the back in proper alignment and protect the spine.

Which one of the following is an assumption required by the argument?

    A. Muscles on opposite sides of the spine that are equally well developed will be enough to keep the back in proper alignment.
    B. Exercising the muscles on opposite sides of the spine unequally tends to lead to unbalanced muscle development.
    C. Provided that one exercises the muscles on opposite sides of the spine equally, one will have a generally healthy back.
    D. If the muscles on opposite sides of the spine are exercised unequally, one's back will be irreparably damaged.
    E. One should exercise daily to ensure that the muscles on opposite sides of the spine keep the back in proper alignment.

13. Most of the students who took Spanish 101 at the university last semester attended every class session. However, each student who received a grade lower than B minus missed at least one class session.

Which one of the following statements about the students who took Spanish 101 at the university last semester can be properly inferred from the information above?

    A. At least some of the students who received a grade of A minus or higher attended every class session.
    B. Most, if not all, of the students who missed at least one class session received a grade lower than B minus.
    C. Most of the students received a grade higher than B minus.

D. At least one student who received a grade of B minus or higher missed one or more class sessions.

E. More than half of the students received a grade of B minus or higher.

14. Editorialist: News media rarely cover local politics thoroughly, and local political business is usually conducted secretively. These factors each tend to isolate local politicians from their electorates. This has the effect of reducing the chance that any particular act of resident participation will elicit a positive official response, which in turn discourages resident participation in local politics.

Which one of the following is most strongly supported by the editorialist's statements?

A. Particular acts of resident participation would be likely to elicit a positive response from local politicians if those politicians were less isolated from their electorate.
B. Local political business should be conducted less secretively because this would avoid discouraging resident participation in local politics.
C. The most important factor influencing a resident's decision as to whether to participate in local politics is the chance that the participation will elicit a positive official response.
D. More-frequent thorough coverage of local politics would reduce at least one source of discouragement from resident participation in local politics.
E. If resident participation in local politics were not discouraged, this would cause local politicians to be less isolated from their electorate.

15. Economist: Every business strives to increase its productivity, for this increases profits for the owners and the likelihood that the business will survive. But not all efforts to increase productivity are beneficial to the business as a whole. Often, attempts to increase productivity decrease the number of employees, which clearly harms the dismissed employees as well as the sense of security of the retained employees.

Which one of the following most accurately expresses the main conclusion of the economist's argument?

A. If an action taken to secure the survival of a business fails to enhance the welfare of the business's employees, that action cannot be good for the business as a whole.
B. Some measures taken by a business to increase productivity fail to be beneficial to the business as a whole.
C. Only if the employees of a business are also its owners will the interests of the employees and owners coincide, enabling measures that will be beneficial to the business as a whole.
D. There is no business that does not make efforts to increase its productivity.
E. Decreasing the number of employees in a business undermines the sense of security of retained employees.

16. While tablet computer sales have increased steadily over the last 2 years, we can expect a reversal of this trend in the near future. Since they became popular in the marketplace 5

years ago, 60 percent of tablet computers sold have been purchased by people from 18 to 25 years of age, and the number of people in this age group is expected to decline steadily over the next 15 years.

Which of the following, if true, would most seriously weaken the argument?

   A. New technology will make new computing options available over the next 15 years.
   B. Most people under the age of 18 have never purchased a tablet computer.
   C. Sales of tablet computers to small businesses has declined over the past 2 years.
   D. Most purchasers of tablet computers over the past 2 years have been over the age of 25.
   E. The number of different types of tablet computers available is likely to increase in the near future.

17. Those who go to college are wasting their money. The vast majority of college graduates are employed in fields that do not require their specializations, while others are unemployed. Further, contrary to common belief, the average college graduate is not paid substantially more than the average worker who is not a college graduate.

Which of the following, if true, most weakens the argument?

   A. The average college graduate has more debt than the average non graduate
   B. College graduates are more likely to be employed than those who are not college graduates
   C. Very few college graduates say they regret attending college
   D. Certain professions highly prefer or require a college degree as a condition of employment, while no employers prefer an employee not be a college graduate
   E. There are more college graduates now than at any other time in history

18. It is immoral for a government to enter a war unless its own citizens have been attacked. To avoid taking immoral action, governments should receive international approval before entering a war in another country, no matter the cost.

Which of the following, if true, provides the most support for the argument?

   A. There is usually international approval for a government that goes to war after its citizens are attacked
   B. Some governments have caused international turmoil by entering wars without international approval
   C. Governments often save lives by entering wars in other countries
   D. Governments increase casualties by joining wars in other countries
   E. A government will not receive international approval to join a war when its citizens have not been attacked

19. Scholar: Journalists tend to be low-paid workers struggling to meet deadlines. Their editors tend to care less about the accuracy of the story and more about whether the story will sell. It follows that readers should be skeptical of the accuracy of most newspaper articles they read.

Each of the following helps strengthen the argument in the passage above EXCEPT:

A. Many readers feel like they are not being given the whole story when they read newspaper articles.
B. Articles that are most popular with readers tend to be sensationalist and lack accuracy.
C. Lower paid professions tend to attract less qualified people who do not have the necessary background to effectively research a complex issue.
D. Pressure from editors affects the way journalists produce their articles.
E. Time pressure incentivizes journalists to cut corners and exclude certain facts they could not research in time.

20. Recent evidence has conclusively shown that cholesterol levels do not correlate with human lifespan. Despite this new evidence, doctors still advise patients with high cholesterol to take medication and engage in physical activity to reduce cholesterol levels.

Which of the following, if true, would most help resolve this discrepancy?

A. High cholesterol levels are proven be correlated with hypertension disorders.
B. Low levels of cholesterol are proven to increase quality of life.
C. Engaging in extensive physical exercise can stress the human heart.
D. Most medications that doctors prescribe to reduce cholesterol levels are clinically proven to be effective.
E. Many doctors receive large gifts from pharmaceutical companies.

READING COMPREHENSION SECTION

Passage:

To create the Trafficking in Persons (TIPS) Report, the Secretary of State ranks countries according to a system of tiers based on the efforts those countries make against human trafficking. According to the United States, the minimum conditions that a country must meet to be a country in good standing, designated as a Tier 1 country, are somewhat subjective. There must be "serious and sustained efforts to eliminate human trafficking," such as prohibiting and punishing acts of human trafficking, taking measures to deter offenses in the future, creating public awareness, and protecting victims of human trafficking.

Tier 2 countries do not fully comply with the standards for Tier 1 countries, but are making significant efforts to do so. Tier 2 Watch List countries meet the same criteria as Tier 2 countries, but also satisfy one of the following: 1) the number of victims of severe forms of trafficking is very significant or significantly increasing; 2) no evidence can be shown that there are increasing efforts to combat severe forms of trafficking in persons from the previous year; or 3) the finding that a country was making significant efforts to comply with minimum standards was based on that country's commitment to take future steps over the next year. Tier 3 countries do not fully comply with the minimum standards and are not making significant efforts to do so. The penalties for Tier 3 countries include being subject to certain sanctions such as: the withdrawal of non-humanitarian and non-trade related foreign assistance, not receiving funding for educational and cultural exchange programs, and potential U.S. opposition to assistance from international financial institutions such as the World Bank and International Monetary Fund.

The TIPS Report relies on U.S. missions to regularly meet with foreign government officials in order to gain information about human trafficking in countries throughout the world. It is the world's most comprehensive report on human trafficking, and is trusted as an accurate depiction of the policies and laws being used in various countries. Specifically, the TIPS Report evaluates countries' efforts against human trafficking based on the efforts taken in the areas of prosecution, prevention, and protection. The evaluation of a country's prosecution efforts is based on whether laws against human trafficking exist and are actively enforced against perpetrators. Prevention efforts should focus on raising public awareness about human trafficking and rectifying laws that make certain populations more vulnerable to human trafficking than others. Finally, protection efforts seek to address the needs of existing or potential victims.

Questions:

1. It can be inferred from the passage that the primary purpose of the TIPS report is to:

    A. Provide a consistent system for documenting how various countries respond to the issue of human trafficking
    B. Enable to the United States to exercise its power in the arena of humanitarian affairs
    C. Discourage countries from passively accepting the levels of human trafficking within their borders
    D. Motivate countries to implement methods that fight human trafficking by using the prevention, protection and prosecution techniques
    E. Create a system of incentives for countries to fight human trafficking, while also tracking which countries are effectively addressing the issue

2. The author most likely provides an explanation of the tier system used by the TIPS Report in order to:

    A. Show how the United States ranks countries' efforts to combat human trafficking
    B. Simplify a complex problem
    C. Highlight the drastic differences in how human trafficking is addressed throughout the world
    D. Minimize the severity of a serious issue
    E. Demonstrate that different countries handle human trafficking in different ways

3. The primary purpose of the passage is most likely to

A. Describe a type of report produced by the United States
B. Shed light on a complex issue
C. Describe the evolution of a program
D. Compare and contrast different forms of measurement
E. Quantify a qualitative issue

4. Which one of the following best captures the author's attitude toward the TIPS Report?

A. Subtly emotive, as the text deals with a sensitive issue
B. Disinterested in the human trauma that results from human trafficking
C. Enthusiasm for its effectiveness and innovative tactics
D. Objectively descriptive of how the TIPS Report is used to assess countries' actions against human trafficking
E. Admiration for the TIPS Report's ability to be nonpartisan

5. Which of the following is NOT a penalty that a Tier 3 country might be subject to?

A. Being punished by the World Bank
B. Withdrawal of funding for cultural exchange programs
C. Reduction in funding for educational programs
D. U.S. opposition to assistance from the International Monetary Fund
E. Withdrawal of non-trade related foreign assistance

6. The author mentions that U.S. missions regularly meet with foreign officials for all of the reasons EXCEPT:

A. To help cast the TIPS Report in a positive light
B. To suggest that the TIPS Report is politically biased
C. To demonstrate that the U.S. is willing to engage in dialogue with other countries
D. To demonstrate a willingness on the part of the United States to cooperate with other countries
E. To offer insight as to how data is collected

Passage:

1. OBJECTS OF HUMAN KNOWLEDGE. It is evident to anyone who takes a survey of the objects of human knowledge, that they are either IDEAS actually imprinted on the senses; or else such as are perceived by attending to the passions and operations of the mind; or lastly, ideas formed by help of memory and imagination—either compounding, dividing, or barely representing those originally perceived in the aforesaid ways. By sight I have the ideas of light and colors, with their several degrees and variations. By touch I perceive hard and soft, heat and cold, motion and resistance, and of all these more and less either as to quantity or

degree. Smelling furnishes me with odors; the palate with tastes; and hearing conveys sounds to the mind in all their variety of tone and composition. And as several of these are observed to accompany each other, they come to be marked by one name, and so to be reputed as one thing. Thus, for example, a certain color, taste, smell, figure and consistence having been observed to go together, are accounted one distinct thing, signified by the name APPLE. Other collections of ideas constitute a stone, a tree, a book, and the like sensible things, which as they are pleasing or disagreeable excite the passions of love, hatred, joy, grief, and so forth.

2. MIND--SPIRIT--SOUL. But, besides all that endless variety of ideas or objects of knowledge, there is likewise something which knows or perceives them, and exercises diverse operations as willing, imagining, and remembering about them. This perceiving, active being is what I call MIND, SPIRIT, SOUL, or MYSELF, by which words I do not denote any one of my ideas, but a thing entirely distinct from them, WHEREIN THEY EXIST, or, which is the same thing, whereby they are perceived—for the existence of an idea consists in being perceived.

3. HOW FAR THE ASSENT OF THE VULGAR CONCEDED. That neither our thoughts, nor passions, nor ideas formed by the imagination, exist WITHOUT the mind, is what EVERYBODY WILL ALLOW. And it seems no less evident that the various sensations or ideas imprinted on the sense, however blended or combined together (that is, whatever objects they compose), cannot exist otherwise than IN a mind perceiving them. I think an intuitive knowledge may be obtained of this by any one that shall attend to WHAT IS MEANT BY THE TERM "EXIST," when applied to sensible things. The table I write on I say exists— that is, I see and feel it—and if I were out of my study I should say it existed, meaning thereby that if I were in my study I might perceive it, or that some other spirit actually does perceive it. There was an odor, that is, it was smelt; there was a sound, that is, it was heard; a color or figure, and it was perceived by sight or touch. This is all that I can understand by these and the like expressions. For as to what is said of the absolute existence of unthinking things without any relation to their being perceived, that seems perfectly unintelligible. Their ESSE is PERCIPI, nor is it possible they should have any existence out of the minds or thinking things which perceive them.

4. THE VULGAR OPINION INVOLVES A CONTRADICTION. It is indeed an opinion STRANGELY prevailing amongst men, that houses, mountains, rivers, and in a word all sensible objects, have an existence, natural or real, distinct from their being perceived by the understanding. But, with how great an assurance and acquiescence soever this principle may be entertained in the world, yet whoever shall find in his heart to call it in question may, if I mistake not, perceive it to involve a manifest contradiction. For, what are the fore-mentioned objects but the things we perceive by sense? And what do we PERCEIVE BESIDES OUR OWN IDEAS OR SENSATIONS? And is it not plainly repugnant that any one of these, or any combination of them, should exist unperceived?

5. CAUSE OF THIS PREVALENT ERROR. If we thoroughly examine this tenet it will, perhaps, be found at bottom to depend on the doctrine of ABSTRACT IDEAS. For can there be a nicer strain of abstraction than to distinguish the existence of sensible objects from their being perceived, so as to conceive them existing unperceived? Light and colors, heat and cold, extension and figures—in a word, the things we see and feel—what are they but so

many sensations, notions, ideas, or impressions on the sense? And is it possible to separate, even in thought, any of these from perception? For my part, I might as easily divide a thing from itself. I may, indeed, divide in my thoughts, or conceive apart from each other, those things which, perhaps, I never perceived by sense so divided. Thus, I imagine the trunk of a human body without the limbs, or conceive the smell of a rose without thinking on the rose itself. So far, I will not deny, I can abstract—if that may properly be called ABSTRACTION which extends only to the conceiving separately such objects as it is possible may really exist or be actually perceived asunder. But my conceiving or imagining power does not extend beyond the possibility of real existence or perception. Hence, as it is impossible for me to see or feel anything without an actual sensation of that thing, so is it impossible for me to conceive in my thoughts any sensible thing or object distinct from the sensation or perception of it.

Questions:

7. Given the author's account of imagining of the smell of a rose, which one of the following is most analogous to the author's ideas in action?

   A. A man who has been alone for his whole life dreams of a woman.
   B. A bird knows how to fly south in autumn without ever having done so.
   C. A dog chases a rabbit and later dreams of a rabbit chasing him.
   D. Until a man sees another man with power and then dreams of a god, that god does not exist.
   E. A man has to see a chair without legs before he can imagine it.

8. The author of the passage would be most likely to disagree with which of the following statements?

   A. Everything exists independently of mankind.
   B. The self is synonymous with the mind.
   C. Certain things are a conglomeration of specific perception.
   D. Without considerable perception, we cannot reach complicated abstract thought.
   E. Smell is akin to taste.

9. What is the primary function of the passage's final paragraph?

   A. To function as a break from the initial argument
   B. To draw on the third and fourth paragraphs and attempt to pinpoint the source of the problem they deal with
   C. To conclude the author's argument
   D. To discuss a criticism of the argument presented by the author in the third and fourth paragraphs
   E. To discuss the abstract at a level of detail not afforded to it in the other paragraphs.

10. Which of the following is an apt description of the author's assessment of emotions in the passage?

    A. Simply spurious
    B. Extremely complex
    C. Extensive
    D. Brief and lacking detail
    E. Off-topic

11. The underlined phrase "Their ESSE is PERCIPI" as used in the third paragraph most nearly means what?

    A. Their saying is perceiving.
    B. Their attempt is acknowledged.
    C. To see them is to believe in them.
    D. Their essence is production.
    E. Their being is perception.

12. Which one of the following best captures the author's attitude toward abstract thoughts?

    A. They exist only when we put effort into perceiving them.
    B. They are not real.
    C. They are always founded on real perceptions.
    D. They are contradictory to human knowledge.
    E. They are more important than when we perceive senses.

13. Which one of the following most accurately states the main point of the passage?

    A. We perceive things with our senses then assess or transform these perceptions.
    B. Human thinking is mostly sensing things and only sometimes assessing them.
    C. None of these answers accurately convey the main point of the passage.
    D. Men are meant to dream and derive fanciful thoughts from their experienced sensations.
    E. The process of thought does not allow things to exist when we are not near them.

Passage:

The theory that the brilliant colors of flowers and fruits is due to the direct action of light has been supported by a recent writer by examples taken from the arctic instead of from the tropical flora. In the arctic regions, vegetation is excessively rapid during the short summer, and this is held to be due to the continuous action of light throughout the long summer days. "The further we advance towards the north, the more the leaves of plants increase in size as if to absorb a greater proportion of the solar rays. M. Grisebach says that during a journey in Norway he observed that the majority of deciduous trees had already, at the 60th degree of latitude, larger leaves than in Germany, while M. Ch. Martins has made a similar observation as regards the leguminous plants cultivated in Lapland." The same writer goes on to say that all the seeds of cultivated plants acquire a deeper color the further north they are grown, white haricots becoming brown or black, and white wheat becoming brown, while the green color of all vegetation becomes more intense. The flowers also are similarly changed: those which are white or yellow in central Europe becoming red or orange in Norway. This is what occurs in the Alpine flora, and the cause is said to be the same in both—the greater intensity of the sunlight. In the one the light is more persistent, in the other more intense because it traverses a less thickness of atmosphere.

Admitting the facts as above stated to be in themselves correct, they do not by any means establish the theory founded on them; and it is curious that Grisebach, who has been quoted by this writer for the fact of the increased size of the foliage, gives a totally different explanation of the more vivid colors of Arctic flowers. He says, "We see flowers become larger and more richly colored in proportion as, by the increasing length of winter, insects become rarer, and their cooperation in the act of fecundation is exposed to more uncertain chances." (Vegetation du Globe, col. i. p. 61—French translation.) This is the theory here adopted to explain the colors of Alpine plants, and we believe there are many facts that will show it to be the preferable one. The statement that the white and yellow flowers of temperate Europe become red or golden in the Arctic regions must we think be incorrect. By roughly tabulating the colors of the plants given by Sir Joseph Hooker as permanently Arctic, we find among fifty species with more or less conspicuous flowers, twenty-five white, twelve yellow, eight purple or blue, three lilac, and two red or pink; showing a very similar proportion of white and yellow flowers to what obtains further south.

Questions:

14. The author of the passage is most likely _____.

    A. a botanist
    B. an archeologist
    C. a geographer
    D. a chemist
    E. a meteorologist

15. The "recent writer" quoted in the first paragraph believes that _____.

    A. M. Ch. Martins' theory is incorrect
    B. cultivated flowers have lighter colors in the south and darker colors in the north
    C. because light continuously shines on arctic plants during the summer, they grow very quickly
    D. light is less persistent in the north than in the south
    E. the green color of plants becomes more intense in the south

16. This passage is taken from a longer work. Based on what you have read, which of the following would you most expect to find in the paragraphs immediately following those in the passage?

    A. Praise of the useful nature of Hooker's research
    B. Further consideration of the theory of the writer quoted in the first paragraph
    C. A summary of a paper the author wishes to publish on the topic being discussed
    D. A discussion of the historical uses of alpine plants
    E. More evidence as to why Grisebach's theory is the correct one

17. The author brings up Joseph Hooker's research in order to _____.

    A. demonstrate that the colors of flowers change at varying latitudes
    B. disprove the theory of the "recent writer" quoted in the first paragraph
    C. suggest that a follow-up experiment be performed to check his result
    D. provide evidence in favor of the author's theory, which disagrees with all of the previously mentioned theories
    E. support Martins' theory

18. The author's critique of the theory presented in the first paragraph is that _____.

    A. The author does not critique the theory presented in the first paragraph; he wholeheartedly agrees with its claims.
    B. they are true, but do not support the theory established based on them
    C. the facts supporting the theory are false, so the theory is also false
    D. the facts were gathered in an unscientific manner and are thus not reliable, making the theory doubtful
    E. only some of the facts are true, casting doubt on the reliability of the theory as a whole

19. In this passage, the author _____.

    A. agrees with all of the writers and scientists mentioned in the passage
    B. disagrees with Martins but agrees with Grisebach
    C. disagrees with all of the writers and scientists mentioned in the passage
    D. disagrees with Hooker but agrees with Martins
    E. disagrees with the "recent writer" quoted in the first paragraph, but agrees with Grisebach

20. The underlined sentence in the passage tells us that _____.

    A. leaf size is associated with atmospheric moisture levels
    B. the number of leaves on a tree is related to the latitude in which it is found
    C. many northern-dwelling plants have small leaves
    D. the further south you travel, the smaller plants' leaves should be

E. if you take a plant from a northern climate into a southern climate, its leaves will shrink

21. According to the "recent writer" quoted in the first paragraph, what are the two factors that affect light intensity?

  A. Opacity of medium the light is passing through and temperature
  B. Persistence and thickness of atmosphere
  C. Thickness of atmosphere and cloud cover
  D. Temperature and moisture levels
  E. Cloud cover and persistence

Passage:

The first and principal contribution to which I shall ask your attention is the advance made in the United States, not in theory only, but in practice, toward the abandonment of war as the means of settling disputes between nations, the substitution of discussion and arbitration, and the avoidance of armaments. If the intermittent Indian fighting and the brief contest with the Barbary corsairs be disregarded, the United States have had only four years and a quarter of international war in the one hundred and seven years since the adoption of the Constitution. Within the same period the United States have been a party to forty-seven arbitrations—being more than half of all that have taken place in the modern world. The questions settled by these arbitrations have been just such as have commonly caused wars, namely, questions of boundary, fisheries, damage caused by war or civil disturbances, and injuries to commerce. Some of them were of great magnitude, the four made under the treaty of Washington (May 8, 1871) being the most important that have ever taken place. Confident in their strength, and relying on their ability to adjust international differences, the United States have habitually maintained, by voluntary enlistment for short terms, a standing army and a fleet which, in proportion to the population, are insignificant.

The beneficent effects of this American contribution to civilization are of two sorts: in the first place, the direct evils of war and of preparations for war have been diminished; and secondly, the influence of the war spirit on the perennial conflict between the rights of the single personal unit and the powers of the multitude that constitute organized society—or, in other words, between individual freedom and collective authority—has been reduced to the lowest terms. War has been, and still is, the school of collectivism, the warrant of tyranny. Century after century, tribes, clans, and nations have sacrificed the liberty of the individual to the fundamental necessity of being strong for combined defense or attack in war. Individual freedom is crushed in war, for the nature of war is inevitably despotic. It says to the private person: "Obey without a question, even unto death; die in this ditch, without knowing why; walk into that deadly thicket; mount this embankment, behind which are men who will try to kill you, lest you should kill them." At this moment every young man in Continental Europe learns the lesson of absolute military obedience, and feels himself subject to this crushing power of militant society, against which no rights of the individual to life, liberty, and the pursuit of happiness avail anything.

In the War of Independence there was a distinct hope and purpose to enlarge individual liberty. It made possible a confederation of the colonies, and, ultimately, the adoption of the Constitution of the United States. It gave to the thirteen colonies a lesson in collectivism, but it was a needed lesson on the necessity of combining their forces to resist an oppressive external authority. The War of 1812 is properly called the Second War of Independence, for it was truly a fight for liberty and for the rights of neutrals, in resistance to the impressment of seamen and other oppressions growing out of European conflicts. The Civil War of 1861-65 was waged, on the side of the North, primarily, to prevent the dismemberment of the country, and, secondarily and incidentally, to destroy the institution of slavery. On the Northern side it therefore called forth a generous element of popular ardor in defense of free institutions.

In all this series of fighting the main motives were self-defense, resistance to oppression, the enlargement of liberty, and the conservation of national acquisitions. The war with Mexico, it is true, was of a wholly different type. That was a war of conquest, and of conquest chiefly in the interest of African slavery. It was also an unjust attack made by a powerful people on a feeble one; but it lasted less than two years, and the number of men engaged in it was at no time large. Its results contradicted the anticipations both of those who advocated and of those who opposed it. It was one of the wrongs which prepared the way for the great rebellion; but its direct evils were of moderate extent, and it had no effect on the perennial conflict between individual liberty and public power.

The ordinary causes of war between nation and nation have been lacking in America for the last century and a quarter. How many wars in the world's history have been due to contending dynasties; how many of the most cruel and protracted wars have been due to religious strife; how many to race hatred! No one of these causes of war has been efficacious in America since the French were overcome in Canada by the English in 1759. Looking forward into the future, we find it impossible to imagine circumstances under which any of these common causes of war can take effect on the North American continent. Therefore, the ordinary motives for maintaining armaments in time of peace, and concentrating the powers of government in such a way as to interfere with individual liberty, have not been in play in the United States as among the nations of Europe, and are not likely to be. Such have been the favorable conditions under which America has made its best contribution to the progress of civilization.

Questions:

22. The author would be most likely to describe the young men in continental Europe as

_____.

    A. bound by centuries of tradition to sacrifice his life for the good of the state
    B. incompetent, ill-educated, and doomed to a violent life and death
    C. subject to the tyranny of warfare and significantly less free than their American counterparts
    D. justly conditioned to fear chaos and so trained to preserve the established order
    E. overly religious and ignorant of scientific and philosophical developments

23. This essay is most likely _____.

    A. a political speech given by a candidate in a local election
    B. part of a longer essay about the history and progression of warfare
    C. part of a longer essay about the various contributions America has made to the advancement of society and humanity
    D. a stand-alone piece about the American contribution to the declining influence of warfare and tyranny
    E. a response to another essay that was written to attack the contributions made by the United States to advancement of civilization

24. The primary function of the fourth paragraph is to _____.

    A. support the author's primary argument by introducing new evidence that supports the thesis
    B. introduce a foreseen refutation of the author's thesis and downplay the significance of this argument
    C. vehemently disparage the United States' government for turning its back on the mission of personal liberty
    D. confess to one flaw in the author's argument and demonstrate why this flaw is relevant, but not enough to overturn the author's thesis
    E. condemn the Mexican government for their bellicose behavior in the build-up to the Mexican War

25. Which of these criticisms can be most reasonably leveled against the author of this essay?

    A. He relies on faith and references religious evidence to further his thesis.
    B. His writing is idiomatic and informal.
    C. His conclusions are poorly researched and lack definition.
    D. He is biased and ignores or demeans evidence against his argument.
    E. He is overly patriotic and allows his love for his country to inform his opinions.

26. The author's tone in this passage could best be described as _____.

    A. cantankerous and wanton
    B. haughty and courageous
    C. self-absorbed and condescending
    D. congratulatory and optimistic
    E. thoughtful and nationalistic

27. Which of these is not given as a reason why the author believes the war with Mexico was unjust?

A. All of these are given as reasons why the author believes the war with Mexico was unjust.
B. The war with Mexico was not fought for the purposes of self-defense.
C. The war with Mexico was fought to preserve and expand the institution of slavery.
D. The war with Mexico witnessed a stronger country exerting its power against a weaker country.
E. The war with Mexico involved the needless sacrifice of thousands of young American men.

28. The main point of the third paragraph is that _____.

A. America failed to prevent the outbreak of warfare on numerous occasions and so is perhaps less deserving of the praise offered in the first two paragraphs
B. American entanglements with the British have always ended in defeat for the British, proving America's moral superiority
C. America has been embroiled in numerous conflicts in the nineteenth century, but they have all been the fault of someone else
D. In the majority of American conflicts, the primary motivation is self-defense and the preservation of liberty
E. America has emerged triumphant from several wars in the nineteenth century and now does not have to rely on warfare as a means of diplomacy

ARGUMENTATIVE WRITING SECTION

Prompt:

A city government is considering implementing a policy that would make public transportation free for all residents. Proponents argue that this would reduce traffic congestion, lower carbon emissions, and provide equitable access to transportation for low-income individuals. Critics, however, raise concerns about the potential strain on the city's budget and whether such a policy might lead to overcrowding and deteriorated services due to increased demand.

Assignment:

Write an essay in which you argue for or against the city's proposed policy of making public transportation free for all residents. In your essay, discuss the potential benefits and drawbacks of such a policy, considering its impact on traffic congestion, environmental sustainability, budgetary constraints, and the quality of public transportation services.

Answer sheet with explanation

LOGICAL REASONING SECTION

1. **Correct Answer:** A. Neither of the two populations of sockeyes has interbred with the native salmon.

Explanation: The argument asserts that the separation of a genetically uniform group of sockeye salmon into two distinct populations in Lake Clearwater indicates that both populations have "adapted genetically" to their environment. To strengthen this claim, two main objectives are identified: demonstrating that the argument logically follows from the premises or defending it against counterarguments.
Predictions for potential strengthening answers include affirming that distinct populations often adapt to their environments and rejecting counterarguments about the genetic testing of the populations. A strong counterargument could suggest that the populations did not adapt but instead interbred with native salmon, which would undermine the original claim.
Evaluating the answer options reveals that option B fails to clarify the genetic distinction, C does not impact the argument, D contradicts the argument by suggesting no genetic change, and E is irrelevant to the claim.
Ultimately, while none of the answers provide a direct strengthening of the argument, option A effectively defends against a critical counterargument, making it the best choice.

2. **Correct Answer:** E. To what extent does the new drug retain its efficacy when used in combination with the other drugs?

Explanation: The argument is challenged by questioning the necessity of taking both drugs. It suggests that a drug preserving existing bone might suffice, or a drug promoting new bone growth could be effective alone. Concerns arise about potentially excessive bone growth leading to mobility issues.
Among the answer choices, only option E is relevant to assessing the argument. It addresses the clinician's recommendation for taking both drugs by considering whether their combination would diminish efficacy or cause adverse effects. This inquiry aligns with the original objection, indicating that if the combined treatment is harmful, it undermines the recommendation. As the evaluation of the clinician's advice shifts from negative to acceptable based on this consideration, option E emerges as the best question to ask.

3. **Correct Answer:** A.

Explanation: The argument presents a paradox: Jimmy's gas bills increased after he replaced his old gas water heater with a new, highly efficient one. The goal is to find an explanation for this unexpected outcome. Answer A fails to provide an explanation, making it the correct answer to this "EXCEPT" question.

In contrast, answers B, C, D, and E all offer plausible reasons for the increased gas bills. B suggests Jimmy's uncle moved in, potentially increasing gas usage. C indicates additional gas appliances were installed. D points to rising gas prices, and E attributes the increase to colder weather, requiring more gas for heating. These options effectively address the paradox, leaving A as the only choice that doesn't explain the situation.

4. **Correct Answer:** A. It would have been permissible for the chairperson to release the commission's report to the public only if most other members of the commission had first given their consent.

Explanation: The argument concludes that "the chair should not have released the report" based on the premise that the chair didn't consult anyone before doing so. To strengthen this conclusion in a Sufficient Assumption question, an additional premise is needed, suggesting that the chair must consult or obtain consent before releasing a report.
Answer A effectively supports the argument by stating that the chair needs the consent of most members before releasing the report, which aligns with the given premise and leads to the conclusion. Other options (B, C, D, and E) do not strengthen the argument because they introduce conditions or loopholes that either justify the chair's action or fail to prove that consulting others was necessary. Thus, A is the correct answer because it directly reinforces the conclusion.

5. **Correct Answer:** B. Often, cattle or sheep can be raised to maturity on grass from pastureland that is unsuitable for any other kind of farming.

Explanation: The argument claims that eating meat is unethical because the grains used to feed animals could be used to feed humans instead. To weaken this, a counterpoint is needed that suggests eating meat is not necessarily unethical, despite its potential negative consequences.
Answer B effectively weakens the argument by stating that animals consume types of grain that humans can't eat, thereby undermining the premise of the ethicist's argument. Other choices either strengthen the original claim or fail to address the core issue of whether the grain used for animals could be utilized by humans, making B the strongest option for weakening the argument.

6. **Correct Answer:** B. what a life of moderation requires of a person

Explanation: Antonio argues that living a life of moderation means consistently following a middle course without deviations. In contrast, Marla challenges this view, asserting that rigid adherence to moderation is itself a lack of true moderation, as it avoids necessary risks. Their disagreement centers on whether strict consistency in moderation can truly be called "a life of moderation." The correct point of disagreement lies in defining whether unwavering moderation aligns with the concept of living a moderate life.

7. **Correct Answer:** C. On average, there are a few errors in an issue of the journal Periodos. Aisha has finished proofreading all but the last two pages of an issue of this journal but has encountered no errors. So there are probably errors in the pages she has not yet checked in this issue of the journal.

Explanation: The argument contains a flawed reasoning similar to assuming that if an average event hasn't occurred yet, it must happen soon to "balance out" the average. This is like expecting heads to appear after flipping tails multiple times, which misunderstands how averages work and overlooks variance in individual outcomes.

In finding a matching example, choice C perfectly mirrors this flawed logic. It suggests that because there are typically a few errors in the journal, and none have been found so far, the last pages are likely to contain errors. This matches the mistaken belief that an event must occur to maintain an average pattern.

8. **Correct Answer:** B. If the lowest bidder on the sanitation contract is not Dillon, then it is Ramsey. So if the contract goes to the lowest bidder and it does not go to Dillon, then it will go to Ramsey.

Explanation: The argument uses solid reasoning based on an "if/then" structure. It states that if Suarez isn't the most qualified, then Anderson must be, implying that the most qualified candidate must be either Suarez or Anderson. If the most qualified candidate is chosen and it isn't Suarez, it has to be Anderson.
To find a matching example, choice B mirrors this structure by identifying two candidates for a quality (lowest bid) and concluding that if one candidate doesn't get chosen based on this quality, then the other must be selected. This parallel reasoning makes B the correct answer.

9. **Correct Answer:** E. Claiming that a goal that Inez mentions could be pursued without the programs Inez endorses

Explanation: Inez argues that investing in space exploration is essential because it leads to valuable technological advancements. Winona counters by suggesting that instead of investing in space exploration, funding technological advancements directly would be more efficient. Winona's response implies that the goal of technological progress could be achieved more effectively by bypassing space exploration altogether. Therefore, choice E is correct, as it captures Winona's recommendation to remove the intermediary (space exploration) to achieve the same objective.

10. **Correct Answer:** C. an example of a cultural change that did not necessarily have a detrimental effect on the human mind overall

Explanation: Pedantic Turd (P.T.) argues that electronic media likely changes the way we think rather than making us less intelligent. To support this, P.T. draws an analogy to the time when books were first introduced, and some critics claimed that books were making people dumber by reducing the need to memorize long speeches. P.T. uses this historical example to suggest that similar complaints about electronic media might also be unfounded.

The role of the reference to the cranks who complained about books is to provide evidence through an analogous situation. P.T. implies that just as the introduction of books didn't actually reduce intelligence, electronic media probably isn't doing so either. The correct answer is C, as P.T. uses the reference to make a case that technology likely isn't having a net negative effect, based on the historical experience with books.

11. **Correct Answer:** B. The argument relies on the testimony of experts whose expertise is not shown to be sufficiently broad to support their general claim.

Explanation: The question involves identifying a flaw in the argument presented. The argument relies on computer experts making broad claims about the biggest threats to large institutions, but the issue is that these experts may not be qualified to assess threats beyond their specific technological expertise. They might understand unauthorized access to data as a major problem, but they lack the authority to compare it with threats outside their domain, like financial risks.

The correct answer is B, as it identifies this flaw. The experts overstep by making broad statements about threats to institutions without properly qualifying their knowledge to only technological concerns. The other choices either don't align with what the argument actually does or don't point out a relevant flaw.

12. **Correct Answer:** B. Exercising the muscles on opposite sides of the spine unequally tends to lead to unbalanced muscle development.

Explanation: The argument claims that exercising both sides of the back equally is crucial for a healthy back, based on the idea that balanced muscle development is necessary. The reasoning requires an additional assumption that exercising the sides unequally would lead to unbalanced muscle development.

Answer choice B provides the missing link by stating that "exercising opposite sides of the back unequally leads to unbalanced muscle development," which directly connects the argument's premises and conclusion. This fills the gap and strengthens the reasoning, making B the correct answer.

Other answer choices either introduce unnecessary details or assumptions not addressed in the argument, or they misinterpret what is required to maintain a healthy back.

13. **Correct Answer:** E. More than half of the students received a grade of B minus or higher.

Explanation: In analyzing this formal question, real numbers can help clarify the relationships. Assuming a class of ten students, "most" attending all classes implies at least six students attended every class. If "each" student with a grade lower than a B- missed at least one class, then those six who attended every class must have received a B- or higher.

However, the four students who did not attend all classes are not necessarily all receiving grades of C+ or lower - some might, but not necessarily all. Misinterpreting this as a certainty would be a false contrapositive error.

The correct choice, E, aligns with the idea that students who attended all classes did not receive a grade lower than a B-. This is the only option supported by the conditions in the passage, making E the right answer.

14. **Correct Answer:** D. More-frequent thorough coverage of local politics would reduce at least one source of discouragement from resident participation in local politics.

Explanation: The argument contains a gap in reasoning that assumes "if there's a lower chance of a positive official response, we're less likely to participate." However, this isn't explicitly supported by the evidence provided. To find the correct answer in a "Must Be True" question, the key is to select a choice that is necessary for the conclusion to hold, based on the given premises.
Answer D aligns with the idea that more thorough news coverage leads to less discouragement in participation, supporting the argument's chain of reasoning. While it might not align perfectly with the initial prediction, it's the only option that must be true according to the argument's premises. Thus, D is the correct answer.

15. **Correct Answer:** B. Some measures taken by a business to increase productivity fail to be beneficial to the business as a whole.

Explanation: The argument presents a structure where the second sentence is the conclusion, supported by the third sentence as a premise. The second sentence states that "not all productivity increases are beneficial to the business as a whole," while the third sentence provides the reason: attempts to increase productivity can lead to a decrease in the number of employees, harming both dismissed employees and the sense of security for retained ones. Therefore, the second sentence is the main conclusion, supported by the premise in the third sentence.
Answer choices A and C misinterpret the argument's logic, and D provides background information. The correct answer is B, which correctly identifies the main conclusion, with E being the premise that supports it.

16. **Correct Answer:** D. Most purchasers of tablet computers over the past 2 years have been over the age of 25.

Explanation: The correct answer suggests that the predicted demographic shift may not have the impact on tablet computer sales that the author predicts. That is, the author uses 5-year demographic data to predict a reversal in the 2-year tablet sales trend. However, the correct answer suggests that such data is misleading insofar as purchasers in the 18 - 25 demographic were not responsible for driving the 2-year sales trend.

17. **Correct Answer:** B. College graduates are more likely to be employed than those who are not college graduates

Explanation: The argument asserts that college graduates do not have a substantial employment advantage over non-graduates. That assertion is directly undermined if college graduates are more likely to be employed than non-graduates.

18. **Correct Answer:** E. A government will not receive international approval to join a war when its citizens have not been attacked

Explanation: An apparent weakness of the argument is that a government might receive international approval for going to war even when its citizens have not been attacked. If a government could never receive international approval for such a war, then this would no longer be a weakness.

19. **Correct Answer:** A. Many readers feel like they are not being given the whole story when they read newspaper articles.

Explanation: The correct answer does nothing to strengthen the argument presented in the stimulus. The fact that readers do not feel they are getting the whole story does not mean that readers should not trust the newspaper articles they read. This answer only speaks to how readers feel, not the objective reality of whether the newspaper articles are accurate.

20. **Correct Answer:** B. Low levels of cholesterol are proven to increase quality of life.

Explanation: The correct answer helps explain why doctors would advise their patients to reduce their cholestrol levels even if it would not increase their longevity.

READING COMPREHENSION SECTION

1. **Correct Answer:** Create a system of incentives for countries to fight human trafficking, while also tracking which countries are effectively addressing the issue

Explanation: The best answer will cover the two primary purposes behind the TIPS report: to instill change in how countries address the issue of human trafficking, and to also document the issue more effectively. The correct answer choice mentions both of these priorities:
Create a system of incentives for countries to fight human trafficking, while also tracking which countries are effectively addressing the issue

2. **Correct Answer:** Show how the United States ranks countries' efforts to combat human trafficking

Explanation: The tier system is described in order to explain how the United States categorizes different countries according to how they address the issue of human trafficking. Therefore, the correct answer is:
Show how the United States ranks countries' efforts to combat human trafficking
A tempting incorrect answer is: Simplify a complex problem. This is incorrect because while the tier system might have this effect, that was not the author's intended message when describing the tier system.

3. **Correct Answer:** Describe a type of report produced by the United States

Explanation: The entire focus of the text is on the TIPS Report and how it is formulated. Therefore, the best answer is:
Describe a type of report produced by the United States
The incorrect answers are either too broad or only apply to certain parts of the text, rather than the text as a whole.

4. **Correct Answer:** Objectively descriptive of how the TIPS Report is used to assess countries' actions against human trafficking

Explanation: The tone is very objective and descriptive; its intent is simply to communicate information, not to inspire admiration, enthusiasm, or emotion. Additionally, the text is not disinterested. Therefore, the correct answer is:
Objectively descriptive of how the TIPS Report is used to assess countries' actions against human trafficking

5. **Correct Answer:** Being punished by the World Bank

Explanation: While one of the potential consequences of being a Tier 3 country is that the U.S. may pressure the World Bank to limit assistance, the World Bank would not itself punish a Tier 3 country of its own accord. Therefore, the correct answer is:
Being punished by the World Bank

6. **Correct Answer:** To suggest that the TIPS Report is politically biased

Explanation: The author mentions that U.S. missions regularly meet with foreign officials in order to cast the TIPS Report in a positive light, to show a willingness on part of the U.S. to engage in a dialogue and cooperate with other countries, and to offer insight as to how data is collected. The only answer choice that does not reflect this mission is:
To suggest that the TIPS Report is politically biased.

7. **Correct Answer:** A dog chases a rabbit and later dreams of a rabbit chasing him.

Explanation: The specific instance of the rose, which comes in the last paragraph, is this: "I imagine the trunk of a human body without the limbs, or conceive the smell of a rose without thinking on the rose itself." The author's ideas here are that we cannot change something in our minds until we have perceived it. The dog has perceived chasing the rabbit and is therefore following the author's ideas when it dreams that the role between it and the rabbit are changed. At least two of the other answers go against the author's ideas in that no perception occurs. The other two are not analogous to the image of the rose's scent and perhaps go beyond the author's overall argument.

8. **Correct Answer:** Everything exists independently of mankind.

Explanation: It is quite obvious that the statement "Everything exists independently of mankind" is the one argument with which the author would be most likely to disagree. Despite the fact that the author makes no distinction between the thoughts of humans and other living things, we can assume that he is talking with specific reference to humanity. If humans did not exist, then in the author's opinion everything else's existence would perhaps be invalid. If you were to ask the author the famous riddle, "If a tree falls in the woods and no one is around to hear it, does it make a sound?" he would be quite adamant in answering "no."

9. **Correct Answer:** To draw on the third and fourth paragraphs and attempt to pinpoint the source of the problem they deal with

Explanation: We can tell from the paragraphs' clear titles that the author intended to have the fifth paragraph pinpoint the problem discussed in the third and fourth paragraphs. In order, they are titled, "HOW FAR THE ASSENT OF THE VULGAR CONCEDED," "THE VULGAR OPINION INVOLVES A CONTRADICTION," and "CAUSE OF THIS PREVALENT ERROR." The author does in part detail the abstract in this paragraph, but it is not the paragraph's primary function.

10. **Correct Answer:** Brief and lacking detail

Explanation: The author does not fully address emotions in the passage; he only mentions emotions when he says at the end of the first paragraph, "Other collections of ideas constitute a stone, a tree, a book, and the like sensible things, which as they are pleasing or disagreeable excite the passions of love, hatred, joy, grief, and so forth." In relation to the rest of the passage, this is perhaps the briefest address of any subject mentioned. The use of the phrase
"and so forth" emphasizes how brief the assessment of emotions is, as if they may undermine his argument.

11. **Correct Answer:** Their being is perception.

Explanation: The saying "ESSE is PERCIPI" means "to be is to be perceived," and we can interpret this despite it being in a different language. We can either spend time discovering the links between the words
"esse" and "essence" and "percipi" and "perceived," or we can use the author's argument in the preceding sentence to guide us in the right direction: "nor is it possible they should have any existence out of the minds or thinking things which perceive them." Be careful here to read the answers carefully as many of their words look similar but have vastly different meanings.

12. **Correct Answer:** They are always founded on real perceptions.

Explanation: If we look at the last paragraph, which is largely about abstract thoughts, we can see that the author says "my conceiving or imagining power does not extend beyond the possibility of real existence or perception." Abstract thoughts are thus founded in reality according to the author. We could perhaps say that "they exist only when we put effort into perceiving them," however, the author never says this outright.

13. **Correct Answer:** We perceive things with our senses then assess or transform these perceptions.

Explanation: The passage quite clearly states at the beginning that we perceive things, then other parts which may be called "mind, body, or spirit" "[exercise] diverse operations as willing, imagining, and remembering about them." We can say this continues on to the end of the passage as the author discusses in more detail the
"imagining" portion of our perceptions. We cannot say that the statement "Human thinking is mostly sensing things and only sometimes assessing them" is correct, as the word "sometimes" nullifies it. Likewise, the statement "The process of thought does not allow things to exist when we are not near them" is nullified by being a simplified, perhaps inaccurate, argument of a part of the passage, not of the whole passage.

14. **Correct Answer:** a botanist

Explanation: As the title of the passage is "Recent Views as to Direct Action of Light on the Colors of Flowers and Fruits" and its subject is flower color, leaf size, and other scientific phenomena that have to do with plants, trees, and especially flowers, we can safely infer that of the given answer choices, the author is most likely a botanist.
While the author does discuss flowers at different latitudes, which may suggest "geographer," and different atmospheric conditions, which may suggest "meteorologist," he only broaches these topics because of how they intersect with his primary topic of flowers and plants.

15. **Correct Answer:** cultivated flowers have lighter colors in the south and darker colors in the north

Explanation: Answering this question requires you to read the first paragraph very closely and to go back and figure out what exactly the "recent writer" is asserting, whether or not the author of the passage agrees with those assertions. Let's consider each of the answer choices one by one:

"M. Ch. Martins' theory is incorrect" - This cannot be the correct answer, as the "recent writer" is quoted as mentioning M. Ch. Martins to bolster his own assertion about leaf size and latitude.

"light is less persistent in the north than in the south" - This cannot be the correct answer because the author, in referring to the "recent writer," says that "the same writer goes on to say that all the seeds of cultivated plants acquire a deeper color the further north they are grown ... This is what occurs in the Alpine flora, and the cause is said to be the same in both- the greater intensity of the sunlight."

"the green color of plants becomes more intense in the south" - This answer choice cannot be correct because the author, in discussing the "recent writer," says, ""The same writer goes on to say that all the seeds of cultivated plants acquire a deeper color the further north they are grown, white haricots becoming brown or black, and white wheat becoming brown, while the green color of all vegetation becomes more intense."

"because light continuously shines on arctic plants during the summer, they grow very quickly" - The author states, "In the arctic regions, vegetation is excessively rapid during the short summer, and this is held to be due to the continuous action of light throughout the long summer days." Note that this isn't presented as a belief of the "recent writer," but instead as a statement of fact, so this answer choice couldn't be correct for that reason also.

"cultivated flowers have lighter colors in the south and darker colors in the north" - This is the correct answer! We can find evidence supporting it in that the author says (discussing the "recent writer") "The same writer goes on to say that all the seeds of cultivated plants acquire a deeper color the further north they are grown, white haricots becoming brown or black, and white wheat becoming brown, while the green color of all vegetation becomes more intense."

16. **Correct Answer:** More evidence as to why Grisebach's theory is the correct one

Explanation: In the concluding sentences of the passage, the author is asserting that Grisebach's interpretation is the correct one, not that of the "recent writer" quoted in the first paragraph. The author is also bringing up evidence (Joseph Hooker's enumerated observations) to prove his point. One could thus reasonably expect to encounter "more evidence as to why Grisebach's theory is the correct one" if one read on further in the larger text of which this passage is a small part.

17. **Correct Answer:** disprove the theory of the "recent writer" quoted in the first paragraph

Explanation: The author brings up Joseph Hooker's research near the end of the second paragraph, stating, "By roughly tabulating the colors of the plants given by Sir Joseph Hooker as permanently Arctic, we find among fifty species with more or less conspicuous flowers, twenty-five white, twelve yellow, eight purple or blue, three lilac, and two red or pink; showing a very similar proportion of white and yellow flowers to what obtains further south." This immediately follows the sentence, "The statement that the white and yellow flowers of temperate Europe become red or golden in the Arctic regions must we think be incorrect." In this sentence, the author is doubting the veracity of the "recent writer" quoted in the first paragraph. The author then uses Hooker's evidence to disprove the theory of the "recent writer," because if the theory of the "recent writer" were correct, there would be very few white or yellow flowers in the Arctic and many red or golden ones, and Hooker's evidence shows that this is not the case, as most of the Arctic flowers he observed were white. So, the correct answer is that the author uses Joseph Hooker's evidence to "disprove the theory of the 'recent writer' quoted in the first paragraph."

"Provide evidence in favor of the author's theory, which disagrees with all of the previously mentioned scientists" statements" cannot be the correct answer because the author agrees with M. Grisebach.

18. **Correct Answer:** they are true, but do not support the theory established based on them

Explanation: At the start of the second paragraph, the author says, "Admitting the facts as above stated to be in themselves correct, they do not by any means establish the theory founded on them." So, the correct answer is that "[the facts] are true, but do not support the theory established based on them."

19. **Correct Answer:** disagrees with the "recent writer" quoted in the first paragraph, but agrees with Grisebach

Explanation: Answering this question requires you to read closely, as many theories are mentioned throughout the passage and keeping track of them can be quite challenging. In the first paragraph, the writer quotes a "recent writer," who then quotes evidence in the form of observations by M. Grisebach and M. Ch. Martins. In the second paragraph, the writer says that he agrees with the evidence of the "recent writer" (in other words, Grisebach and Martins), but not with the theory the "recent writer" has come up with to explain that evidence. So, the author disagrees with the "recent writer," but agrees with Grisebach, because the author goes on to quote Grisebach's own theory, with which the author agrees.

20. **Correct Answer:** the further south you travel, the smaller plants' leaves should be

Explanation: The underlined sentence is "The further we advance towards the north, the more the leaves of plants increase in size as if to absorb a greater proportion of the solar rays." This has nothing to do with the number of leaves on a plant, so "the number of leaves on a tree is related to the latitude in which it is found" cannot be the correct answer. Similarly, nothing is said about moisture levels in the specified sentence, so "leaf size is associated with atmospheric moisture levels" cannot be correct either. Many northern-dwelling plants have small leaves" reverses the relationship being presented in a way that makes it incorrect; northern plants should have large leaves, not small ones. "If you take a plant from a northern climate into a southern climate, its leaves will shrink" derives too much from the statement; nothing is said about a given set of leaves changing size, just a variation amongst the sizes of many different sets of leaves. This leaves us with one remaining answer choice, the correct one: "the further south you travel, the smaller plants' leaves should be." The specified sentence tells us that if you move north, the leaves of plants you see should get bigger. So, therefore, if you head south, the leaves you see on plants should get smaller. The correct answer states what the sentence is saying in a reverse, but still correct, way.

21. **Correct Answer:** Persistence and thickness of atmosphere

Explanation: The answer to this question is provided in the last two sentences of the first paragraph, where the "recent writer" is being quoted as stating, "This is what occurs in the Alpine flora, and the cause is said to be the same in both—the greater intensity of the sunlight.
In the one the light is more persistent, in the other more intense because it traverses a less thickness of atmosphere." So, the correct answer is "persistence and thickness of atmosphere." While many of the other answer choices may sound plausible, it is important to rely on what is presented in the passage when answering questions like this.

22. **Correct Answer:** subject to the tyranny of warfare and significantly less free than their American counterparts

Explanation: In the conclusion of the second paragraph, the author states, "At this moment every young man in Continental Europe learns the lesson of absolute military obedience, and feels himself subject to this crushing power of militant society, against which no rights of the individual to life, liberty, and the pursuit of happiness avail anything." From this information, and the context of the information in the sentences that precede this quotation, we may determine that the author would describe the young men in continental Europe as subject to the tyranny of warfare, and as a result, less free than their American counterparts.

23. **Correct Answer:** part of a longer essay about the various contributions America has made to the advancement of society and humanity

Explanation: This essay is most likely part of a longer essay about American contributions to the betterment of civilization. The most obvious piece of evidence that supports this is the opening line where the author declares "The first and principal contribution to which I shall ask your attention is the advance made in the United States, not in theory only, but in practice, toward the abandonment of war." The fact that "the abandonment of war" is only the "first and principal contribution" suggests that there are other contributions that the author has made that he will go on to discuss. There is no evidence to support the notion that this essay is given in response to an earlier piece, nor does the essay seem to be about the history and progression of warfare.

24. **Correct Answer:** introduce a foreseen refutation of the author's thesis and downplay the significance of this argument

Explanation: The primary function of the fourth paragraph is to address the problems to the author's overall thesis presented by the Mexican-American War. The author seems to recognize that the causes of the Mexican-American War, and the manner in which it was carried out, represent a hole in his argument. He foresees that someone who might offer a refutation to his thesis would bring up this conflict, so he seeks to downplay the significance of it. You can tell the author believes that the Mexican-American War represents a deviation from his thesis because he says, "[The Mexican-American War] was a war of conquest, and of conquest chiefly in the interest of African slavery. It was also an unjust attack made by a powerful people on a feeble one..." After this quotation, you can see the manner in which the author tries to downplay the conflict: "... but it lasted less than two years, and the number of men engaged in it was at no time large... its direct evils were of moderate extent, and it had no effect on the perennial conflict between individual liberty and public power."

25. Correct Answer: He is biased and ignores or demeans evidence against his argument.

Explanation: Of these answer choices, it is most reasonable to criticize this author because he is heavily biased and tends to diminish the significance of evidence that goes against his argument. This is most clearly seen in the paragraph about the Mexican-American War. We cannot say that the author's writing style is overly idiomatic or that his conclusions are poorly researched because there is no evidence to support these conclusions. Likewise the author makes no mention of God or faith, so this answer choice makes little sense. The only incorrect answer that could reasonably be selected is "He is overly patriotic and allows his love for his country to inform his opinions." But, we do not actually know the author is American; the correct answer is a much closer fit to the problems that can be identified with this essay.

26. Correct Answer: congratulatory and optimistic

Explanation: The primary tone of this passage is definitely optimistic. The author is discussing the positive changes that have been wrought by the American approach to warfare and seems extremely optimistic about what will happen in the future. This can be seen, for example, when the author states in the last paragraph, "Looking forward into the future, we find it impossible to imagine circumstances under which any of these common causes of war can take effect on the North American continent." We may also observe a congratulatory tone in the author's writings. He is rather distinctly praising the United States for its influence, and seems to believe that the advancement of society is no accident: "Therefore, the ordinary motives for maintaining armaments in time of peace, and concentrating the powers of government in such a way as to interfere with individual liberty, have not been in play in the United States as among the nations of Europe, and are not likely to be. Such have been the favorable conditions under which America has made its best contribution to the progress of civilization." You might be able to call this essay "haughty," "condescending," or "nationalistic," but none of these properly capture the tone and feel of the essay.

27. Correct Answer: The war with Mexico involved the needless sacrifice of thousands of young American men.

Explanation: This question asks which of these reasons was "not given," so the evidence must be directly stated, rather than simply inferred. We know that the author believes the war with Mexico was fought in the interests of slavery and not fought in the interests of self-defense because in the fourth paragraph the author declares,
"[The war with Mexico] was a war of conquest, and of conquest chiefly in the interest of African slavery." Likewise, we know that it witnessed a stronger country exerting its power against a weaker country because the author states, "It was also an unjust attack made by a powerful people on a feeble one." However, the author does not directly reference the sacrifice made by the young American men who died on the battlefield. We may infer from the author's earlier arguments that he would object to this sacrifice, but it is not given as a reason in the essay. Be careful not to infer where no inferences should be made.

28. **Correct Answer:** in the majority of American conflicts, the primary motivation is self-defense and the preservation of liberty

Explanation: The main point of the third paragraph is actually most succinctly defined at the beginning of the fourth paragraph. In the third paragraph, the author describes the various wars that the United States was involved in and the reasons why those wars broke out, with his overarching thesis being that the wars were fought for liberty and independence. At the beginning of the fourth paragraph, the author states, "In all this series of fighting the main motives were self-defense, resistance to oppression, the enlargement of liberty, and the conservation of national acquisitions." This is the conclusion he wishes the reader to take from the third paragraph.

ARGUMENTATIVE WRITING SECTION

Prompt Recap:
A city government is considering implementing a policy that would make public transportation free for all residents. Proponents argue that this would reduce traffic congestion, lower carbon emissions, and provide equitable access to transportation for low-income individuals. Critics, however, raise concerns about the potential strain on the city's budget and whether such a policy might lead to overcrowding and deteriorated services due to increased demand.

Introduction:

The topic of providing free public transportation has sparked a significant debate within urban planning and public policy circles. Proponents argue that making public transportation free could address various urban challenges, including reducing traffic congestion, lowering carbon emissions, and ensuring equitable access for all socioeconomic groups. On the other hand, critics are concerned about the financial sustainability of such a policy and the potential decline in service quality due to increased demand. In this essay, I argue in favor of making public transportation free, emphasizing its potential benefits for urban environments and social equity.

Body Paragraph 1: Benefits of Free Public Transportation

170

Free public transportation offers numerous benefits, particularly in reducing traffic congestion and environmental impact. With fewer people relying on personal vehicles, the city could see a significant reduction in traffic, which in turn would lower greenhouse gas emissions. This shift not only contributes to environmental sustainability but also improves the quality of life for residents by reducing commute times and air pollution. Additionally, free public transportation ensures that low-income individuals have access to reliable transportation, which can enhance their ability to seek employment, access healthcare, and participate fully in the community.

Body Paragraph 2: Potential Drawbacks and Criticisms

Despite these benefits, there are valid concerns about the feasibility and sustainability of free public transportation. One major criticism is the potential financial burden on the city's budget. Funding such a policy would require substantial investment, possibly leading to higher taxes or cuts to other public services. Moreover, making public transportation free could lead to overcrowding, as the system may struggle to accommodate the surge in demand. Overcrowded buses and trains could diminish the quality of service, making the experience less pleasant and potentially driving users back to personal vehicles, thus negating the policy's intended benefits.

Body Paragraph 3: Addressing Counterarguments

While the concerns regarding budgetary strain and service quality are valid, they can be mitigated through careful planning and phased implementation. For instance, the city could explore alternative funding mechanisms, such as congestion pricing for private vehicles, which would not only generate revenue but also further discourage car use. Additionally, the city could gradually roll out the policy, starting with certain demographics or geographic areas, allowing for adjustments based on demand. Investing in infrastructure improvements before implementing free transportation could also help prevent overcrowding and maintain service quality.

Conclusion:

In conclusion, while the implementation of free public transportation presents challenges, the potential benefits in terms of reducing traffic congestion, lowering carbon emissions, and promoting social equity make it a policy worth pursuing. With strategic planning and a focus on sustainability, the city can overcome the financial and logistical hurdles, making public transportation a viable and valuable public service for all residents. This policy not only aligns with environmental goals but also ensures that all citizens, regardless of income, have access to essential services, thereby fostering a more inclusive and connected community.

Practice Test 6: Full-length simulated exam practice tests

LOGICAL REASONING SECTION

1. Over the past ten years, insurance premiums have increased, resulting in a large decrease in insurance enrollment across the country. Insurance company revenues, however, have progressively increased in each of the ten years during this period, and industry analysts predict further increases in years to come.

Which one of the following, if true, offers the best explanation for the situation described above?

    A. Insurance companies donate substantial sums of money to political campaigns.
    B. The rise of concierge medicine exceeds the number of those enrolling in traditional insurance in most high-income areas.
    C. Most insurance companies raise their premiums every three years.
    D. The decrease in the number of people enrolling for health insurance over the past ten years has been more than offset by the increases in insurance premiums.
    E. More individuals are seeking a subsidy for their health care.

2. Plug-in hybrid vehicles are much more cost-effective than vehicles powered by traditional gasoline engines. These hybrid vehicles cost only twice as much as gasoline vehicles in the same class, but consume only 1/10 of the gasoline while traveling an equal distance. Despite hybrid manufacturers' exhaustive efforts to publicize the advantages of plug-in hybrid vehicles, industry analysts predict that these hybrid vehicles will sell poorly.

Each of the following, if true, provides support for the industry analysts' prediction EXCEPT:

    A. Plug-in hybrid vehicles will come with financing plans that are not provided for traditional gasoline vehicles.
    B. A foreign automaker is about to reveal a vehicle powered exclusively by solar technology that costs less than a gasoline vehicle in the same class.
    C. Plug-in hybrids only come in pastel body colors, colors that most people find unappealing.
    D. Most car purchasers focus on the short-term sticker price of the vehicle rather than the long-term savings from fuel economy.
    E. A car manufacturer of vehicles powered exclusively by gasoline engines has launched an advertising campaign claiming that the cost of charging a plug-in hybrid vehicle costs more than filling the tank of a gasoline vehicle.

3. Marie: Local charities need to proactively recruit volunteers. Otherwise, they are likely to continue being understaffed. The functioning of these charities depends on volunteers, and

people will only volunteer if they know there is a need. If charities can let enough people know about that need, people will volunteer.

Tony: The charities also need more funding. Without funds, it does not matter how many volunteers sign up to help charities. If charities do try to recruit more volunteers, they will have to find new tactics because people know the need is great.

Marie and Tony most likely disagree about whether

    A. people know there is a need for volunteers
    B. the functioning of charities depends on volunteers
    C. local charities are understaffed
    D. local charities should try to recruit volunteers
    E. there is a need for increased funding

4. It has been scientifically established that all dogs bark. As a result, any animal that barks is a dog. So, if a person hears an animal bark, that person can safely conclude that the animal is a dog.

Which of the following arguments most closely parallels the flawed reasoning above?

    A. High interest debt should sometimes be avoided. As a result, some debt that should be avoided is high interest debt. So, a person can safely conclude that high interest debt should be avoided.
    B. Only high interest debt is debt that should be avoided. Debt that is not high interest should not be avoided.
    C. All high interest debt should be avoided. Debt that is not high interest need not be avoided. So, people should prefer low interest debt.
    D. If all high interest debt should be avoided, and if some debt is high interest, then some debt should be avoided.
    E. All debt that should be avoided is high interest debt because all high interest debt should be avoided. Debt that should be avoided must be high interest debt.

5. Economist: All hamburger joints must offer fries and drinks to maximize their revenue. The Burger Shack is a hamburger joint. Because it offers fries and drinks, its revenue is clearly being maximized.

The flawed reasoning in which one of the following is most similar to that in the economist's argument?

    A. Every traffic jam is caused by two factors: impatient driving and lack of available roads. In the city of San Calistranus, there are plenty of available roads and few impatient drivers. So, clearly, there are few traffic jams in San Calistranus.
    B. It will never snow unless the temperature is below 40 degrees and there is sufficient humidity. On Thursday there was sufficient humidity, but the temperature was 45 degrees, so it didn't snow.

C. Successful campaigning relies on two factors: powerful action committees and sufficient exposure. Sarah Strong was a congressional candidate in the last election. She must have had a powerful action committee and sufficient exposure, because she ran a successful campaign.

D. For a video game to sell well, it must include both a memorable character and lots of action. Arkham's Revenge is a video game that has been selling well. Therefore, it must have a memorable character and lots of action.

E. Every piano teacher needs to have a clear course of instruction and a patient personality to succeed. Beverly, a piano teacher, has both of these, so she is undoubtedly successful.

6. Bill: Popular musicians today cannot find much success through the traditional routes. Since nearly all of their songs are now available for easy access on streaming web sites and services, they cannot hope to make money by selling albums. Now they must focus on live shows, and must increase the shows' ticket prices if they hope to gain any profit.

Karen: Why do you think success should only be measured in terms of direct sales? Much of the job of musicians is to publicize themselves, and any exposure they can get is useful in the long run, even if initially they don't receive immediate royalties. This was true even before the digital age.

Karen responds to Bill's argument by

A. misrepresenting the argument's premises and conclusion
B. presenting evidence that directly contradicts Bill's offered evidence
C. casting doubt on Bill's knowledge about the concept of proper marketing
D. suggesting an alternative standard to evaluate the point being discussed
E. showing that the argument is fundamentally flawed in its method of reasoning

7. James: Public schools should require students to wear uniforms. Studies have shown that both violence and bullying can be curtailed if such measures are taken.

Violet: I don't agree. Those same studies show that in schools where uniforms are required, there was still an average of 11.6 reported episodes of gang-related incidents and 8.4 reported bullying incidents per month. With those kinds of numbers, uniforms are clearly not worth the loss of student self-expression.

Violet responds to James' argument in which one of the following ways?

A. She disputes one of James' premises and argues that its refutation justifies disregarding James' conclusion.
B. She criticizes a flaw in James' reasoning and shows how his premises, even when taken at face value, fail to justify his conclusion.
C. She notes an inherent ambiguity in the word "violence" and argues that such a term cannot be effectively quantified.

D. She cites statistics showing that uniforms actually increase, rather than decrease, gang-related violence and bullying in schools that require uniforms.

E. She challenges James' conclusion by noting that the value of self-expression is such that it outweighs most concerns regarding violence against the individual.

8. The growth of coffee shops raises interesting questions about the desire to spend time with other people. Coffee shops are wildly popular but it is not clear why. Sure, people love coffee, but they don't need to sit in a coffee shop to drink it. Further, while coffee shops try to create pleasant study environments, it seems unlikely that people sit for hours for the music over the speakers and the pictures on the walls. Besides, as coffee shops have become more popular, public and school libraries have become less popular. Is it possible that the real coffee shop appeal is the opportunity to be around other people?

Which of the following most accurately states the primary point of the passage?

A. It is unclear why coffee shops are popular, but the answer could be that they provide a way for customers to be around other people
B. Customers are drawn to coffee shops even though they are filled with other people and do not have uniquely appealing atmospheres
C. The atmosphere of coffee shops should be more appealing than that of libraries
D. It is unclear why coffee shops are so popular because they do not seem to have any unique advantages
E. Coffee shops are more popular than they once were despite the fact that they appear to have little to offer customers

9. While factory unions provide accountability for employers and job security for employees, they also present some hazards. First, unions always increase costs of production by adding bureaucracy. Second, unions sometimes serve the elitist purpose of providing high pay and benefits for union members while non-members fail to find any employment.

Which of the following is the most logical conclusion to the passage?

A. Unions serve a valuable role, but also increase costs of production and sometimes increase elitism.
B. Unions provide critically important services to factory employees.
C. Unions provide valuable services, but sometimes increase costs of production and always serve elitist purposes.
D. Unions sometimes cause the hazards of elitism and increased costs of production.
E. Unions serve a valuable role, but sometimes increase costs of production and increase elitism.

10. Most dachshunds have legs less than four inches long. Most dachshunds have long faces. Some animals with long faces make great pets. If an animal has legs less than four inches long, then it will not be a fast runner. Some animals are friendly.

If the statements above are true, then which one of the following must be true?

    A. Most animals with long faces are Dachshunds.
    B. Most great pets have long faces.
    C. Most animals are friendly.
    D. Most animals with long faces make great pets.
    E. Some animals with legs less than four inches long have long faces.

11. Some of the college athletes playing football are also playing rugby, but none of them are playing soccer. Yet some of the soccer players are also playing rugby. For this reason, many coaches refer to rugby as the catch-all sport.

Which one of the following statements follows logically from the statements above?

    A. There are some rugby players who play neither soccer nor football.
    B. Some of the soccer players playing rugby also play football.
    C. There are some rugby players who play soccer but not football.
    D. Most rugby players also play either soccer or football.
    E. Most football players play only football and no other sport.

12. Jim: My friends say I am putting my life in danger by snowboarding recklessly. But I have done some research, and apparently skiers have much lower accident rates than snowboarders. So, trading in my snowboard for a a pair of skis would lower my risk of having an accident.

Jim's argument is most vulnerable to criticism on which of the following grounds?

    A. The argument confuses the causes of a problem with the appropriate solutions to that problem.
    B. The argument relies on information from a source that may be biased.
    C. The argument fails to take into account that Jim's friends are medical professionals.
    D. The argument relies on a sample that is too narrow.
    E. The argument assumes that a correlation between two phenomena is evidence that one is the cause of the other.

13. Computers have finally reached their maximum potential for processing information. For fifty years, computer processing capabilities have steadily improved each year. Although some years saw greater advancements than others, each year saw at least some progress. That pattern was broken last year when computer processing capabilities failed to improve at all.

The argument is most vulnerable to which of the following criticisms?

    A. It assumes, without providing support, that if information processing capabilities improve in a given year, those capabilities have not reached their maximum potential

B. It assumes that computer processing capabilities failed to make any progress over the last year.
C. It fails to address the possibility that some of the previous fifty years saw no progress in information processing capabilities
D. It assumes, without providing support, that if information processing capabilities fail to improve in a given year, those capabilities cannot improve in the future
E. It fails to account for the possibility that information processing capabilities improved somewhat over the last year, even though there has been greater improvement in other years

14. Live theater has been in competition with more modern media options for years. Today, there are a vast number of entertainment options and there is easy access to high quality entertainment technology, such as sophisticated home theater systems. Fewer people watch live theater than in the past. As a result, live theater has lost the competition with modern media.

Which of the following, if true, would allow the conclusion to be logically drawn?

A. Live theater has lost the competition with modern media only if it has fewer viewers than in the past
B. Home theater systems provide the same entertainment quality as live theater
C. In the past, there were very few entertainment options other than live theater
D. Some people who once attended live theater now use sophisticated home theater systems
E. Live theater performances are not performed as often as they once were

15. Movie producers complain that movie critics find it easier to write reviews about movies they dislike than to write reviews about movies that they like. Regardless of whether this hypothesis is true, most movie reviews are devoted to movies that critics find distasteful. Therefore, most movie reviews are devoted to movies other than the best movies.

The conclusion above is properly drawn if which of the following is assumed?

A. A movie that garners attention from critics can become more widely known than if it had not received this attention.
B. All movie critics have difficulty finding movies that they find tasteful.
C. The best movies are those that critics find tasteful.
D. None of the movie critics likes to write about movies that they find extremely distasteful.
E. The greatest movies are not recognized until after the death of the movie producer.

16. It is important that each driver have an insurance policy before driving on the road. Otherwise, people may not be compensated when they are injured in car accidents. Everyone injured in accidents deserves to be compensated.

The argument assumes which of the following?

    A. Those who are injured in accidents are never at fault for those accidents
    B. Compensation always requires monetary payment
    C. All car accidents result in injuries
    D. If every driver is insured, every person injured in an accident will be compensated
    E. No one who is in an accident but is uninjured deserves to be compensated

17. The production of pencil sharpeners can no longer be profitable. This is because various factors have decreased demand for pencil sharpeners. First, pens are used far more than they once were. Second, those who use pencils often use mechanical pencils. Finally, increased use of electronics has decreased the need for handwriting.

The argument depends on which of the following assumptions?

    A. Production of pencil sharpeners cannot be profitable if there is a decreased demand for them compensated
    B. Availability of mechanical pencils has increased
    C. Anything that can be accomplished with pencils can also be accomplished with electronics
    D. Students no longer prefer pencils over pens for math calculations
    E. Pencil sharpeners are only in demand for the purpose of sharpening pencils

18. Businesses that invest in renewable energy tend to view profit as secondary to social responsibility. Investments in renewable energy are also very risky and several have been known to cause their company very large losses. Therefore, it is a bad idea for you to invest in renewable energy.

Which on the following, if true, most weakens the argument presented above?

    A. Many investment strategies dictate that you should diversify your portfolio.
    B. Most businesses do not invest in renewable energy.
    C. Typically, companies that have very big losses go bankrupt within a year.
    D. Companies that focus on social responsibility first tend to have lower profits.
    E. Companies that invest in renewable energy compensate for their high risk by diversifying the energy sources they use.

19. Teacher: While standardized testing is appropriate for adults and high school students, it should not be used with younger children. The variety of curricula, as well as the fact that many elementary school-aged children are home schooled or attend private schools, make a single standard of measurement nearly impossible at that age. While some would argue that children's innate abilities can be isolated from their learned knowledge, experience shows that these distinctions are nearly impossible to make until children reach their teenage years.

Which one of the following, if true, would most support the teacher's argument?

A. Standardized tests are becoming increasingly important for college admission, often outweighing a student's high school grade point average.
B. Most elementary school children who attend private schools are taught the same subjects as those who attend public schools.
C. Standardized IQ tests, which are crafted to take age into account, are commonly given to children as young as three years old.
D. By the time they reach their junior year of high school, nearly all students have taken a class in algebra, though some take such classes as early as the seventh grade.
E. Many believe that the human brain's capacity for learning does not fully develop until a person is at least sixteen years old.

20. Jane: Nowadays 3D effects are seen as a distracting gimmick that most people no longer appreciate. The recent trend toward producing more 3D movies is not a good financial strategy for movie studios. In fact, I and my friends refuse to attend movies in 3D, and I know many others that feel the same way.

Bill: But you fail to take into account the fact that 3D ticket prices are higher than 2D ticket prices. The difference in price offsets the lower attendance at 3D movies. I, for one, appreciate having the choice between 2D and 3D films.

The dialogue provides the most support for the claim that Jane and Bill disagree about whether

A. ticket price differentials between 2D and 3D movies are reasonable
B. it is financially wise for movie studios to continue producing movies in 3D
C. people appreciate 3D effects in movies less now than they used to
D. movie studios ought to offer audiences the option to choose between 2D and 3D films
E. 2D movies are superior to 3D movies in overall quality

READING COMPREHENSION SECTION

Passage:

We cannot inquire far into the meaning of proverbs or traditional sayings without discovering that the common understanding of general and abstract names is loose and uncertain. <u>Common speech is a quicksand.</u>

Consider how we acquire our vocabulary, how we pick up the words that we use from our neighbors and from books, and why this is so soon becomes apparent. Theoretically, we know the full meaning of a name when we know all the attributes that it connotes, and we are not justified in extending it except to objects that possess all the attributes. This is the logical ideal, but between the ought to be of Logic and the is of practical life, there is a vast difference. How seldom do we conceive words in their full meaning! And who is to instruct us in the full meaning? It is not as in the exact sciences, where we start with knowledge of the full meaning. In Geometry, for example, we learn the definitions of the words used, "point," "line," "parallel," etc., before we proceed to use them. But in common speech, we hear the words applied to individual objects; we utter them in the same connection; we extend them to other objects that strike us as like without knowing the precise points of likeness that the convention of common speech includes. The more exact meaning we learn by gradual induction from individual cases. The individual's extension of the name proceeds upon what in the objects has most impressed him when he caught the word: this may differ in different individuals; the usage of neighbors corrects individual eccentricities. The child in arms shouts "Da" at the passing stranger who reminds him of his father; for him at first it is a general name applicable to every man; by degrees he learns that for him it is a singular name.

It is obvious that to avoid error and confusion, the meaning or connotation of names, the concepts, should somehow be fixed; names cannot otherwise have an identical reference in human intercourse. We may call this ideal fixed concept the Logical Concept. But in actual speech we have also the Personal Concept, which varies more or less with the individual user, and the Popular or Vernacular Concept, which, though roughly fixed, varies from social sect to social sect and from generation to generation.

When we come to words of which the logical concept is a complex relation, an obscure or intangible attribute, the defects of the popular conception and its tendencies to change and confusion are of the greatest practical importance. Take such words as "monarchy," "civil freedom," "landlord," "culture." Not merely should we find it difficult to give an analytic definition of such words; we might be unable to do so, and yet flatter ourselves that we had a clear understanding of their meaning.

It was with reference to this state of things that Hegel formulated his paradox that the true abstract thinker is the plain man who laughs at philosophy as what he calls abstract and unpractical. He holds decided opinions for or against this or the other abstraction, "freedom," "tyranny," "revolution," "reform," "socialism," but what these words mean and within what limits the things signified are desirable or undesirable, he is in too great a hurry to pause and consider.

The disadvantages of this kind of "abstract" thinking are obvious. The accumulated wisdom of mankind is stored in language. Until we have cleared our conceptions, and penetrated to the full meaning of words, that wisdom is a sealed book to us. Wise maxims are interpreted by us hastily in accordance with our own narrow conceptions. All the vocabulary of a language may be more or less familiar to us, and yet we may not have learnt it as an instrument of thought.

Questions:

1. The author's tone in this passage could best be described as _____.

    A. nonchalant and withdrawn
    B. demanding and meticulous
    C. authoritative and assured
    D. pessimistic and ambivalent
    E. haughty and condescending

2. The underlined clause "Common speech is a quicksand" could be most reasonably assumed to mean which of the following?

    A. It is easy to get lost in English due to the abundance of words used to describe the same thing.
    B. The definitions of English words are being altered by academic dictates.
    C. The definition of English words and phrases are often vague and debatable.
    D. English expressions are confusing.
    E. English regional vernacular is being lost.

3. Which of these bests restates the author's meaning in the underlined selection, "It is obvious that to avoid error and confusion, the meaning or connotation of names, the concepts, should somehow be fixed: names cannot otherwise have an identical reference in human intercourse"?

    A. The meaning and connotation of names can be fixed, so that human intercourse will proceed without confusion and error.
    B. It is of fundamental importance that the meaning of words and names be understood universally by all people to prevent debate and unnecessary arguments.
    C. If words and names are to mean the same thing to all people, than the meanings and implications of those words must be somehow conclusively determined.
    D. Trying to avoid error and confusion by fixing the meaning of words would eliminate the variety and beauty of the English vernacular language.
    E. It is apparent that the meaning of names and words cannot be fixed in human interaction because such an undertaking is beyond the scope of any one person or institution.

4. How does the Personal Concept differ from the Vernacular Concept as defined by the author?

    A. It is impossible to say, as the author does not define what he means by the Vernacular Concept.
    B. The Personal Concept is highly unpredictable, whereas the Vernacular Concept is easy to understand.
    C. The Vernacular Concept allows for identical usage across human intercourse, whereas the Personal Concept varies by individual.
    D. The Personal Concept is rigidly defined, whereas the Vernacular Concept is loose and fluid.
    E. The Vernacular Concept varies by social group or generation, whereas the Personal Concept varies by individual.

5. Which of these bests summarizes the main point of the sixth paragraph?

A. Hegel's "abstract" thinking is not applicable to the author's argument because it ignores the preconceptions that blind each individual to the true meaning of words and names.
B. Our individual preconceptions blind us to the true meaning of words and prevent us from accurately penetrating the combined knowledge of humanity.
C. None of these answers accurately summarizes the point of the sixth paragraph.
D. In order to fix the problems associated with "abstract" thinking we must collectively focus on deep thinking and a scientific classification of words and names.
E. We acquire words through natural means and as such the meanings and definitions of those words will always differ greatly from person to person.

6. Which of these best captures the main idea of the second paragraph?

A. We learn the meaning of most words organically and as a result the exact definition and application of those words will differ from person to person.
B. Babies learn words without being intentionally taught them and seem to develop incorrect assumptions about the meanings of certain words.
C. It is impossible to define the vast majority of words because people have their own personal ideas about how each thing could best be described.
D. People learn the meaning of words best when those words are specifically and rigidly defined.
E. People learn words before they really understand them and if we want to have consistency in language we must teach the word and its correct meaning simultaneously.

Passage:

The United Nations Convention on Contracts for the International Sale of Goods (CISG) can help countries throughout the world have a more uniform way of navigating the challenging waters of international law surrounding trade. It is not uncommon for two countries to have adopted different laws on international trade that conflict with each other. This becomes a serious problem when trade disputes arise. To help make this concept more tangible, consider the following hypothetical.

Suppose China ships three million dollars' worth of electronics to Uganda using standard bulk shipping transportation methods via a commonly traveled sea route. However, the packaging isn't secured in a manner sufficient to withstand unforeseen weather conditions. As a result, the goods become damaged in transit and are no longer fit for resale. Given that two countries are involved in this transaction–China and Uganda–the question arises as to which country's trade laws will apply to resolve the matter at hand.

In this scenario, it is fortunate that both China and Uganda are parties to the CISG, which provide for a uniform set of laws governing trade. Such laws cover which party would be responsible for the damaged goods in this scenario. As a result, there will be no dispute as to whether China's or Uganda's trade laws apply. Given that both countries are parties to the CISG, the laws set forth by the CISG would be applicable.

However, not all countries are parties to the CISG. One example is Rwanda. Even though Rwanda is not a party to the CISG, the fact of the matter is that CISG laws can still apply to it. The CISG applies to trade between countries so long as one of those countries is a party to the CISG (unless the parties expressly specify that the CISG will not apply to their specific trade arrangement). Several of Rwanda's main trade partners, such as the United States, China, Belgium, and Uganda, are parties to the CISG, so the laws of the treaty will apply in those trade agreements. Meanwhile, there is a different story when it comes to Rwanda's trade agreements with Kenya, Swaziland, Tanzania, and Thailand, which are not parties to the CISG. Due to these countries' lack of membership in the CISG, if a problem ever arose in a trade agreement between Rwanda and one those countries, it would be unclear as to which country's laws would apply.

There has been <u>heated discussion</u> as to whether Rwanda should sign the CISG. The United Nations Development Program takes the stance that it would behoove Rwanda to join. Whether or not Rwanda decides to become a member, the CISG will still apply to a large portion of its trade agreements, as about 100 countries are in fact CISG members, with a strong portion of those members also being trade partners with Rwanda. On the flip side, some Rwandan politicians believe that valuable autonomy would be lost if Rwanda assented to the CISG. However, given the potential benefits that Rwanda stands to gain from the CISG, these fears do not merit forgoing such a valuable opportunity.

Questions:

7. Which of the following, if true, best supports the author's contention that Rwanda should become a member of the CISG?

  A. Participation fees for becoming a CISG member can hinder certain countries from joining.
  B. Status as a CISG member can deter non-CISG countries from engaging in trade arrangements.
  C. Becoming a CISG member can sometimes delay the processing of trade agreements because additional protocols are set in place for members to follow.
  D. Even if a country is a CISG member, commercial trade disputes are just as likely to occur.
  E. Disputes over which country's laws to apply in commercial trade situations can chill future trade arrangements with other countries, even those which belong to the CISG.

8. The author would most likely agree with which of these statements?

  A. It would be to Rwanda's benefit to join the CISG.
  B. The CISG has a narrow window of applicability.
  C. Although joining the CISG has benefits, Rwanda ultimately should not join the CISG.
  D. There are positive and negative aspects that Rwanda should weigh and balance when deciding whether to join the CISG.
  E. It is imperative that Rwanda join the CISG in order to avoid impending trade disputes that could prove to be disastrous.

9. The primary purpose of the second paragraph is to _____.

    A. provide an example that makes an abstract concept easier to understand
    B. demonstrate the deleterious effects that can result from a trade dispute
    C. suggest that China and Uganda should join the CISG
    D. directly support the author's thesis
    E. indirectly offer a counter-argument to the author's thesis

10. Which of the following is the main purpose of the article?

    A. To explain how the landscape of international trade has evolved in recent years
    B. To explain why Rwanda should become a member of the CISG
    C. To provide a broad overview of Rwanda's trading practices
    D. To weigh and balance the reasons why Rwanda should join the CISG versus why Rwanda should not join the CISG
    E. To argue that countries should always heed the recommendations of the United Nations Development Program

11. The use of the underlined phrase "heated discussion" in the context of the last paragraph of the passage most closely means _____.

    A. combative discourse
    B. unfair exchange
    C. emotional conversation
    D. strong debate
    E. intense persuasion

Passage:

With the American people, and through them all others, familiarity with the buffalo has bred contempt. The incredible numbers in which the animals of this species formerly existed made their slaughter an easy matter, so much so that the hunters and frontiersmen who accomplished their destruction have handed down to us a contemptuous opinion of the size, character, and general presence of our bison. And how could it be otherwise than that a man who could find it in his heart to murder a majestic bull bison for a hide worth only a dollar should form a one-dollar estimate of the grandest ruminant that ever trod the earth? Men who butcher African elephants for the sake of their ivory also entertain a similar estimate of their victims.

By a combination of unfortunate circumstances, the American bison is destined to go down to posterity shorn of the honor which is his due, and appreciated at only half his worth. The hunters who slew him were from the very beginning so absorbed in the scramble for spoils that they had no time to measure or weigh him, nor even to notice the majesty of his personal appearance on his native heath. In captivity, he fails to develop as finely as in his wild state, and with the loss of his liberty, he becomes a tame-looking animal. He gets fat and short-bodied, and the lack of vigorous and constant exercise prevents the development of bone and muscle which made the prairie animal what he was.

From observations made upon buffaloes that have been reared in captivity, I am firmly convinced that confinement and semi-domestication are destined to effect striking changes in the form of Bison americanus. While this is to be expected to a certain extent with most large species, the changes promise to be most conspicuous in the buffalo. The most striking change is in the body between the hips and the shoulders. As before remarked, it becomes astonishingly short and rotund, and through liberal feeding and total lack of exercise, the muscles of the shoulders and hindquarters, especially the latter, are but feebly developed.

Both the live buffaloes in the National Museum collection of living animals are developing the same shortness of body and lack of muscle, and when they attain their full growth will but poorly resemble the splendid proportions of the wild specimens in the Museum mounted group, each of which has been mounted from a most careful and elaborate series of post-mortem measurements. It may fairly be considered, however, that the specimens taken by the Smithsonian expedition were in every way more perfect representatives of the species than have been usually taken in times past, for the simple reason that on account of the muscle they had developed in the numerous chases they had survived, and the total absence of the fat which once formed such a prominent feature of the animal, they were of finer form, more active habit, and keener intelligence than buffaloes possessed when they were so numerous. Out of the millions that once composed the great northern herd, those represented the survival of the fittest, and their existence at that time was chiefly due to the keenness of their senses and their splendid muscular powers in speed and endurance.

Under such conditions it is only natural that animals of the highest class should be developed. On the other hand, captivity reverses all these conditions, while yielding an equally abundant food supply.

Questions:

12. Which of the following, if true, most undermines the author's thesis?

    A. Not all captive bison developed the weak form described by the author.
    B. Some animals closely related to bison grow larger when kept in captivity.
    C. Wild bison who are underfed do not develop the same muscle tone as those who are not underfed.
    D. Bison who are idle in the wild look more like other wild bison than captive bison.
    E. Bison who are active in captivity look more like wild bison than other captive bison.

13. Which of the following, if true, would most undermine the author's thesis?

    A. A professional elephant hunter was well-known for his moving, poetic descriptions of the power and stature of elephants.

B. A captive bison raised in the wild does not show any of the symptoms (small size, underdevelopment) described by the author.
C. Bison raised at another zoo grew up to be short and underdeveloped.
D. Professional bison hunters would often measure especially large animals they had killed for record keeping purposes.
E. Immediately following the start of systematic bison hunting, unusually large and powerful individual bison died out, never to be seen again.

14. Which of the following best describes the role of the underlined passage at the end of the last paragraph within the passage as a whole?

A. It anticipates objections that could be raised against the author's thesis.
B. It is a piece of evidence used to strengthen the author's thesis by showing an important similarity between two seemingly disparate cases.
C. It is an assumption whose truth is not assured by the available evidence.
D. It introduces a necessary condition for one of the author's secondary conclusions.
E. It is a sufficient condition for the passage's primary conclusion.

15. Which of the following best describes the purpose of the third paragraph?

A. An empirical statement whose causes will be explained elsewhere in the passage
B. A delineation of certain necessary conditions needed for the author's conclusion to be true
C. An anticipation of certain objections to the author's thesis
D. Introducing a complex premise that supports a conclusion noted earlier
E. Drawing a secondary conclusion used to support the primary conclusion of the passage

16. Which of the following best describes the primary purpose of this passage?

A. Relating empirical observations on the effects of overfeeding and lack of exercise
B. Explaining how a well-known piece of anomalous data can be accounted for using current theories
C. Proposing a new theoretical model to account for an important exceptional case the prevailing model cannot explain
D. Correcting and accounting for misperceptions and biases in observations that underlie a popular conception of a specie's traits
E. Describing the effects of environmental change on an animal species

Passage:

Most books on the philosophy of religion try to begin with a precise definition of what its essence consists of. Some of these would-be definitions may possibly come before us in later portions of this course, and I shall not be pedantic enough to enumerate any of them to you now. Meanwhile the very fact that they are so many and so different from one another is enough to prove that the word "religion" cannot stand for any single principle or essence, but is rather a collective name. The theorizing mind tends always to the oversimplification of its materials. This is the root of all that absolutism and one-sided dogmatism by which both philosophy and religion have been infested.

Let us not fall immediately into a one-sided view of our subject, but let us rather admit freely at the outset that we may very likely find no one essence, but many characters which may alternately be equally important to religion. If we should inquire for the essence of "government," for example, one man might tell us it was authority, another submission, another police, another an army, another an assembly, another a system of laws; yet all the while it would be true that no concrete government can exist without all these things, one of which is more important at one moment and others at another. The man who knows governments most completely is he who troubles himself least about a definition that shall give their essence. Enjoying an intimate acquaintance with all their particularities in turn, he would naturally regard an abstract conception in which these were unified as a thing more misleading than enlightening. And why may not religion be a conception equally complex?

Questions:

17. The author includes the various descriptions of "government" in order to _____.

    A. show that government is a more interesting subject than religion
    B. show that the difficulty of defining religion is unique to the study of religion
    C. show that government is a very different concept to define, more so than religion
    D. show how concepts other than religion are as difficult to define in simple terms
    E. show how "religion" and "government" often mean the same thing

18. Which one of the following best describes the author's attitude toward religion?

    A. Fascinated by it as a subject of inquiry
    B. Reverential towards its more traditional aspects
    C. Preferring a more orthodox orientation toward the subject
    D. Annoyed by its inherently confusing nature
    E. Dismissive of people who are religious

19. The "absolutism and one-sided dogmatism" the author references in the second paragraph indicate that the author believes some people incorrectly view philosophy and religion as _____.

    A. subjects not worthy of critical study
    B. subjects that are not to be studied by people with rigid belief systems
    C. subjects that are only of interest to specialists
    D. subjects with clear correct and incorrect answers to their inquiries
    E. subjects that can be studied easily and simply

20. The author's description of "religion" as "rather a collective name" indicates that
_____.

    A. the author believes that religion cannot be defined by one single term or sentence
    B. that each religion must be defined individually and not as a group
    C. defining anything as varied as religion is a useless exercise that no serious person should undertake
    D. religion is only a valid concept if it has a cooperative element
    E. developing a clear definition is the first step in studying any subject

21. The author's most likely response to a government recognizing religion as any belief system with regular rituals would be which of the following?

    A. Such a definition excludes many groups that could legitimately be called religions.
    B. The definition of religion should be simpler and more concrete than the government's definition.
    C. The government must take such action to appropriately define religion.
    D. Religion is not the kind of subject which a government should be defining in any way whatsoever.
    E. An official authority defining religion will do a great deal of good in advancing a clear definition.

22. The author's main point is best summarized by which of the following statements?

    A. "Religion" can be easily reduced to its most basic elements for ease of definition.
    B. "Religion" is a concept which should not be defined, as it is not worthy of study.
    C. "Religion" should only be talked about carefully because it is a subject that can easily offend people.
    D. "Religion" is a concept that is not easy to define with a simple statement of basic characteristics.
    E. "Religion" is a concept very similar to the concept of "government."

Passage:

Coleridge left Cambridge in 1794 without taking his degree, and presently we find him with the youthful Southey—a kindred spirit who had been fired to wild enthusiasm by the French Revolution—founding his famous Pantisocracy for the regeneration of human society. "The Fall of Robespierre," a poem composed by the two enthusiasts, is full of the new revolutionary spirit. The Pantisocracy was to be an ideal community that combined farming and literature; work was to be limited to two hours each day. Moreover, each member of the community was to marry a good woman and take her with him. The two poets obeyed the latter injunction first, marrying two sisters, and then found that they had no money to pay even their traveling expenses to the new utopia.

During all the rest of his career a tragic weakness of will takes possession of Coleridge, making it impossible for him, with all his genius and learning, to hold himself steadily to any one work or purpose. He studied in Germany; worked as a private secretary, till the drudgery wore upon his free spirit; then he went to Rome and remained for two years, lost in study. Later he started The Friend, a paper devoted to truth and liberty; lectured on poetry and the fine arts to enraptured audiences in London, until his frequent failures to meet his engagements scattered his hearers; was offered an excellent position and a half interest (amounting to some £2000) in the Morning Post and The Courier, but declined it, saying "that I would not give up the country and the lazy reading of old folios for two thousand times two thousand pounds—in short, that beyond £350 a year I considered money a real evil." His family, meanwhile, was almost entirely neglected; he lived apart, following his own way. Needing money, he was on the point of becoming a Unitarian minister, when a small pension from two friends enabled him to live for a few years without regular employment.

A terrible shadow in Coleridge's life was the apparent cause of most of his dejection. In early life he suffered from neuralgia, and to ease the pain began to use opiates. The result on such a temperament was almost inevitable. He became a slave to the drug habit; his naturally weak will lost all its directing and sustaining force, until, after fifteen years of pain and struggle and despair, he gave up and put himself in charge of a physician, one Mr. Gillman of Highgate. Carlyle, who visited him at this time, calls him "a king of men," but records that "he gave you the idea of a life that had been full of sufferings, a life heavy-laden, half-vanquished."

The shadow is dark indeed; but there are gleams of sunshine that occasionally break through the clouds. One of these is his association with Wordsworth and his sister Dorothy, out of which came the famous Lyrical Ballads of 1798. Another was his loyal devotion to poetry for its own sake. With the exception of his tragedy Remorse, for which he was paid £400, he received almost nothing for his poetry. Indeed, he seems not to have desired it; for he says: "Poetry has been to me its own exceeding great reward; it has soothed my afflictions; it has multiplied and refined my enjoyments; it has endeared solitude, and it has given me the habit of wishing to discover the good and the beautiful in all that meets and surrounds me." One can better understand his exquisite verse after such a declaration. A third ray of sunlight came from the admiration of his contemporaries; for though he wrote comparatively little, he was by his talents and learning a leader among literary men. Wordsworth says of him that, though other men of the age had done some wonderful things, Coleridge was the only wonderful man he had ever known. Of his conversation it is recorded: "Throughout a long-drawn summer's day would this man talk to you in low, equable but clear and musical tones, concerning things human and divine; marshaling all history, harmonizing all experiment, probing the depths of your consciousness, and revealing visions of glory and terror to the imagination."

Questions:

23. The passage provides evidence to suggest that the author would be most likely to assent to which one of the following proposals?

A. Coleridge was wise in declining the job at the Morning Post.
B. Coleridge was a greater poet than Wordsworth.
C. If Coleridge hadn't encountered some of his early misfortunes, he could have been truly great.
D. Carlyle's assessment of Coleridge was incorrect.
E. Coleridge and Southey broke off their friendship when their experiment failed.

24. Given Carlyle's account of Coleridge, which one of the following is most analogous to his opinion?

A. A sycophant finally reaching the greatness he has long grovelled for
B. A diver who has found a magnificent pearl that is too deep for her to reach
C. A tyrant defeated at the end of his life
D. An aged emperor who has never seen peace in his kingdom.
E. A giant waiting for knights to come fight him

25. Based on how he is described in the passage, Wordsworth would be most likely to agree with which of the following statements?

A. The weight of the things Coleridge did outweigh who he was.
B. The distinction between what we say and what we do can only be written down.
C. Wordsworth did not know many nice people.
D. Coleridge was greater as a person than the greatness of great works.
E. Coleridge did more wonderful things than any other person.

26. The primary purpose of the passage is most likely _____.

A. to explore Coleridge's work with Wordsworth
B. to introduce a biography
C. to discuss Coleridge's view of poetry
D. to give a short summary of the life of an influential man
E. to act as part of an argument against opiates

27. The primary function of the third paragraph is _____.

A. to show that Coleridge trusted in modern medicine
B. to explore the contemporary issue of addiction and art
C. to show that Coleridge was afflicted by addiction but resolved to be cured of it
D. to condemn Coleridge for his addiction
E. to show the respect of writers like Carlyle for Coleridge

28. Which of the following is mentioned by the passage as a possible consequence of the French Revolution?

190

A. The reform of Western society
B. Coleridge and Southey's friendship
C. The development of ideas that would later be included in Lyrical Ballads
D. The development of Coleridge's early radical views
E. The descent of France into anarchy

ARGUMENTATIVE WRITING SECTION

Prompt:

A tech company is considering implementing a mandatory remote work policy for all its employees. Proponents argue that remote work increases productivity, reduces costs, and allows for a better work-life balance. Critics, however, are concerned that it may lead to decreased collaboration, weaker company culture, and difficulties in managing teams.

Assignment:

Write an essay in which you argue for or against the tech company's proposed mandatory remote work policy. In your essay, discuss the potential benefits and drawbacks of such a policy, considering its impact on productivity, company culture, employee satisfaction, and management challenges.

Answer sheet with explanation

LOGICAL REASONING SECTION

1. **Correct Answer:** D. The decrease in the number of people enrolling for health insurance over the past ten years has been more than offset by the increases in insurance premiums.

Explanation: Here, the author describes two simultaneous trends that, at first blush, seem to contradict one another. Insurance premiums have increased, which have led to a decrease in insurance enrollment.
This first part is logical. However, interestingly, revenues for insurance companies have continued to rise despite the decreased enrollment. The correct answer choice must provide additional revenue that compensates for the decrease in revenue from decreased enrollment. Only the answer choice: "The decrease in the number of people enrolling for health insurance over the past ten years has been more than offset by the increases in insurance premiums" provides this increased revenue that would explain this phenomenon.

2. **Correct Answer:** A. Plug-in hybrid vehicles will come with financing plans that are not provided for traditional gasoline vehicles.

Explanation: This EXCEPT question is looking for the one answer choice that does not support the prediction that plug-in hybrid vehicles will sell poorly. The answer choice: "Plug-in hybrid vehicles will come with financing plans that are not provided for traditional gasoline vehicles" will either have no effect or a positive effect on the sales of plug-in vehicles. In either scenario, the answer choice does not support the argument and is the correct answer choice. All the other answer choices support the argument.

3. **Correct Answer:** A. People know there is a need for volunteers

Explanation: There is no indication in the passage that Marie and Tony disagree about whether there is a need for volunteers or for funding, though they appear to disagree about the magnitude of the needs. Neither is there a direct conflict about whether charities should recruit. The parties only explicitly disagree about whether people know there is a need.

4. **Correct Answer:** E. All debt that should be avoided is high interest debt because all high interest debt should be avoided. Debt that should be avoided must be high interest debt.

Explanation: The argument assumes that if all A are B, then all B must be A.
That is the central flaw of the argument because it may be true that all dogs bark and that seals also bark. Similarly, although it may be true that all high interest debt should be avoided, there may be other debt that should be avoided as well. It is important to note that the reasoning can be parallell even when the order of the argument may be slightly different.

5. **Correct Answer:** E. Every piano teacher needs to have a clear course of instruction and a patient personality to succeed. Beverly, a piano teacher, has both of these, so she is undoubtedly successful.

Explanation: The correct answer choice is the only one which commits the fallacy of affirming the consequent. In other words, both it and the original argument improperly assume the converse of their conditional statements. We know that the Burger Shack needs to offer fries and drinks to maximize its revenue, but we do not know that its revenue is necessarily maximized if it offers them.
Likewise, we do not know whether Beverly is a successful piano teacher simply because she has a clear course of instruction and a patient personality.

6. **Correct Answer:** D. Suggesting an alternative standard to evaluate the point being discussed

Explanation: Karen does not argue against Bill's conclusion directly, but rather offers an alternate standard by which to evaluate the commercial "success" of musicians. Thus, Karen does not claim Bill's reasoning is fallacious nor that any of his premises are incorrect; she merely reframes the argument by focusing on one of its key terms.

7. **Correct Answer:** A. She disputes one of James' premises and argues that its refutation justifies disregarding James' conclusion.

Explanation: Violet's primary disagreement with James is with his idea that "both violence and bullying can be curtailed" if uniforms are required at schools. She cites statistics showing that they will not be curtailed, thus disputing his premise. With that premise disregarded, she argues that his conclusion does not follow in light of the loss of student self-expression that wearing uniforms entails. The remaining answer choices do not correctly characterize Violet's response.

8. **Correct Answer:** A. It is unclear why coffee shops are popular, but the answer could be that they provide a way for customers to be around other people

Explanation: The first and last sentences of the passage raise the issue of whether people attend coffee shops to be around other people.
Instead of stating a firm conclusion, the purpose of the passage is to raise that possible explanation by ruling out others.

9. **Correct Answer:** A. Unions serve a valuable role, but also increase costs of production and sometimes increase elitism.

Explanation: There are two keys to this question. First, the passage does not reach a firm, positive or negative conclusion about unions, instead suggesting that there are considerations on both sides. Second, the passage discusses two negative traits, but specifies that the first "always" occurs and the second "sometimes" occurs.

10. **Correct Answer:** E. Some animals with legs less than four inches long have long faces.

Explanation: The answer is correct because there are overlapping "most" statements. From the stimulus, we can conclude that some animals with legs less than four inches long have long faces.

11. **Correct Answer:** A. There are some rugby players who play soccer but not football.

Explanation: Only three assertions are made in the paragraph: 1) no players play both football and soccer; 2) some players play both football and rugby; 3) some players play both soccer and rugby. There must be, therefore, a subset of players who play both soccer and rugby but not football.

12. **Correct Answer:** E. The argument assumes that a correlation between two phenomena is evidence that one is the cause of the other.

Explanation: The fact the skiers have lower accident rates than snowboarders may not have any bearing on whether either activity is safer for Jim. That is, just because skiing is more correlated with safety than snowboarding does not mean that skiing is inherently safer than snowboarding; it is possible that skiers, as a group, tend to act less recklessly than snowboarders making the activity appear safer. In such a scenario, if Jim continues his reckless ways as a skier, he may be no better off than if he had continued to snowboard.

13. **Correct Answer:** D. It assumes, without providing support, that if information processing capabilities fail to improve in a given year, those capabilities cannot improve in the future

Explanation: The argument's primary assertion is that information processing capabilities will not improve in the future (have reached maximum potential). It supports this by claiming that no advancements were made last year, but fails to address why that claim supports the conclusion. That there have been advancements in years past is not enough without an additional premise.

14. **Correct Answer:** A. Live theater has lost the competition with modern media only if it has fewer viewers than in the past

Explanation: The argument concludes that live theater has lost a competition with modern media. The conclusion does not logically follow from the assertions in the argument as they are presented. It is not clear how the competition would be lost. The additional premise allows the conclusion to be drawn.

15. **Correct Answer:** C. The best movies are those that critics find tasteful.

Explanation: This argument misses the important link between critics not liking a movie and that movie not being one of the best movies.
However, this conclusion would be valid if we have the assumption provided in the correct answer choice, "The best movies are those that critics find tasteful." This assumption links the best movies with the movies that critics find tasteful. Thus, with this assumption, the conclusion works: If most movie reviews are devoted to movies that critics find distasteful, and the best movies are the movies that critics find tasteful, then it follows that most criticism is devoted to movies other than the best movies.

16. **Correct Answer:** D. If every driver is insured, every person injured in an accident will be compensated

Explanation: If injured people might not be compensated even if every driver has insurance, then the argument's conclusion does not follow.

194

17. **Correct Answer:** A. Production of pencil sharpeners cannot be profitable if there is a decreased demand for them compensated

Explanation: The argument's assertion is that production of pencil sharpeners cannot be profitable. The argument does not link this assertion to the rest of the argument, however. Instead, it supports the claim that demand has decreased. The argument assumes that decreased demand has made production of pencil sharpeners unprofitable.

18. **Correct Answer:** E. Companies that invest in renewable energy compensate for their high risk by diversifying the energy sources they use.

Explanation: Only the correct answer shows how one of the arguments use to justify not investing in renewable energy companies could in fact be wrong. This weakens the argument by removing one of the pillars that support it.

19. **Correct Answer:** D. By the time they reach their junior year of high school, nearly all students have taken a class in algebra, though some take such classes as early as the seventh grade.

Explanation: Since the argument explicitly listed varying curricula as a reason to delay standardized testing, showing that nearly all high school juniors have taken algebra by then (and not all in the same grade) directly supports the argument. Giving a standardized test containing algebra is, in fact, more appropriate when all the students taking the test are familiar with it. The remaining answer choices either provide little relevant support or weaken the argument rather than strengthening it.

20. **Correct Answer:** B. It is financially wise for movie studios to continue producing movies in 3D

Explanation: Bill's rebuttal to Jane's argument is that studios can make up for the lower attendance at 3D films through increased ticket prices.
Hence, he does not agree with Jane that producing 3D movies "is not a good financial strategy for movie studios." The remaining answer choices do not contain statements about which Jane and Bill necessarily disagree, even though the topics may have been mentioned in the dialogue.

READING COMPREHENSION SECTION

1. **Correct Answer:** authoritative and assured

Explanation: The author's tone in this passage is authoritative and assured. You can tell is it authoritative because the author speaks with an academic and commanding voice. You can tell it is assured because the author leaves little room for debate or opposition; he does not question himself or relate the opposite sides of the debate to his argument. Rather, he states his points as if they are fact. Failing this approach, you could also eliminate the other answer choices for how they fail to capture the tone of the author.

The author could not be called "demanding" because although he is commanding in his use of language and his certainty, he is not urging the reader to make a change, but rather simply illuminating what he believes should happen with regard to words and names. You certainly could not call the author's tone

"nonchalant" or "ambivalent" because he clearly cares deeply about the subject matter. And, while the author might be a little bit haughty, he never approaches condescension.

2. **Correct Answer:** The definition of English words and phrases are often vague and debatable.

Explanation: This phrase is used very early in the passage, in the opening lines of the introduction. In context, the author states, "We cannot inquire far into the meaning of proverbs or traditional sayings without discovering that the common understanding of general and abstract names is loose and uncertain. Common speech is a quicksand." To best determine the answer, it is best to understand the introduction as it relates to the entire essay, as authors usually introduce the main point of their essay early in the introduction.

The primary point of the essay is to discuss the problems with ambiguity in the application of words and names, so when the author says that "common speech is a quicksand," it is reasonable to assume that he means common speech alters and varies the meanings of words rapidly to create words and phrases that are vague and debatable.

3. **Correct Answer:** If words and names are to mean the same thing to all people, then the meanings and implications of those words must be somehow conclusively determined.

Explanation: In the context in which the author uses this quotation, he is discussing the difference between what he defines as the "Logical Concept," which is when words and names have a defined meaning for all speakers, and the "Personal" and "Vernacular Concept," which is where words differ from individual to individual and social group to social group. It is clear from the author's tone and conclusions throughout the paragraph and passage that he believes a "Logical Concept" of words needs to exist in order for language to be universally applied and understood. From this conclusion, we can easily determine the meaning of the underlined text. He wishes to underscore the importance of having a fixed meaning for words and names so as to avoid error and confusion in speech. The correct answer best summarizes this meaning.

Some of the other answer choices might seem reasonable, but crucially, they are conclusions that the author reaches at different points in the essay. The answer choice "The meaning and connotation of names can be fixed, so that human intercourse will proceed without confusion and error" is incorrect because of the word "can"; the author is closer to saying it ought to be done, rather than it can be done. Likewise, the answer choice "It is of fundamental importance that the meaning of words and names be understood universally by all people to prevent debate and unnecessary arguments" is incorrect because the author does not mention debate and disagreement in this particular passage.

This is a difficult question to answer because so many of the answer choices seem like possible alternatives, but when tasked with deciphering the meaning of a certain excerpt, it is important to use the rest of the essay for context, but to also focus on the exact words the author uses when translating the correct answer.

4. **Correct Answer:** The Vernacular Concept varies by social group or generation, whereas the Personal Concept varies by individual.

Explanation: Answering this question requires you to read critically and understand the definitions attributed by the author to various terms he creates. In the third paragraph, he describes what he means by the Personal Concept and the Vernacular Concept, so it really is just a matter of reading carefully. Of the Personal Concept, the author says, "in actual speech we have also the Personal Concept, which varies more or less with the individual user," and of the Vernacular Concept, the author says,
"the Popular or Vernacular Concept, which, though roughly fixed, varies from social sect to social sect and from generation to generation."

5. **Correct Answer:** Our individual preconceptions blind us to the true meaning of words and prevent us from accurately penetrating the combined knowledge of humanity.

Explanation: The main point of the sixth paragraph is best captured in the following few sentences: "The accumulated wisdom of mankind is stored in language. Until we have cleared our conceptions, and penetrated to the full meaning of words, that wisdom is a sealed book to us. Wise maxims are interpreted by us hastily in accordance with our own narrow conceptions." Here, the author discusses how people's individual preconceptions blind them to the true meaning of words, and draws his conclusions on how this individual approach to definition and meaning prevents people from accessing to combined wisdom of humanity. The other answer choices either summarize the wrong paragraph, or else do not properly penetrate to the heart of the author's argument in this paragraph.

6. **Correct Answer:** We learn the meaning of most words organically and as a result the exact definition and application of those words will differ from person to person.

Explanation: The second paragraph begins with the author stating, "Consider how we acquire our vocabulary, how we pick up the words that we use from our neighbors and from books." We thus know that the second paragraph is going to be a consideration of how we acquire words and definitions for things. The author goes on to state, "We hear the words applied to individual objects; we utter them in the same connection; we extend them to other objects that strike us as like without knowing the precise points of likeness that the convention of common speech includes." This tells us that the author believes we learn words "organically," or naturally. Finally, the author says, "The individual's extension of the name proceeds upon what in the objects has most impressed him when he caught the word: this may differ in different individuals." This tells us that the author believes the result of our organic learning is that the exact definition and application of words differs from person to person. The other answer choices either summarize a small part of the paragraph, or else they draw incorrect conclusions from the author's writing.

7. **Correct Answer:** Disputes over which country's laws to apply in commercial trade situations can chill future trade arrangements with other countries, even those which belong to the CISG.

Explanation: Given that the purpose of CISG is to reduce disputes over trade between countries, the correct answer is, "Disputes over which country's laws to apply in commercial trade situations can chill future trade arrangements with other countries, even those which belong to the CISG." This is the correct answer because the inference can be made that if the CISC is reducing disputes between countries, and that there is a weaker chance of future trade arrangements being chilled.

8. **Correct Answer:** It would be to Rwanda's benefit to join the CISG.

Explanation: The correct answer is, "It would be to Rwanda's benefit to join the CISG." A tempting wrong answer is "It is imperative that Rwanda join the CISG in order to avoid impending trade disputes that could prove to be disastrous." However, this is not correct because the author does not take such an extreme position. While the author believes it would be in Rwanda's favor to join the CISG, there is no indication that the author foresees disastrous results if Rwanda foregoes joining.
The other answer choices state positions that are directly contrary to the author's arguments: "The CISG has a narrow window of applicability," is wrong because the author argues that the CISG is broadly applicable.
"Although joining the CISG has benefits, Rwanda ultimately should not join the CISG," is wrong because the author states that Rwanda should join the CISG.
"There are positive and negative aspects that Rwanda should weigh and balance when deciding whether to join the CISG," is wrong because the author does not argue that Rwanda should weigh and balance positives and negatives, but rather states that Rwanda should simply join.

9. **Correct Answer:** provide an example that makes an abstract concept easier to understand

Explanation: The purpose of the second paragraph is to "provide an example that makes an abstract concept easier to understand." In fact, the second paragraph discusses the scenario of a trade arrangement between Uganda and China in order to show the practial applications of the CISG. The purpose of the second paragraph is also signaled in the last sentence of the first paragraph, which reads, "To help make this concept more tangible, consider the following hypothetical."

10. **Correct Answer:** To explain why Rwanda should become a member of the CISG

Explanation: The article is written with a heavy-handed favoritism towards Rwanda becoming a member of the CISG. This is especially apparent in the opening and closing paragraphs. Therefore, the correct answer is "Explain why Rwanda should become a member of the CISG."

11. **Correct Answer:** strong debate

Explanation: The phrase, "heated discussion" appears in the last paragraph in this sentence: "There has been heated discussion as to whether Rwanda should sign the CISG." Given the context in which the phrase appears, it seems to mean that strong arguments are being made both for and against membership in the CISG. As such, "strong debate" is the best answer, as the discoure is not emotional, is not characerized as being combative, nor unfair, and there is no indication that "intense persuasion" is being utilized.

12. **Correct Answer:** Bison who are idle in the wild look more like other wild bison than captive bison.

Explanation: The author's main explanation for why captive bison are smaller than normal and the bison in the Smithsonian collection are larger than normal hinges on the amount of exercise and activity animals living in both environments had. According to the author, wild bison living at the end of the bison hunts survived more chases and had more activity than was usual, meaning only the finest specimens survived, while captive bison were deprived of exercise and activity. Thus, if a wild bison that did not exercise and was not active looked more like other wild bison, some other factor besides exercise would have to be found to explain the difference in appearance between wild and captive bison.

13. **Correct Answer:** Immediately following the start of systematic bison hunting, unusually large and powerful individual bison died out, never to be seen again.

Explanation: The credited answer is the only one that addresses the author's central thesis - that the accounts and examples we have of bison are all in some way different from the norm of bison that existed in the wild-targeting his assumption that the mounted bison, being examples of the last, fittest survivors, are unusual in their size and fitness. If no unusually large bison had existed since the bison hunts first began, then it could not be possible that the last survivors of the bison hunts would be unusually large. Thus, the National Museum specimens he mentions could not be anomalous examples in the way he describes.

14. **Correct Answer:** It is a piece of evidence used to strengthen the author's thesis by showing an important similarity between two seemingly disparate cases.

Explanation: By showing that both wild bison and captive bison are fed the same amounts of food, the author removes one possible cause (disparity in feeding) that might account for captive bison being fatter or wild ones being larger, and attempts to strengthen his case that the cause of this difference is due to the factors he mentions. In removing other possible variables, the author strengthens the causal chain that he argues is responsible for the change in appearance in captive bison. It should be noted that this statement is related to the causal, rather than strictly logical, order of the author's argument; it is not a necessary or sufficient condition, nor is it an anticipation of possible counterarguments, but rather an explanation that certain possible variables are more-or-less constant across all cases under consideration, meaning some cause other than over- or underfeeding must be responsible for the differences in appearance between captive and wild bison.

15. **Correct Answer:** An empirical statement whose causes will be explained elsewhere in the passage

Explanation: The third paragraph primarily describes the difference in form seen in captive bison - a set of empirical observations based not in logic or argumentation but in experiential evidence. The author does not proceed to lay out an argument in this section, nor does he attempt to define or delineate terms and conditions; rather, this section describes a set of observations made by the author about a certain class of animals, observations he will attempt to explain elsewhere in the passage.

16. **Correct Answer:** Correcting and accounting for misperceptions and biases in observations that underlie a popular conception of a specie's traits

Explanation: The passage focuses on how well-known accounts of wild bison, bison found in captivity and mounted specimens all diverge for various reasons and in different ways from how wild bison generally looked and acted; thus, the passage's purpose is best described as focusing on correcting biases and misperceptions.
While some of the alternative responses are supported by the passage (given that Hornaday does discuss his observations on the effects of environmental change and captivity on American bison), they are subordinate points and purposes used to support his main aim, counteracting and correcting the effects of the
"combination of unfortunate circumstances" that he believes could cause "the American bison ... to go down to posterity shorn of the honor which is his due, and appreciated at only half his worth"

17. **Correct Answer:** show how concepts other than religion are as difficult to define in simple terms

Explanation: When the author invokes the many different ways "government" is defined, he is doing so to show that his point about the complexities around defining "religion" can happen in other areas.
In particular, the author wishes to show that the multifaceted way "government" can be defined means that a rigid approach to "religion" will not produce a suitable definition.

18. **Correct Answer:** Fascinated by it as a subject of inquiry

Explanation: While the author of this passage is certainly not enthralled by religion, particularly its more traditional elements, he is somewhat respectful of "religion" as a concept. What most intrigues the author is religion's complexity and the way it can be defined on a number of different levels. This indicates that the author appreciates religion as a subject of inquiry.

19. **Correct Answer:** subjects with clear correct and incorrect answers to their inquiries

Explanation: The author's argument in this passage is that religion is a multifaceted and complex subject that should be looked at in a new way. The "absolutism and one-sided dogmatism" he derides in the passage should be viewed as representing positions with which he disagrees. Additionally, the invocation of "absolutism and one-sided dogmatism" paints people who hold beliefs that fall into these categories as opposing the author's view of religion's definition.

20. **Correct Answer:** the author believes that religion cannot be defined by one single term or sentence

Explanation: The use of the phrase "rather a collective name" is an indication by the author that he is not satisfied with any definition given for religion. In particular, he uses such an ambiguous phrase to show that any singular definition of "religion" is bound to not work appropriately, and that religion must be defined by more than a simple sentence or single word.

21. **Correct Answer:** Such a definition excludes many groups that could legitimately be called religions.

Explanation: The author's main point is that "religion" is a concept that needs a multifaceted and fluid definition. If a government defined religion with broad yet simplified terms, the definition would go against what the author views an appropriate definition. One cause of such a definition would be that some groups would not be encompassed in the government's official definition.

22. **Correct Answer:** "Religion" is a concept that is not easy to define with a simple statement of basic characteristics.

Explanation: The author is attempting to be quite careful in defining "religion," largely because he wants to have a deeper conversation about the idea of "religion." As this serves the purpose of beginning a more nuanced discussion, the author is making an argument for religion as a valuable course of study and one which should be studied carefully. The author's discussion of "government" in the second paragraph is used as a parallel to his point about "religion."

23. **Correct Answer:** If Coleridge hadn't encountered some of his early misfortunes, he could have been truly great.

Explanation: The author specifically focuses on the misfortunes of Coleridge's early life as points that may have influenced his later life, particularly his addiction to opiates. We can suggest from this that the author would assent to the proposal that Coleridge may have been able to be more productive and therefore of greater literary significance and influence had he not encountered such misfortunes during his youth. Of the other statements, only the one about Wordsworth can be really considered and even then, there is not enough evidence to support it.

24. **Correct Answer:** An aged emperor who has never seen peace in his kingdom.

Explanation: Carlyle's account is mentioned at the end of the third paragraph: "Carlyle, who visited him at this time, calls him 'a king of men, but records that 'he gave you the idea of a life that had been full of sufferings, a life heavy-laden, half-vanquished." So, Coleridge was a great man who had never been able to enjoy or revel in his greatness due to a lack of mental and physical peace. Of the analogies, the closest to this is that of the emperor who has never seen peace throughout his reign.

25. **Correct Answer:** Coleridge was greater as a person than the greatness of great works.

Explanation: The passage states that Wordsworth said "though other men of the age had done some wonderful things, Coleridge was the only wonderful man he had ever known." This does not suggest that Coleridge was the only nice person he had ever known or that Coleridge did more wonderful things than any other person; instead, it means that Coleridge was great as a person where others only achieved greatness in their works.

26. **Correct Answer:** to give a short summary of the life of an influential man

Explanation: The passage is quite simply a short summary of the life of Coleridge, who, by the author's account, can be considered an influential man in the world of literature. It cannot be the introduction to a biography; the title of the piece tells us this much, but also the analysis is too quick. There is no depth to the consideration of the man's life; only highlighted points are discussed. Likewise, the subjects of Wordsworth, opiates, and Coleridge's view of poetry only occur at a few points in the passage and not enough is really said of them for them to be part of the main point of the passage.

27. **Correct Answer:** to show that Coleridge was afflicted by addiction but resolved to be cured of it

Explanation: The most important thing to do when answering this question is to simply state the facts. The fact is that the third paragraph shows Coleridge was afflicted with an addiction which probably affected his life seriously and was at one point resolved to cure it.

The other statements are all either lacking in simplicity or are too simplistic.

28. **Correct Answer:** The development of Coleridge's early radical views

Explanation: Of the statements provided as answer choices, there is only one that is supported by the text. This is "the development of Coleridge's early radical views." We cannot say that Southey and Coleridge became friends because of the French Revolution as that much is not stated by the text. Likewise, we may know it to be true that the French Revolution caused reforms in Western society and that France descended into anarchy for a time, but these points are not mentioned by the text.

ARGUMENTATIVE WRITING SECTION

Prompt Recap:

A tech company is considering implementing a mandatory remote work policy for all its employees. Proponents argue that remote work increases productivity, reduces costs, and allows for a better work-life balance. Critics, however, are concerned that it may lead to decreased collaboration, weaker company culture, and difficulties in managing teams.

Introduction:

The debate over whether a tech company should implement a mandatory remote work policy touches on significant aspects of productivity, company culture, and employee satisfaction. Proponents assert that remote work can boost productivity and offer employees greater work-life balance, while critics worry about potential declines in collaboration and difficulties in maintaining a strong company culture. This essay argues that while remote work offers several advantages, the potential drawbacks, particularly in terms of collaboration and culture, must be carefully considered.

Body Paragraph 1: Benefits of Remote Work

Remote work has several clear benefits, particularly in terms of productivity and cost savings. By allowing employees to work from home, the company can reduce overhead costs, such as rent and utilities, associated with maintaining large office spaces. Employees also benefit from greater flexibility in managing their personal and professional lives, leading to higher job satisfaction and potentially increased productivity. Studies have shown that employees who work remotely often report being able to focus better without the distractions commonly found in an office environment. This can lead to more efficient work processes and a better output, which is a significant advantage for any tech company aiming to remain competitive.

Body Paragraph 2: Challenges of Remote Work

Despite these benefits, remote work also poses significant challenges. One of the main concerns is the potential for decreased collaboration and weaker company culture. In a remote work environment, spontaneous brainstorming sessions and informal communication, which are often the breeding ground for innovation, can be difficult to replicate. Additionally, managing teams remotely can introduce challenges in ensuring all members are engaged and working cohesively. Without the physical presence that an office provides, managers may struggle to build and maintain a sense of community and shared purpose within their teams. This could lead to feelings of isolation among employees and a gradual erosion of the company's culture.

Body Paragraph 3: Addressing Counterarguments

While critics raise valid concerns about remote work, these challenges can be mitigated with the right strategies. For instance, companies can invest in collaborative tools that facilitate communication and project management in a remote setting. Regular virtual meetings, team-building activities, and clear communication guidelines can help maintain a strong company culture even when employees are not physically together. Furthermore, a hybrid model, where employees split their time between remote work and office work, could offer a balanced solution, allowing the company to reap the benefits of remote work while still fostering a collaborative and cohesive work environment.

Conclusion:

In conclusion, while a mandatory remote work policy presents both benefits and challenges, it is essential for the tech company to weigh these factors carefully. The potential for increased productivity and cost savings is compelling, but not at the expense of collaboration and company culture. By implementing strategies to address the downsides of remote work or considering a hybrid approach, the company can find a balanced solution that meets the needs of both the organization and its employees. Ultimately, the success of such a policy will depend on the company's ability to adapt and innovate in its approach to managing a remote workforce.

CHAPTER 7: Costs, locations and Test day preparation

Exam Costs and Fees

When considering the financial aspects of taking the exam, it's important to be aware of the various fees associated with the process. The primary cost is the registration fee, which covers the basic exam itself. The current registration fee for the LSAT is $238 (August 2024). However, additional fees can quickly add up, depending on your circumstances.

The base registration fee is the first and most obvious cost. This fee grants you access to the test, but it's essential to register by the specified deadline to avoid late registration fees. These additional fees are imposed if you miss the initial registration window, and they can significantly increase the overall cost of taking the exam. Late registration is often a result of unforeseen circumstances, but planning ahead can help you avoid this unnecessary expense.

Beyond registration, other fees may apply if you need to send your score reports to multiple law schools. Most registration packages include a certain number of score reports, but if you plan to apply to more schools than the allotted number, you'll need to pay extra for each additional report. This cost can add up, especially for applicants who are casting a wide net in their law school applications.

Another possible expense is the fee for changing your test date or location. If your plans change after you've registered, you may need to reschedule your test. This can happen for various reasons, such as personal conflicts or a realization that another test date better aligns with your study schedule. The rescheduling fee, though not as substantial as the registration fee, is another cost to consider when budgeting for the exam.

In some cases, candidates may also incur fees for specific services, such as hand-scoring requests if they wish to challenge their results. While these instances are rare, they represent another layer of potential cost that could arise during the testing process.

To mitigate these expenses, it's crucial to plan your registration carefully. Registering early, ensuring that you're prepared for the test date, and selecting the correct test location can help minimize additional fees. Moreover, thoroughly reviewing all the details before finalizing your registration can prevent costly changes down the line.

For candidates facing financial difficulties, there may be fee waivers available. These waivers can significantly reduce the cost of registration and associated fees, making the exam more accessible. It's worth exploring these options if you believe you qualify, as they can ease the financial burden.

In summary, while the base registration fee is the primary cost associated with the exam, additional fees for late registration, extra score reports, and rescheduling can quickly add up. Careful planning and attention to deadlines are key to minimizing these expenses. Understanding the full scope of potential costs will help you budget effectively and ensure that you're fully prepared for the financial commitments involved in taking the exam.

Test Locations and Options

When planning to take the LSAT, choosing the right testing location is a key part of your preparation process. The options for where and how to take the exam have evolved, particularly in response to recent global changes. Candidates can now choose between remote testing, in-person testing centers, and international testing locations, offering flexibility to accommodate diverse needs and preferences.

Remote Testing:

Remote testing has become an increasingly popular option, especially in the wake of the COVID-19 pandemic. This option allows candidates to take the exam from the comfort of their own homes. The flexibility of remote testing is one of its greatest advantages. Candidates can avoid the stress and logistics of traveling to a testing center, which can be particularly beneficial for those who live far from designated testing locations or have mobility issues.

However, remote testing requires a reliable internet connection, a quiet and private space, and a computer that meets the technical requirements set by LSAC. Candidates must also be comfortable with the remote proctoring process, which involves monitoring through video and audio to ensure the integrity of the exam. For some, the presence of a virtual proctor may feel intrusive or add to test anxiety, so it's important to consider whether this setting is conducive to your best performance.

Additionally, those opting for remote testing should prepare for potential technical issues. It is advisable to perform system checks well in advance and have contingency plans in place, such as an alternative location with a stable internet connection, to mitigate any unforeseen challenges.

In-Person Testing Centers:

For many, taking the exam at an in-person testing center remains the preferred choice. These centers are equipped with all necessary facilities, including computers that meet LSAC's specifications and environments designed to minimize distractions. Testing centers can offer a more controlled and familiar setting, which can be comforting for those who prefer a traditional exam experience.

In-person testing is ideal for candidates who may not have a suitable environment at home for remote testing or who feel more comfortable in a formal testing setting. These centers are located throughout the country, making them accessible for most candidates. However, it's important to register early, as spots can fill up quickly, especially in popular or urban locations.

Another advantage of in-person testing is the support available on-site. Test administrators are present to assist with any issues that arise during the exam, such as technical difficulties or procedural questions, providing a safety net that can help alleviate stress.

International Testing Locations:

For candidates outside the United States, international testing locations provide an opportunity to take the exam in a setting that meets LSAC's rigorous standards. These locations are strategically placed in various countries to accommodate the growing number of international applicants to U.S. law schools.

Choosing an international testing center may involve more logistics, such as travel arrangements and understanding local regulations. Additionally, some locations may have different registration deadlines or fee structures, so it's crucial to be aware of these details well in advance.

International candidates who cannot access a testing center nearby may also be eligible for remote testing, subject to LSAC's guidelines. However, it's important to verify the availability of remote testing in your country and ensure that all technical and logistical requirements can be met.

Choosing the Best Option:

Selecting the right testing location depends on your individual circumstances and preferences. If you value convenience and have a conducive environment at home, remote testing might be the best choice. For those who prefer a more controlled and supportive setting, an in-person testing center may be more suitable. International candidates should consider both the accessibility of testing centers and the feasibility of remote testing in their region.

No matter which option you choose, early registration is key to securing your preferred testing location. Consider your personal comfort, technical capabilities, and any logistical concerns when making your decision. Each testing option has its own set of advantages and challenges, so choose the one that aligns best with your needs to set yourself up for success on test day.

Test Environment Protocols: In-Person and Remote

Understanding the protocols for the test environment, whether in-person or remote, is essential for candidates preparing for the LSAT. These protocols ensure a fair and secure testing experience, aligning with the rigorous standards expected in such a high-stakes exam. Both in-person and remote test environments have specific procedures and guidelines that candidates must follow, and understanding these protocols can help alleviate anxiety and allow for better focus on the test itself.

In-Person Test Environment Protocols:

For candidates opting to take the LSAT in-person at a designated testing center, the experience is designed to be as uniform and controlled as possible. Upon arrival, test-takers are typically required to present a valid government-issued photo ID to verify their identity. This step is crucial in maintaining the integrity of the exam, ensuring that the person registered for the test is the one actually taking it.

Once inside the testing center, candidates are usually asked to leave personal belongings in a secure area, as only essential items are allowed in the testing room. This typically includes the ID, pencils or pens, and an eraser. Test-takers are also allowed to bring a snack or drink, which must be stored in a clear plastic bag and can only be accessed during designated breaks.

The testing environment itself is strictly monitored. Proctors are present to enforce rules and provide instructions throughout the exam. They ensure that the test is conducted in a quiet and orderly manner, free from any distractions. Candidates must remain seated during the test and can only leave the room during scheduled breaks. Any disruptive behavior or violation of test protocols, such as attempting to access prohibited materials, can result in immediate dismissal from the test and potential cancellation of scores.

In-person testing centers are equipped with all the necessary materials, such as scratch paper and test booklets. The physical setup usually involves individual desks or cubicles spaced to minimize the risk of cheating. The atmosphere is designed to be as conducive as possible to concentration, with lighting, temperature, and noise levels controlled to create an optimal testing environment.

Remote Test Environment Protocols:

For those who choose the remote option, the testing environment shifts from a controlled public setting to the privacy of one's home or another suitable location. Remote testing has gained popularity due to its convenience, but it comes with its own set of protocols to ensure fairness and security.

Before the test day, candidates are required to install specific software that enables remote proctoring. This software is used to monitor the candidate's computer activity and, in some cases, the testing environment through the webcam. The system typically requires a room scan at the beginning of the test to ensure that the space is free from prohibited items, such as books, notes, or electronic devices. The software also tracks eye movement, keyboard activity, and other behaviors to detect any potential cheating.

Identity verification remains a critical part of the remote testing process. Candidates must show their ID to the webcam for verification before the test begins. The proctoring software may also take periodic photos or videos during the test to confirm that the same person is taking the exam throughout.

One of the significant differences between remote and in-person testing is the level of control over the environment. While in-person testing centers offer a standardized setting, remote test-takers must ensure that their environment is suitable for taking the exam. This includes securing a quiet room where interruptions are unlikely, ensuring a stable internet connection, and setting up a workspace that complies with the testing requirements. Candidates are advised to test their equipment and internet connection well in advance of the test day to avoid technical issues that could disrupt the exam.

During the remote LSAT, candidates are typically not allowed to leave their seat, except during scheduled breaks, and must adhere to strict guidelines regarding what can be on their desk. The remote proctor monitors the test-taker in real-time, and any suspicious activity can result in the test being flagged for further review.

Adapting to the Environment:

Whether taking the test in person or remotely, candidates should familiarize themselves with the specific protocols well before the test day. Understanding these rules helps prevent any last-minute surprises and allows candidates to focus entirely on performing their best during the exam. Preparing the test environment, whether by selecting the right testing center or setting up a quiet, controlled space at home, is a critical part of the preparation process.

By thoroughly understanding the test environment protocols for both in-person and remote LSAT options, candidates can better manage their test day experience, reduce anxiety, and ensure that they adhere to all the rules and guidelines, paving the way for a successful examination.

Registration and Test Day Procedures

Preparing for the LSAT involves several key steps, starting with the registration process, scheduling the test, and understanding the procedures that will take place on test day. Each of these steps is crucial to ensure a smooth and successful test-taking experience.

Registration and Scheduling:

The first step in the LSAT journey is registering for the exam. Registration is typically completed online through the official Law School Admission Council (LSAC) website. Candidates must create an account, where they can manage all aspects of their LSAT journey, including registration, scheduling, and accessing scores. It's important to register as early as possible to secure a preferred testing date and location. Early registration also provides ample time to prepare for the test, both academically and logistically.

When registering, candidates are prompted to select their preferred test date and location. The LSAT is offered multiple times a year, and test dates can fill up quickly, especially in popular locations. Therefore, early registration is advised to avoid the disappointment of having to choose a less convenient date or location. Additionally, candidates should be aware of registration deadlines, as late registration incurs additional fees. The cost of registering for the LSAT is generally around $215, but this fee may vary slightly, so checking the current rate on the LSAC website is recommended.

Once registered, candidates receive confirmation and instructions on how to proceed with scheduling. The LSAT offers flexibility in terms of test format, with options to take the exam either in-person at a designated testing center or remotely from home. Each option has its own set of procedures and requirements, so understanding these details well in advance is essential.

Test Day Procedures:

Test day procedures begin well before the actual exam. Candidates should familiarize themselves with what to expect, starting with the time and location of their test. For those taking the test in person, it's advisable to visit the testing center beforehand to reduce anxiety on test day. Remote test-takers should ensure that their computer and internet setup meets the technical requirements, and it's a good idea to perform a system check provided by the LSAC to confirm everything is functioning correctly.

On the day of the test, candidates must arrive at the testing center or log in to the remote testing platform well in advance of the scheduled start time. For in-person testing, arriving at least 30 minutes early is recommended to allow time for check-in procedures, which include presenting a valid government-issued photo ID and LSAT admission ticket. Only a few essential items, such as identification and approved testing materials, are allowed in the testing area. All other personal belongings, including bags and electronic devices, must be stored as directed by the testing center staff.

Remote test-takers must ensure they are in a quiet, private space free from interruptions. The LSAT's remote proctoring system uses live proctors who monitor the test environment through the candidate's webcam. Any disruptions or violations of test day rules can result in the cancellation of the test and, in some cases, further disciplinary action.

Regardless of the testing format, it's crucial to remain calm and focused throughout the exam. The LSAT is a timed test, and maintaining a steady pace while carefully managing time for each section is key to success. Breaks are limited, so candidates should make sure they are comfortable and ready to focus for the duration of the test.

In summary, the process of registering, scheduling, and preparing for test day involves several important steps that must be carefully managed. Early registration, understanding the specific procedures for the chosen testing format, and being thoroughly prepared on the day of the exam are all essential components of a successful LSAT experience. By following these guidelines, candidates can approach the LSAT with confidence, knowing that they are well-prepared for both the logistical and academic challenges of the test.

Accommodations, Special Requests and Retaking the LSAT

Navigating the process of requesting accommodations, making special requests, and considering the possibility of retaking the LSAT involves a series of steps that require careful planning and attention to detail. Understanding these aspects is crucial for candidates who may need additional support during the test or who are contemplating a second attempt to improve their scores.

Accommodations and Special Requests:

For many candidates, the standard LSAT format may not be sufficient to ensure an equitable testing experience. To address this, the LSAC provides accommodations for test-takers with documented disabilities. These accommodations are designed to level the playing field, allowing all candidates an equal opportunity to perform to the best of their abilities.

The process of requesting accommodations begins with submitting documentation that verifies the need for specific adjustments. This documentation typically includes a recent evaluation from a qualified professional, such as a psychologist or physician, who can attest to the candidate's disability and the necessity of the requested accommodations. Common accommodations include extended time, additional breaks, a separate testing room, and the use of assistive technology such as screen readers or braille materials.

Candidates should apply for accommodations well in advance of their test date. The LSAC has specific deadlines for submitting these requests, and it's crucial to adhere to these timelines to avoid delays or denials. Once a request is submitted, it undergoes a review process where the LSAC evaluates the documentation and determines the appropriate accommodations. The candidate is then notified of the outcome, and any approved accommodations are implemented for their scheduled test.

In addition to accommodations, some candidates may have special requests that do not fall under the typical accommodations umbrella. These could include requests related to religious observance, such as needing to test on a different day due to a religious holiday, or other personal circumstances that require specific arrangements. These requests should also be submitted as early as possible, accompanied by a clear explanation of the need and any relevant supporting documents.

Retaking the LSAT:

For many, the decision to retake the LSAT arises from a desire to improve their score and enhance their law school applications. Retaking the test can be a strategic move, but it's essential to approach it with a clear plan and realistic expectations.

Before deciding to retake the LSAT, candidates should thoroughly analyze their previous performance. This includes reviewing the score report to identify specific areas of weakness and determining whether these areas can be improved with additional study. It's important to consider whether the initial score accurately reflects the candidate's abilities or if external factors, such as test-day anxiety or inadequate preparation, played a significant role in the outcome.

Candidates who decide to retake the test should develop a focused study plan that addresses their weaknesses. This may involve enrolling in a prep course, working with a tutor, or dedicating more time to practice exams under timed conditions. The goal is to refine test-taking strategies and build confidence in the areas that previously posed challenges.

When scheduling a retake, it's also important to consider the timing of law school application deadlines. Candidates should ensure that their new score will be available in time for schools to consider it during the admissions process. Additionally, it's worth noting that while many law schools consider the highest score, some may take an average of multiple scores or review the entire testing history, so understanding the policies of each prospective school is critical.

The LSAC allows candidates to take the LSAT up to three times in a single testing year (from August 1 to July 31), five times within the current and five past testing years, and a total of seven times over a lifetime. These limits are in place to prevent candidates from taking the test excessively without significant improvement. If a candidate's scores plateau or decline with multiple attempts, it may be time to reassess their preparation strategies or consider whether their score range is in alignment with their law school goals.

Whether navigating the process of requesting accommodations or contemplating a retake, it's crucial to approach these decisions with careful planning and realistic expectations. By understanding the available resources and strategically planning their LSAT journey, candidates can better position themselves for success in their law school admissions process.

Mental and Physical Preparation: Managing Anxiety and Well-being

Preparing mentally and physically for the LSAT is just as important as the study sessions themselves. This phase of preparation ensures that you are not only equipped with the knowledge to tackle the exam but also in the right mindset and physical state to perform optimally. Managing anxiety and maintaining well-being are critical components of this process.

Understanding the Role of Anxiety:

Anxiety is a common response to high-stakes exams like the LSAT. While a certain level of stress can be motivating and improve performance by heightening focus and alertness, excessive anxiety can be detrimental. It can cloud judgment, impair memory, and reduce the ability to think critically under pressure.

One of the first steps in managing anxiety is recognizing it as a natural reaction. Acknowledging your feelings without judgment can help prevent them from escalating. It's important to remember that anxiety, in manageable amounts, is a sign that you care about your performance and that it can be harnessed as a tool for success.

Techniques for Managing Anxiety:

There are several strategies to help manage anxiety effectively, both in the lead-up to the exam and on test day. Developing a routine that includes regular relaxation techniques can significantly reduce stress levels. Deep breathing exercises, for instance, are a simple yet powerful way to calm the nervous system. Taking slow, deep breaths can activate the parasympathetic nervous system, which counteracts the fight-or-flight response induced by anxiety.

Another effective technique is mindfulness meditation. Practicing mindfulness helps in staying present and reduces the tendency to ruminate on past failures or future uncertainties. It teaches the mind to focus on the current task, which can be particularly useful during long study sessions or when facing difficult questions on the test.

Visualization is another tool that can be employed. Visualizing success—seeing yourself confidently answering questions and finishing the test—can help reduce fear and build a positive mental outlook. This form of mental rehearsal conditions the brain to approach the exam with confidence rather than dread.

Importance of Physical Well-being:

Physical health plays a critical role in mental clarity and focus. Regular exercise is known to reduce stress levels by releasing endorphins, the body's natural mood lifters. Engaging in physical activity, even something as simple as a daily walk, can improve sleep, increase energy levels, and enhance cognitive function—all of which are essential for peak performance on test day.

Nutrition also cannot be overlooked. A balanced diet, rich in fruits, vegetables, whole grains, and lean proteins, fuels the brain and body. Avoiding excessive caffeine and sugar is particularly important, as these can lead to energy crashes and heightened anxiety. Hydration is equally crucial; dehydration can lead to fatigue and difficulty concentrating.

Sleep is another vital component of physical preparation. Lack of sleep can impair memory, decision-making, and the ability to cope with stress. Establishing a regular sleep routine in the weeks leading up to the exam ensures that you're well-rested and able to function at your best.

Developing a Test Day Routine:

Establishing a routine for the day of the test can also help manage anxiety. Plan your morning so that it is calm and free of last-minute rushes. This might include a light, nutritious breakfast and some light stretching or a short walk to wake up the body and mind.

It's also beneficial to have a mental checklist of things to bring to the test center or have ready for a remote test. Being prepared with all necessary materials—such as your ID, admission ticket, and approved supplies—reduces the potential for added stress.

Staying Calm During the Exam:

Once the exam begins, anxiety management continues. Start by reading the instructions carefully and take a moment to center yourself. If you find yourself becoming anxious during the test, employ the deep breathing techniques you've practiced. Remember that it's okay to take a brief pause to refocus before continuing.

Pacing yourself is crucial; rushing through questions can increase mistakes and elevate stress. Trust in the preparation you've done and approach each question methodically.

Managing anxiety and maintaining well-being are integral to performing well on the LSAT. By incorporating relaxation techniques, prioritizing physical health, and establishing a solid test day routine, you can approach the exam with confidence and clarity. Remember that preparation is not just about mastering content but also about preparing your mind and body to perform under pressure. By focusing on these aspects, you set the stage for a successful test day.

Score Reporting and Strategic Test Management

Score reporting and strategic test management are critical aspects of the LSAT preparation process, playing a pivotal role in how candidates approach the test and utilize their scores to maximize their chances of law school admission. Understanding these components in detail can help test-takers develop a more informed and strategic approach to their LSAT journey.

Score Reporting:

After completing the LSAT, your score is typically released approximately three weeks after your test date. When registering for the LSAT, you can choose which law schools will automatically receive your score once it is available. This process is managed through your LSAC (Law School Admission Council) account, where you can view your score and decide if you want to release it to additional schools.

It's important to note that all LSAT scores from the past five years are included in your score report unless you specifically choose to cancel a score within a specified period after the test. This means that if you retake the exam, the new score will be sent alongside previous scores, giving law schools a full picture of your testing history. For some applicants, multiple scores can demonstrate improvement and resilience, while others may prefer to cancel lower scores to focus on higher performances.

Score reports also include your percentile rank, which shows how your score compares to those of other test-takers. For instance, a score in the 90th percentile indicates that you scored higher than 90% of test-takers. This percentile ranking can be just as important as the scaled score itself, as it provides context for law schools to interpret your performance relative to other applicants.

Strategic Test Management: Maximizing Your LSAT Performance:

Managing the LSAT strategically begins with understanding the implications of your score and how it will be perceived by law schools. One key element of this is deciding whether to retake the exam. Given that law schools receive all your scores from the last five years, the decision to retake should be made carefully. If you are confident that you can significantly improve your score, retaking the LSAT could be advantageous. However, if the improvement is likely to be marginal, it may be more strategic to focus on other parts of your application, such as your personal statement or letters of recommendation.

Another aspect of strategic test management involves the timing of your test. Choosing when to take the LSAT should align with your law school application timeline. Early test dates allow you to assess your score and decide whether a retake is necessary before application deadlines. Additionally, taking the test earlier in the admission cycle can reduce stress, allowing ample time for other application components.

Preparation strategies should also be tailored to maximize your score potential. Focus on areas where you have the most room for improvement, especially since the test now includes two sections of Logical Reasoning. Practicing under timed conditions is crucial, as it builds the endurance needed to maintain focus throughout the test. Furthermore, simulating test conditions during practice sessions can help you develop effective time management skills, ensuring that you can navigate each section efficiently.

Finally, mental preparation is just as important as mastering the content. The LSAT is a demanding test, and managing stress and anxiety through relaxation techniques or mindfulness can significantly impact your performance. Remember, the goal is not only to prepare academically but also to ensure that you approach the test with a calm and focused mindset.

By considering these factors in your preparation, you can approach the LSAT with confidence, knowing that you have a comprehensive strategy in place to maximize your performance and enhance your law school application.

APPENDICES

Common Pitfalls and How to Avoid Them

When preparing for the LSAT, it's common for test-takers to encounter a range of pitfalls that can hinder their performance. Understanding these challenges and how to navigate them is crucial for success. Below are some common pitfalls students face and strategies to avoid them.

Overemphasis on Timing:

One of the most significant pitfalls is becoming overly focused on timing. While managing time effectively is essential, an excessive focus on speed can lead to careless mistakes. Many students rush through questions, fearing they won't finish the section, which often results in misreading questions or skipping critical steps in reasoning. The key is to balance speed with accuracy. Practice pacing yourself with timed drills, but ensure that your primary focus remains on understanding and answering each question correctly. Developing a rhythm during practice can help maintain this balance on the test day.

Neglecting Weak Areas:

Another common mistake is spending too much time on strengths and neglecting weaker areas. It's natural to gravitate towards sections where you feel more confident, but this approach can leave you vulnerable. The LSAT requires a well-rounded skill set, and consistently low performance in one area can significantly impact your overall score. To avoid this, regularly assess your performance across all sections and dedicate extra time to areas where you struggle. For instance, if logical reasoning questions pose a challenge, focus on breaking down argument structures and practicing those specific question types until they become more manageable.

Ignoring the Importance of Reviewing Mistakes:

Simply practicing questions without reviewing mistakes is a missed opportunity for growth. Many students complete practice tests and move on without thoroughly analyzing what went wrong. This oversight prevents you from learning from your errors, making it likely you'll repeat them. Instead, after each practice session, spend time reviewing incorrect answers. Understand why your choice was wrong and why the correct answer is right. This process not only reinforces the right approach but also helps identify patterns in your mistakes, enabling you to adjust your strategy accordingly.

Overloading with Study Materials:

The abundance of study resources available can be overwhelming, and some students fall into the trap of using too many materials at once. This can lead to information overload, confusion, and burnout. It's better to focus on a few high-quality resources and use them effectively. Choose materials that align with your learning style and stick with them. Consistency in practice with familiar materials allows for deeper understanding and better retention of strategies.

Inadequate Preparation for the Test Day Environment:

Another pitfall is failing to simulate the test day environment during practice. The LSAT is a high-pressure exam, and many students experience anxiety that affects their performance. Preparing for this by simulating the test environment can make a significant difference. Take full-length practice tests in a quiet space, under timed conditions, and with minimal interruptions. This approach helps acclimate you to the conditions of test day, reducing anxiety and improving focus.

Misunderstanding Question Types:

Each section of the LSAT features distinct question types that require specific approaches. A common pitfall is failing to recognize these question types and applying the wrong strategy. For example, treating a "must be true" question as though it were an assumption question can lead to incorrect answers. Familiarize yourself with the different question types, their common traps, and the best strategies for each. Practice identifying them quickly during practice sessions so that on test day, you can immediately recognize and approach each question type correctly.

Avoiding these common pitfalls requires a balanced and thoughtful approach to LSAT preparation. By focusing on understanding the material, practicing strategically, and learning from mistakes, you can significantly improve your chances of success. Preparing well also means recognizing your weaknesses, addressing them head-on, and maintaining a steady pace rather than rushing. With careful preparation and mindfulness of these common challenges, you can navigate the LSAT with greater confidence and achieve your desired score.

Frequently Asked Questions

How Should I Begin Preparing for the LSAT?

Starting your LSAT preparation can feel overwhelming, but it's essential to approach it systematically. Begin by taking a diagnostic test to assess your strengths and weaknesses. This will help you identify which sections require more focus. Once you have a clear understanding of where you stand, create a study plan that allocates time to each section based on your needs. Consistent practice, especially with full-length timed exams, will help you build endurance and familiarity with the test format.

What Study Materials Should I Use?

Choosing the right study materials is crucial for effective preparation. High-quality resources include official LSAT prep books, online courses, and practice tests released by the Law School Admission Council (LSAC). It's advisable to use a combination of these resources to cover different aspects of the test. Official materials are particularly valuable because they offer the most accurate representation of the questions you'll encounter on the exam. Additionally, consider using digital platforms that offer adaptive learning and personalized feedback.

How Important is Timing During the LSAT?

Timing is a critical aspect of the LSAT, as the exam is designed to test not only your reasoning skills but also your ability to apply them under time constraints. Each section is timed, and managing this effectively is key to maximizing your score. Practice taking sections under timed conditions to develop a sense of pacing. Remember, while it's important to work quickly, accuracy should not be sacrificed. Developing a balance between speed and precision is essential.

Can I Retake the LSAT if I'm Not Satisfied with My Score?

Yes, you can retake the LSAT if you're not satisfied with your score. Many students take the test more than once to improve their results. LSAC allows you to take the LSAT up to three times in a single testing year, five times within the current and five past testing years, and a total of seven times over a lifetime. However, before deciding to retake, carefully consider your previous performance, the areas where you can improve, and how much time you can dedicate to further preparation.

What Should I Bring on Test Day?

On test day, it's important to be prepared with all the necessary materials. For in-person testing, you'll need to bring a valid government-issued ID, your admission ticket, and a few pencils (if you're taking the test in a paper-based format). If you're taking the test remotely, ensure that you have a reliable computer, a stable internet connection, and a quiet environment. In both cases, make sure you're familiar with the test day procedures outlined by LSAC, such as the check-in process and the rules regarding breaks.

How Do I Handle Test Anxiety?

Test anxiety is a common challenge for many LSAT takers. Managing it effectively involves both mental and physical preparation. Regular practice under test-like conditions can help reduce anxiety by making the exam feel more familiar. Additionally, mindfulness techniques such as deep breathing, meditation, and positive visualization can help you stay calm and focused. Ensuring that you get enough sleep, eat well, and exercise regularly in the days leading up to the test can also make a significant difference in your performance.

How Are LSAT Scores Reported to Law Schools?

LSAT scores are typically reported to law schools through the LSAC's Credential Assembly Service (CAS). When you register for the LSAT, you can select the schools where you'd like your scores sent. Once your scores are available, they will be automatically sent to these schools as part of your application file. Law schools will see all of your LSAT scores, as well as an average score if you have taken the test multiple times, although many schools focus on your highest score.

What is the Best Way to Simulate Test Day Conditions During Practice?

To simulate test day conditions, it's important to take full-length practice tests under timed conditions in a quiet environment. Mimicking the timing and pacing of the actual test can help you develop stamina and become comfortable with the test format. Make sure to take these practice tests at the same time of day as your scheduled LSAT to adjust your body and mind to the test timing. Additionally, follow the same break schedule that you will have on test day to replicate the experience as closely as possible.

How Can I Improve in Specific Sections Where I am Weak?

Identifying your weak areas is the first step toward improvement. Once you've pinpointed the sections or question types where you're struggling, focus your studies on these areas. Use targeted practice materials that concentrate on these sections, and review explanations for any questions you get wrong to understand your mistakes. Consider seeking additional resources, such as tutoring or online courses, that offer specialized instruction in those areas. Revisit these sections regularly to track your progress and adjust your study plan as needed.

Are There Any Resources for Students with Disabilities?

Yes, LSAC offers various accommodations for students with disabilities to ensure they have an equal opportunity to succeed on the LSAT. These accommodations may include extended time, additional breaks, the use of assistive technology, or a separate testing room. To apply for accommodations, you will need to submit documentation that supports your request. It's recommended to start this process early, as it can take time to gather the necessary documentation and receive approval from LSAC.

What Should I Do if I Encounter Technical Issues During a Remote Test?

If you encounter technical issues during a remote LSAT, it's crucial to remain calm and follow the procedures outlined by LSAC. You should have contact information for technical support readily available before the test begins. If the issue disrupts your test, LSAC may allow you to reschedule the exam without additional fees. Ensure that your testing environment meets the technical requirements, such as having a stable internet connection and a functioning computer, to minimize the risk of issues.

How Many LSAT Scores Do Law Schools Consider?

Most law schools consider all of your LSAT scores, but many place the greatest emphasis on your highest score. It's important to research the specific policies of the schools you are applying to, as some may average your scores, while others may focus on the most recent or highest score. Knowing this can help you strategize whether to retake the test.

Can I Cancel My LSAT Score After Taking the Test?

Yes, you can cancel your LSAT score if you believe it does not reflect your best performance. You must submit a score cancellation request within six calendar days after the test date. However, keep in mind that law schools will see that you canceled a score, though they won't know what the score was. Consider this option carefully, as it is irreversible.

What's the Difference Between the LSAT and the GRE?

Some law schools now accept the GRE in place of the LSAT. The LSAT is specifically designed to assess skills relevant to legal education, such as logical reasoning, reading comprehension, and writing. The GRE, on the other hand, is a general graduate admissions test that covers verbal reasoning, quantitative reasoning, and analytical writing. If you are considering using the GRE for law school admissions, research which schools accept it and how it fits into your overall application strategy.

How Early Should I Arrive at the Test Center on Test Day?

For in-person testing, it's recommended to arrive at the test center at least 30 minutes before the scheduled start time. This allows time for check-in procedures, such as verifying your identification and securing your personal belongings. Arriving early can also help you settle in and reduce pre-test anxiety. For remote testing, ensure you're logged in and ready to begin at least 15 minutes before the test start time to complete any necessary system checks.

Are There Any Restrictions on What I Can Bring to the Test Center?

Yes, there are specific restrictions on what you can bring to the test center. Typically, you are allowed to bring your ID, admission ticket, pencils, and a highlighter. Items like electronic devices, books, and bags are usually not permitted in the testing room and must be stored in a designated area. It's essential to review LSAC's guidelines for a comprehensive list of permitted and prohibited items to avoid any issues on test day.

Understanding these aspects of the LSAT process can help you approach your preparation and test day with greater confidence and clarity. Each step, from selecting study materials to managing test day logistics, plays a crucial role in your overall success.

Made in United States
Troutdale, OR
12/23/2024

27187419R10124